Paul Wood is a doctor of psychology, motivational speaker, leadership and personal development specialist, media personality, husband and father. At 18, he was in prison and his life was completely off the rails. In his work today, Paul uses his subsequent journey from delinquent to doctor to illustrate the process of transformational change and how we can strive to be the best possible versions of ourselves. Paul contributes regularly to the media and works with a number of charities that focus on helping young men avoid prison or reintegrate effectively on release. He lives in Wellington, New Zealand.

www.paulwood.com

HOW TO ESCAPE FROM PRISON

DR PAUL WOOD

HarperCollins*Publishers*

HarperCollins*Publishers*

First published in 2019
by HarperCollins*Publishers* (New Zealand) Limited
Unit D1, 63 Apollo Drive, Rosedale, Auckland 0632, New Zealand
harpercollins.co.nz

HarperCollins*Publishers*
Unit D1, 63 Apollo Drive, Rosedale, Auckland 0632, New Zealand
Level 13, 201 Elizabeth Street, Sydney NSW 2000
A 53, Sector 57, Noida, UP, India
1 London Bridge Street, London, SE1 9GF, United Kingdom
Bay Adelaide Centre, East Tower, 22 Adelaide Street West, 41st floor, Toronto,
   Ontario M5H 4E3, Canada
195 Broadway, New York NY 10007, USA

A catalogue record for this book is available from the National Library of New Zealand.

ISBN: 978 17755 4119 6 (paperback)
ISBN: 978 17754 9150 7 (ebook)

Cover design by HarperCollins Design Studio
Front and back cover photographs by Simon Woolf
Typeset in Sabon LT by Kirby Jones
Printed and bound in Australia by McPherson's Printing Group
The papers used by HarperCollins in the manufacture of this book are a natural,
recyclable product made from wood grown in sustainable plantation forests. The fibre
source and manufacturing processes meet recognised international environmental
standards, and carry certification.

This book is dedicated to the memory of my mother, Mary Jean Wood (née Thomas). I just wish you'd lived to meet my wife, Mary-Ann, and your grandchildren, Brax and Gordy. They would have loved you so much.

CONTENTS

PROLOGUE

The walls were pink and were crowding in on me. There was nothing in the space except a bench with a blanket, and a stainless steel toilet. The door had a small hole through which, every now and then, an eye would peer at me. Then the eye would disappear and I'd be alone again.

I was numbed by the drugs I had taken earlier that fateful day, but not so numb that I couldn't remember the events in detail, and not so numb that I couldn't feel the first, panicky stirrings of withdrawal. Every addict is prone to the gnawing imperative of their cravings. For me, as for most addicts, drugs were an escape from reality. I had never needed the means to escape reality more than I needed them now. But part of that inexorable reality was the knowledge there would be no escape, physical or mental.

From time to time, panic or restlessness would drive me to my feet, and I would pace from wall to wall: one, two, three paces, turn around; one, two, three paces back. Experiencing no relief, I would curl up on the bench again.

I lay there, balled up, feeling trapped, buffeted by waves of sick realisation. Everyone who has ever made a major mistake in their lives — and that's everyone — knows the feeling when you suddenly become conscious of the terrible momentum of time, and how it can't be halted, let alone reversed.

Sometime after midnight, there was a clatter of keys in the lock.

'Someone here to see you,' the cop said.

I was handcuffed and led to an interview room. Sitting there on one side of the cheap Formica table, his eyes downcast and his shoulders hunched, was my father. He looked up as I entered, handcuffed and wearing the white paper overalls they give you when they take your clothes for forensic analysis. I slumped into the chair opposite him, and the cop took up a position next to the door.

'What happened?' Dad asked.

I didn't know how to answer. I wanted to tell him that whatever he had heard, it wasn't true. Or I wanted to tell him that it hadn't happened the way the police had likely told him it had. I wanted to say it wasn't my fault. I wanted to say sorry, to apologise for heaping another blow on top of the blow he had just suffered. I wanted to promise to make amends for the hurt and misery I could see in his eyes.

I don't think I said anything.

Something was itching above my eyebrow. I lifted my hand and scratched. I saw Dad glance at the cuffs. I felt something crusty where I was scratching. I looked at my fingernail and recognised dried blood beneath it. I saw other flecks of blood on my arms, and smears of blood on my wrists where I had tried to wash them. I felt sick.

'I can't talk about it,' I said, nodding in the direction of the cop. 'Not until I've spoken to a lawyer.'

2

When Dad had gone, my two older brothers came in, one at a time. I didn't have much to say to them, either, especially since it had occurred to me that they were only being let in to see me because the police thought I might open up to them. They wished me good luck. My older brother Jon gave me some prison advice: 'Keep your head down and don't stand out. Be a grey man; someone nobody notices.'

Back in the cell, I realised that's what I had become: a grey man. All that promise and potential had been snuffed out, and I was just a husk. The faint excitement someone my age — I was just 18 — should feel in contemplating their many possible futures was gone. I knew what my future held: prison. I didn't know how long I would be spending there, but I knew it was going to be many years. It might as well have been the rest of my life.

*

My name is Paul Wood, and I am a free man.

What I didn't know then but have come to realise is that I had been in prison for many years before I was ever locked up. It's one of the rich ironies of my life's journey that I had to go to prison to learn how to be free. Now it's my privilege to help others break out of their own prisons.

What I also came to realise while I was physically incarcerated was that most of the people I was inside with, and a hell of a lot of people walking around outside who assume they're free, are locked up in mindsets that prevent them from living full, authentic lives. They are imprisoned by their beliefs about their limitations, about who they are supposed to be and what they are or aren't supposed to feel. That's as much of a waste of human potential as anything the criminal justice system has to offer.

What is a 'mental prison'? It's a set of distorted or misguided beliefs that condition our view of ourselves and the choices available to us, that prevent us from seeing clearly (or at all) what we might achieve if we chose to live freely. As a teenager, I had a narrow, crippled, mistaken view of what it was to be a man. I chose to associate with people who held antisocial views and who reinforced my negative mindset. I dropped out of school, firmly believing I was immune to the benefits of education and was wasting my time there. I took drugs, because they helped me avoid experiencing the confusion and the emotional distress that I didn't think I was supposed to feel as a man. I was, in short, in prison. Other people's prisons might differ from mine, but if they view the world and themselves through a clouded lens, then the freedom they imagine they have is an illusion, or at least a poor shadow of what it might be.

While most people would consider my life changed in the few short minutes during which I took another person's life, it didn't, really. Prison suited the kind of person I thought I was. I was surrounded by relentless negativity. People in there shared my own, unarticulated view of myself: that I was worthless and belonged in a place like the one in which I found myself. I had no problem getting hold of the drugs I thought I needed to get through, minute by minute, day by day. Going to prison didn't alter my behaviour and it would never force me to change for the better. Choosing to change would have to come from me.

I was lucky, in so far as the opportunity to choose to make changes came when I had matured enough to recognise it, through a chance association with people who thought I had potential and the opportunity to better myself through education. But luck wasn't everything. There was a lot of hard work involved as well. I can't pretend I broke out of my mental prison through my own unaided efforts, but if I'd waited for other people to rescue me, well, I'd still be there.

In recent years, I have been using my own experience and my training in psychology to help people to perceive the architecture of the mental prisons in which they languish, and show them how to break out. I have been helping people realise that the stress and hardships we encounter in life just provide the resistance required for growth, and that such adversity is a challenge to be embraced if we really want to unlock our potential. This is what this book is all about, too.

Much of what I write here is a prison memoir. Much of it is based on an account of my experiences I wrote while still in prison, just before I was due to be released. It's been amusing — and not a little unsettling — to compare my current recollections of my time in prison with what I wrote when I was much nearer to events, and presumably recording them more accurately. This has been a lesson in what psychologists call the 'constructive power of memory'.

Some of the material makes for rough reading, just as it was pretty tough to write. For those who have a low tolerance for such things, a warning: there is bad language. There seems to be no point in pretending prison is less foul than it is.

I chose to write about my time in prison precisely because it was so brutal and devoid of hope. My situation while incarcerated was a particularly drastic illustration of the consequences of my disordered thinking. Disordered thinking landed me there. I was surrounded by disordered thinking and, in my opinion, the entire prison system is the product of disordered thinking about the problem of crime and criminals.

The point? Well, there are two points. One is to draw attention to what a former prime minister and minister of finance declared the justice system as being: 'a moral and fiscal failure'. But the main point, and the purpose in the context of this book, is to make *you* feel better. For the majority of people who will read this book, and the majority of people who undertake my personal and professional development programmes, you aren't in a situation as dire as the one I found myself in. My situation seemed hopeless, but there are plenty of people in situations significantly worse, which helped me gain perspective. Perhaps your comparison with this period of my life will help you do the same. This book will ask you to look at your worldview, the mindset you wake up with each day and it will ask you this question: what's your prison?

And once you have identified your prison, this book will set out for you five steps with which you can break free. It won't be easy, but then life's not supposed to be easy and nothing worth having is ever secured without a struggle. You will lapse and fail along the way. But another key message this book will strive to make is that failure is a normal and vital part of improvement, as it presents an opportunity to do better. In the end, that's what our lives are about: getting better. We aren't out to be good at the things we do: we're out to be better at them. To strive to be good at something is to compare ourselves to some standard outside ourselves and outside our control. To aim to be better is to work on the element that we can control: our selves. That is the unceasing battle, to better ourselves, and this is the battle through which we stand to live a life with the greatest possible meaning, satisfaction and purpose.

It will be worth the fight — take it from one who knows: Paul Wood, a free man.

PART ONE

Build Your Prison

The mind is its own place, and in itself
Can make a Heav'n of Hell, a Hell of Heav'n.

—John Milton (1608–1674)

CHAPTER ONE

The Wrong Road

We all live in our own little rooms. They are built of various blocks, some bequeathed to us by nature: our gender, our physiology, our personality type; some by nurture, such as the culture we're born into, and the kind of upbringing we have in the crucial early childhood years; some by subsequent experience. The rooms are imaginary, but they are also real. They enclose, enfold and define us. We view the world from our windows, and our lives take paths determined by the doors we walk through.

The technical term for these rooms is 'schemata'. It's the way our perception of reality, and therefore the choices that are available to us, are determined by the range of factors mentioned above. We're generally not aware of them, of the limitations they impose upon us, any more than a fish is aware of the water in which it swims. But sometimes, there are bars on the windows and the doors are locked. Our minds aren't much better than prison cells.

The placebo effect provides a good example of how powerful the stories we tell ourselves about the world can be. The stories we tell ourselves about ourselves are no different. Often the limitations we perceive we are under become real — not because they are true limitations, but because we believe they are true and that they constrain us. Similarly, the way in which we can unlock our potential can often be as simple as changing the story we tell ourselves about the people we are and the potential we have. This change is not a simple matter. In most cases it can be a life's project.

When you first start trying to identify the stories you tell yourself — what psychologists call your 'mental model', the paradigm or set of unexamined beliefs which condition your view of the world — a good place to begin is at the beginning. Who did you grow up thinking you needed to be to belong and to be accepted, to be considered worthy of love and attention, to be seen and valued in the world?

*

I was born at St Helen's Hospital in Newtown, Wellington, in April 1977. I'm the third of us four boys: Jon is six years older than me, Andrew is four years older and Chris is four years younger. My dad, Brian Henry Wood, hailed from the East End of London. He was a boy during World War II. He didn't tell us a hell of a lot about the war, but in later years he told me bits and pieces. He was evacuated from London when it was widely believed the Germans were about to begin a bombing campaign, but he was there when the Germans did launch the Blitz. He remembers watching dogfights between aircraft in the skies overhead as he walked to school, and picking up shrapnel. Although he never really said anything about this experience when we were kids, there was evidence of its impact: he was strongly opposed to our wearing black clothes, for example, as it reminded him of the Gestapo.

When he was 16, he joined the merchant marine as an apprentice. He probably had many adventures in this trade. He told me a few. On his first voyage, his ship was nearly sunk by a huge wave near the Horn of Africa. Another time, his vessel was steaming up the Saigon River to deliver ammunition to the French, who were involved in a war with the Indochinese (now known as the Vietnamese); the crew had to keep their heads down due to the constant risk of coming under fire from the jungle.

Dad rose steadily through the ranks and by the time he was 28 and had sat and passed the tests for his Foreign-Going Master's ticket, like a lot of other British seamen, he realised he had reached a dead end. The British economy, and the maritime industry in particular, were still rebuilding, and opportunities were few and far between. You basically had to wait for someone to die for a captain's position to come available. Dad had visited New Zealand on one of his voyages and liked the place. He made the decision to emigrate, and took a position with the Waterfront Commission, an agency set up by the New Zealand government to mediate between shipowners and the unions. Soon after settling in Wellington, he met and married my mum.

Mum, Mary Jean Thomas, was the fourth child of seven siblings. Her father, Norman, was also a seafarer. I don't know much about my maternal grandmother, Flora, other than that she and Norman divorced in 1961 and she used to try and whack whoever was closest if any of us boys were annoying her. Mum lived most of her life in Wellington. When she was 12 years old she was sent to boarding school at Wairarapa College. I don't know much about this part of her life, or much of her life at all really. Unfortunately, she died before I was old enough or mature enough to get to know her as a person. That said, I always remember her as a kind and gentle woman and know she had that reputation among my friends, too. I also remember that she had a great sense of humour and her laugh was a familiar sound in the house. Once all of us boys had started school, she worked at the BNZ as a teller and later a retail banker. My parents' marriage always seemed a happy one to me. Mum and Dad would kiss each other hello when they saw each other after work, and I never heard them raise their voices at each other.

My childhood was a Boy's Own idyll. I certainly didn't have what I would consider a hard upbringing. We lived beyond the fringes of Wellington city on the road out to Makara beach, where Dad had a few acres. There was a paddock grazed by sheep and rabbits, a pine forest that climbed the steep hillside behind the house, a stream stocked with eels, and even an abandoned gold mine on the next-door property. From the moment I was big enough to walk, I followed my brothers everywhere as they built forts, lit fires, fished for eels and hunted the rabbits with homemade bows and arrows. We were given plenty of freedom. We had a border collie named Maggie, and as long as someone could see Maggie, they had a pretty good idea where the toddler (me) was.

Once, a neighbour lost control of a heavy gorse roller that weighed several tonnes. It had detached from his bulldozer and plunged down the hillside into the bush. My brothers and I went on a mission to find it, and I remember the thrill we had when we located it in the streambed. On another occasion, when there had been a scrub fire, we were poking about in the ashes and Jon came across the charred corpse of a possum. He lifted a nearby rock and dropped it on the animal. The possum was crispy on the outside, but liquefied within, and the horrible stuff inside

14

spurted everywhere, mostly on Andrew. We yelled with horror and delight.

*

Growing up as the junior member of a tribe of three, I spent much of my time tagging along on my brothers' adventures, but like most younger siblings, I also became accustomed to being on the receiving end of some rough stuff. A couple of early anecdotes still make me smile when I think of them. When I was around three years old, Jon and Andrew tied me to a post in the horse paddock and I was there for what felt like hours before it was noticed I was missing and someone came looking for me. Another time — I wasn't much older — when Dad was sitting on the veranda with a neighbour having a drink, my brothers came and found me just as I was getting out of the bath. They began whipping me with thin lengths of bamboo and told me to run along the veranda in front of the grown-ups. I refused, but that didn't stop them whipping me.

Mostly, this kind of stuff was considered 'boys will be boys'-type behaviour and I certainly don't remember it as traumatic. It was all just part and parcel of growing up as a middle child in the early 1980s. We weren't often disciplined, but when we were, it was strictly within the norms of the day. Mum would give us a smack on the bum for misdemeanours, and for more serious offences she would get out the wooden spoon. Any misdeed too grave for her tariff of punishments and she would issue the dreaded: 'Wait until your father gets home.' Not that Dad was much of a disciplinarian. In the heat of the moment he would give you the occasional whack on the backside with his left hand, or twist your ear, but this was never prolonged.

Fortunately for us he concurred with his own mother's insistence that a grown man should never use his superior strength to a child's disadvantage. The shame you felt having to explain to him what you had done tended to be the worst bit. Mum did most of the hands-on parenting, I suppose. Dad was a quiet, retiring man who was very comfortable in his own company. When he wasn't at work he would often open the newspaper with a flourish at the breakfast table and sit behind it like a wall, responding to any attempts to engage him in conversation with a repertoire of non-committal noises: 'Mmmm', 'Huh', 'Aha'. Because I didn't know how to get the attention I craved from Dad, I suppose (looking back) I fastened on my older brother Jon instead. I idolised him, and tried to impress him in the only way that I knew how: by being tough and brave.

*

I was a socially confident child by the time I started at Makara Model School, which is another way of saying I was cocky and cheeky. I was never a particularly emotional or sensitive kid, yet I was someone who made friends pretty quickly. I remember a couple of them, Lexie and Guy, and there were plenty of others. But soon after I'd started — it can't have been more than six months — Mum and Dad decided we needed to move over the hill to Karori to make things easier for Mum, who did all the running around getting Jon and Andrew to school and sports. Dad found a section in a new subdivision on the outskirts of the suburb, where Wellington peters out into rugged, scrubby hills, and work started on a new house with the help of one of my uncles, who did the bulldozing. In the meantime, we shifted into a rented house near Karori mall and I started at Karori West

School. I hadn't been there long when one day I raced a couple of my new mates down from a tree we had climbed, the branch I was holding broke and I fell like a sack of spuds. I won the race, but at a price. I broke my arm and my leg. Looking back, I can see I was what they call in the literature a 'high sensation-seeker'.

It was probably because of this, and the fact I had grown up in the company of my older brothers, that I made friends with some of the older, tougher kids at school. My friend Fish was typical of the set I was drawn to. He was a couple of years older and lived not far from me, and when I was around six years old, he took me on what was my first burglary. We went to a local kindy and he threw a brick through the window. We stole some Blu-tack, and still to this day I remember the feeling of being somewhere I shouldn't have been. He was an accomplished shoplifter, and he would take me along as he raided dairies or the supermarket for cigarettes, which he would then smoke.

There was a group of us — Fish, Colin, Martin — who would regularly shoplift jelly crystals from the supermarket and walk down the creek munching on them. Inevitably we came under suspicion, the school was notified and we were summoned one by one to the headmaster. When my turn came, I was given the choice of the strap or having my parents called.

No contest. I held out my hand and received six whacks from the Education Department-issue strip of half-inch-thick leather.

It wasn't much later that corporal punishment was banned from New Zealand schools, but old habits died hard for some teachers at Karori West. Even once it had become illegal, the odd blow with a broomstick would be delivered by one of the older teachers, and some still sought your attention in class by throwing wooden blackboard dusters at you. My most memorable breach of the new rules by a teacher occurred when my friend Colin and

I had been sent to the corridor for some general misdemeanour. Colin then made the mistake of delivering a Nazi-style salute to the Jewish teacher who had sent us out. We must have been about ten years old at the time and I am sure Colin had no idea of what he was doing, but the teacher completely lost control and before he knew what had hit him, Colin found himself pinned to the wall by the throat.

This should give you an idea of how much more normal violence was in those days. That said, while a degree of violence seemed acceptable, thuggish behaviour was not. My brothers and I played war games, and more or less assumed we would have careers built around a life of adventure and combat against baddies — we'd join the infantry, we reckoned, and then Special Forces. Our grandparents in England understood this and sent us Action Man figures and kid-sized army fatigues. Jon, Andrew and I all got into martial arts. First up, we did judo, a relatively defensive discipline focused upon grappling and throwing rather than striking. I loved it. I loved the physical contact. And with bigger brothers as sparring partners, I was inspired by the philosophy of using a bigger, stronger opponent's advantages against him. Judo is all about mental and physical efficiency, and even though Dad was the one who encouraged judo, I still remember his reaction to us bringing home Rising Sun badges after having the opportunity to train with the Japanese judo team when they visited New Zealand. His experience in World War II meant there was no way he was having those in the house and they were promptly binned.

Soon Jon learned of a more staunch martial art called kempo. Often considered the first hybrid martial art, kempo used a range of striking techniques as well as the throws, grapples, chokes and twists we were accustomed to, all in line with the notion that a fighter should be equipped to adapt their style to the requirements of the fight. The primary local dojo was in Paraparaumu, but a satellite had opened nearby. Jon and I both joined and trained three times a week in addition to our regular judo training. When we weren't training we watched martial arts movies and staged competitions at home. These often included my friend Richard, who had moved down to Wellington from the Far North and also trained in kempo. It wasn't long before I knew I wanted to be a ninja, and we spent a fair bit of time up on Wrights Hill where there was a fort built during World War II, when it was feared the Japanese might invade. There was a gun emplacement, and beneath it, a labyrinth of concrete tunnels. These had been blocked off with steel doors, but you could get in where the steel had been wrenched or cut open. We spent hours up there, ninja-ing around in the dark.

Not surprisingly, we soon acquired a reputation for being pretty tough. We weren't bullies, in that we considered it beneath our dignity to pick a fight with those smaller, younger or weaker than ourselves — we practised violence with a code. Jon would never pick fights with people; he was just very good at finishing the fights that found him. He was someone who would stand up for others who were being bullied and wouldn't go beyond the violence required of him in a situation. Unfortunately, much of that nuance was lost on me as I observed Jon. It became my goal to be known as the toughest kid in my year at school, and I actively sought opportunities to fight bigger, older kids. Fighting was a common way to measure yourself where I grew up. I remember having full-on fights with friends — without animosity, but just in the interests of seeing how we each measured up. My younger brother recently reminded me of the arranged fights that used to occur for this purpose down at the cricket nets of Karori Park, an area of Karori he and his friends fondly referred to as the 'wild west'. Mum and Dad knew nothing about this, because it was rare for me to come home with cuts or bruises. When I got in a fight, I usually won. One of the few times I didn't and only time Dad became aware of my fighting and put a stop to it was when I was 12 years old and had just had orthodontic braces put on my teeth (at great expense to my parents). A guy I considered a friend headbutted me in the mouth without warning. It knocked my front teeth out, flattened my whole bottom row of teeth, and left me unconscious on the footpath. When I woke up I mumbled my intention for retribution and stumbled home. Dad asked me what had happened and I told him I had fallen over while dancing and hit my face on the curb. He took me straight to the local medical centre and the doctor on duty put on a glove and then pulled my bottom row of teeth back into place before reinserting the top two teeth, which had come out from their roots but had remained hanging from the new braces. Dad didn't buy my story about falling over. I can't remember whether he got the truth out of me or otherwise found out what had happened, but once he did, he went and spoke to the other father to let them know he expected that to be the last of it.

I occasionally got into fights at home too. Not with Jon, though; he was not only a natural and well-trained fighter but also my hero in this respect. Andrew, on the other hand, was closer in age, but just bigger and older enough to make the contests pretty uneven. In most of our battles, I tended to try to land a telling blow then run for the only room in the house that had a lock on the door — the bathroom — and take refuge in there. The bathroom door was soon pocked with multiple holes punched or kicked by angry older siblings while their younger brother cowered on the other side.

'You kids!' Mum would shout. 'Go outside if you want to fight!'

When parents weren't around to intervene, might became right, and you earned the chance to have a say — what channel we watched on TV, for example — by fighting for it. School friends were sometimes too intimidated by my brothers to come around to our place. I found out from my mate Richard that his parents had been told by a teacher not to let him associate with me because I came from a violent family. I thought it was rubbish at the time. My parents certainly weren't violent and I didn't think it applied to us boys either. In fact, the only time it ever dimly occurred to me that we might be slightly unusual with respect to violence was one day when we had a kid come and stay with us as a billet as part of a school exchange. He and I were watching telly when Andrew came in and changed the channel. We squared off and started fighting. Punches and grapples were getting me nowhere, so I went into the kitchen and came back with a long serrated bread knife. As our horrified house guest looked on, I advanced on Andrew, taking experimental swipes at him as he effortlessly danced and dodged out of the way. The kid jumped up and ran off to his room, crying.

I looked at Andrew. Andrew looked at me.

'What's up with him?' he said, jerking a thumb after him. I shrugged.

'Boys,' Mum later explained, 'not everyone is as violent as you.'

At the time I interpreted Jon's interest in developing his martial arts skills as a means to be a good fighter and a tough guy, but I now realise Jon was always someone who wanted to challenge himself and it just so happened that much of this energy was directed towards martial arts. A few years later, Jon was arrested and charged with assault after one such a test of his progress. When his day in court came, the magistrate studied the innocent-looking teenager before him and the three tough young men he was supposed to have knocked unconscious in an alleyway.

'Him, against the three of them?' he said to the prosecuting sergeant, making no effort to conceal his scorn.

The case was dismissed. Later Jon told me the police had chosen to prosecute this case only because he was my brother and they wanted to get at me.

Jon's ability to win a fight against multiple opponents was exactly the sort of thing I considered cool growing up, and the sort of thing I aspired to. I thought this was what it meant to be a man. I thought that having courage and being tough meant you could and would take on all comers, use violence to solve your problems, stand on your own two feet and never need the support of others. My view of masculinity these days is, in many respects, the opposite of this. Now I believe that to be a man and to be courageous is being able to solve problems without violence, showing vulnerability and asking for support when you need it; being able to accept and own the emotions that make you feel weak; and being open and willing to share your life with others rather than trying to be an island unto yourself.

*

When I was 12, Mum was diagnosed with breast cancer. I didn't really know what was going on and was scared to find out, so her sickness and treatment occurred on the periphery of my consciousness. She had a mastectomy, followed by a course of radiotherapy that made her hair fall out and left her exhausted all the time. I wish I could say mum's sickness motivated me to provide more help around the house and do what I could to make her and Dad's life easier, but instead I started gravitating towards some of the rougher people in my neighbourhood. Mum and Dad were so focused on her treatment and recovery they didn't notice, or if they did, they lacked the time and energy to do anything about it. Looking back, I just don't think they had any idea where the small steps I was taking off the path were leading me.

I was a physically big kid — about six feet tall by the time I hit my teens. I also looked a lot older than I was, which meant that by the age of 13 I could buy alcohol with my brother's driver's licence — this was before photo ID became the norm. I started hanging out with a tougher, older crew than my school mates. Some were from families already mixed up in gangs and crime, in some cases over multiple generations. Most of these kids were petty criminals themselves, but I had no reason to hold this against them. Instead, the fact these cool kids — tough guys, graffiti artists, breakdancers — accepted me was a real thrill. While there would be the odd theft and property crime, most of the mischief we got up to was purely for entertainment, excitement and adventure. We would always be on the streets and whenever the police would pull over to speak to us we would run away in different directions. We weren't normally up to anything, but the adrenaline rush of having the police out of their car and chasing us in a footrace was hard to beat! We all knew the area well and I became very skilled at jumping fences and racing through people's property to avoid capture. Running away from the police was mostly viewed as a game, especially when we hadn't been doing anything at the time, but it led me to view other types of law-breaking as exciting ways to test myself and satisfy my craving for thrills. (Today my advice to parents in this situation would be to adopt a 'broken windows' policy towards their teen and his or her peer group. That means don't let the small things go; don't let the questionable associations stand, even if they are only questionable. To do so is to invite a progression towards greater miscreance and associated outcomes.)

Some of the guys I was hanging out with were on the fringes of gangs and I was soon a member of the Home Boys, a bunch of teens who were prospects — apprentices, if you like — for the 21s, a gang of young men who were peers with my older brother Jon. There were several of these gangs around at the time. Inevitably, I got on the wrong side of one of them, the TKs — the 'Tropical Kings' — mostly Pacific Islanders from Rongotai College. I started getting threatening phone calls at home, which led to an arranged fight between myself and Ian, a member of the TKs, a muscular sixth former from Rongotai. I was wiry and tough, but I was still only a third former.

'I hear you're talking shit about the TKs,' he said over the phone. 'I'm gonna bust your face for that.'

'Like to see you try,' I answered.

With a show of apoplectic rage, he promised to smash me, kill me — all the usual threats. We arranged to meet a few days later to have a fight at a secluded spot on the campus of the Teachers' Training College in Karori.

On the day before the rumble, I was walking through the Karori shops deep in thought when I felt a hand on my shoulder. It was Andrew Saunders, the local community cop. He fixed me in his steely gaze and said: 'Are you going to be alive after tomorrow?'

'Yeah,' I shrugged.

He nodded, and let me go.

When the day and time came, the TK crew arrived by bus from the city. I wasn't there to meet them, but Jon was. One of the TK guys was mouthing off, challenging anyone who wanted to fight. Jon took him up on it, and promptly broke his ribs with a side kick and threw him on the ground.

That didn't make the TKs any fonder of the Wood boys. By the time they arrived at the training college, I was there with my crew. There were probably fifty people there, some supporting Ian, some supporting me, and lots just there for the gladiatorial entertainment. I squared up to my opponent. I had a plan, and I wasted no time in executing it. I kicked Ian as hard as I could in the nuts and swung my fist into his face. Both blows had zero effect. I later learned he was wearing a cricketer's box, and as for the punch: well, he was a big guy, and I was still just a kid.

He retaliated by returning the favour, kicking me in the nuts so hard it lifted me off the ground. It's amazing what you can cope with when it feels like you're fighting for your life, and I did what I could to defend myself, but I was only saved from a severe beating by the sound of sirens approaching fast. Everyone scattered before the cops arrived, except me. The best I could do was crawl into the bushes and hide. As the adrenaline faded from my bloodstream, pain like I'd never felt before swamped me and I lay there, doubled up and heaving my guts out. With the brawlers broken up and everyone dispersed, the cops didn't hang around, but soon after they'd gone, I heard a car pull up. Footsteps approached the area where I was lying.

'Paul?'

It was my dad, face like thunder.

I crawled out of my hidey hole.

I'd hardly ever seen him this pissed off. As it turned out, he didn't know about the brawl — I'd left a candle burning in my bedroom, and it had started a small fire. In fact, Dad and Mum had no idea of the extent of fighting we were engaged in, or any of the other criminal behaviour I was starting to immerse myself in.

The whole episode had a sequel. The guy whose ribs Jon broke apparently told his older gang member relatives that he had been minding his own business with his girlfriend when he was jumped by the Wood brothers. Well, they weren't standing for that. A carload of them came up to Karori looking for us. They didn't find us, but they did see a group of our mates hanging out on the benches outside the library. They piled out of the car, attacked the three guys who were there and shoved one of them into their car, where they continued to beat him as they drove.

'You're gonna show us where those fucken Woods live,' they told him.

When they got to our house, they hid in the shrubs and bushes outside our house while my poor mate was sent to knock on the door and get us outside. None of us were home. It was my mum who answered the door to a bruised and bleeding teen.

'What's happened to you?' she asked.

'There's some guys out here who are going to give Jon and Paul a hiding,' he replied.

Mum told him to come into the house and wait and then marched outside.

'I know you're out there,' she yelled. 'Come out, you boys.'

Several heavies stood up from the shrubbery, holding weapons of various descriptions.

After swearing at and abusing my mum, they hopped in their car and drove away. Later that week Jon and some others from our crew headed into town and found the TKs in the spacies parlour where they hung out.

'I'm Jon Wood. I hear you guys are looking for me and someone wants to fight me. Well, here I am.'

None of them were quite so tough then.

*

As we got older, the toys used in the games we were playing became more dangerous. I remember one day when I was about 14, I was at home, grounded because I'd been arrested on suspicion of burgling the Karori library (I had), and Jon came home covered in blood. He'd been at a party, and had been bottled.

'Come on,' he said.

I grabbed the first weapon I could find — a claw hammer — and we headed out to settle the score. As it turned out, the bottling had been done by the brother of one of Jon's friends. By the time we got there Jon's emotions had cooled and he decided not to escalate the situation. Looking back on it now, I recognise it as an example of Jon doing the right thing rather than the easier, more violent thing, but I was so focused on how tough Jon was that I completely missed this lesson and assumed it was about delaying retaliation rather than turning the other cheek. Not too many nights after this, Jon came home bleeding again. He'd gate-crashed someone's twenty-first in the Ngaio Community Hall with two other friends, and several people had jumped them. They'd been bottled multiple times. We grabbed baseball bats and drove to Ngaio. There, we found the crowd from the hall drifting up the street, being followed unhurriedly by police in riot gear and carrying batons. We went ahead of the police and set about hunting down the guys who had used bottles on Jon and his friends then giving them a good beating.

This was all par for the course for me, in those days. Violence was just part of who I was. It was how I defined masculinity: to be a man, you had to be tough and uncompromising. The only emotion you could show was anger. You never showed weakness. Part of me wishes I could reach back in time and shake my younger self and tell him that being a man is about owning and managing your emotions, and that having them is normal, just a function of how your brain works. Strength, I would tell him, lies not in denying weakness but in being able to make yourself vulnerable through leaning into and managing your weaknesses. But another part of me knows I wouldn't have listened.

Around this time, I fell in with a guy I'll call Fagan, because like the Dickensian character, he wasn't adverse to getting others to commit crimes for his profit. Meeting Fagan and choosing to hang out with him was one of those small choices that had significant repercussions for my future.

Fagan was a couple of years older than me, and from a family with a history of intergenerational crime. At that stage, he wasn't a patched member of a gang — someone who had completed their 'apprenticeship' and had a patch on their vest to prove it — but he had gang affiliations and would later get his patch. I can see now he was probably also a psychopath. He seemed to delight in setting up situations where the stakes could run as high as life and death, purely, as far as I could tell, for his own amusement. Once, he told me that a drug dealer he knew of, who lived and plied his trade from a block of flats in the inner-city suburb of Newtown, was going to be away. Fagan was interested in the stash of drugs and cash he kept in the apartment, and he wanted me to go and burgle the place.

'If you had any balls, you'd do it,' he remarked.

That's all it took, in those days. Any challenge to my manhood, and I'd be up for whatever was suggested. My mother's generation used to talk about children who were 'easily led' and that was me. It was probably blindingly obvious to everyone that I had a desperate need for approval. To a psychopath like Fagan, the knowledge was like a remote control. He pushed the buttons and I did just about anything he wanted.

I walked down the dingy hall of the block of flats to the door of the apartment. I had a bag of tools and was an accomplished burglar by now, so the door wouldn't present much of a challenge to me. But as a preliminary precaution, I tried the door handle, and to my surprise, it turned.

'Sweet,' I thought.

Fagan had told me the drugs and money were in the bedroom, so I sauntered in that direction. I entered the lounge, which was on my route. The drug dealer, a huge man, was sitting there on the couch, his arm slung around a woman sitting next to him. I stopped dead. They both stared at me.

'What the fuck?' he said, menacingly.

'Where's Uncle Norm?' I replied.

'*What*?'

'This is Uncle Norm's place, isn't it?' I said.

They kept staring at me. My youth, and my shock and surprise, probably saved me.

'No, it's not. There's no Norm here, so fuck off.'

I fucked off gladly.

Another time, Fagan said he wanted me to come along with him while he spun some sort of deal in Dannevirke, near Hawke's Bay. We drove up there and parked outside a house, a run-down place with the curtains tightly drawn against the sunshine. Fagan pulled a shotgun from under his seat and handed it to me.

'I'm going in there,' he said. 'Watch the windows. If I don't give the signal within ten minutes, you'd better come in and shoot anything that moves.'

'What signal?' I said, stunned by the cool, lethal weight of the gun in my hands.

'I'll move a curtain,' he said.

He went and knocked. The door opened and a face briefly peered out at me from the dim interior past his shoulder. Then the door closed behind him, and I was left sweating. Minutes passed. Then, to my profound relief, a curtain in the designated window twitched and Fagan gave me the thumbs-up. I poked the gun back under the seat and went to the door. Fagan let me in and introduced me to the occupant of the house: his brother.

I never knew what to make of all that.

Yet another time, a guy I knew to have been a good mate of Fagan's committed suicide, according to Fagan because of injuries he'd sustained when he was attacked with a baseball bat. Soon afterwards, Fagan, another mate and I were in Mid City nightclub, in Courtenay Place (I was still well underage, but I was tall and had Jon's driver's licence with me).

Fagan nudged me.

'Over there,' he said. 'That's one of the arseholes that attacked Mark.'

I looked where he pointed.

'We're going to take him out as soon as he leaves,' Fagan said. 'You up for that? You got the balls?'

I needed no further encouragement. Someone went out to the car and came back with a couple of knives and a set of nunchaku. We watched until the man left, whereupon we followed.

'Go on,' Fagan said.

I sped up. My target sensed I was there and turned to face me. I punched him in the face, but as in the stoush with Ian, I lacked the size and bulk to make it count. He made to fight back, so I whipped the knife out. He continued to advance on me, so I tried to stab him in the neck. Fortunately, the blade was broken off at the tip, so it had no sharp point and didn't penetrate.

We were right outside a pub, and dozens of people were watching.

'Come on,' my mate said. 'We'd better get the fuck out of here. They'll be calling the cops.'

We ran off. As we did, one of us dropped the other knife by mistake — a great big ugly Ginsu thing. The bloke I'd cut grabbed it and chased us. He managed to catch my mate and give him three deep wounds in the butt and lower back.

We got in a taxi and I gave the driver our address. On the way, I told the driver I needed to throw up. The driver pulled over and stopped: I opened the door, leaned out and pretended to puke while I dropped the knife in the gutter.

We hadn't got much further when I began to worry about my friend, who was very pale and beginning to lose consciousness.

'My mate's hurt,' I said. 'We need to get him some help.'

The driver turned around and headed for the Wellington Free Ambulance base in Thorndon.

Because he had a warrant out for his arrest for escaping custody — he had been in court in Whanganui facing firearms and cultivation charges when he'd simply jumped out of the dock and done a runner — my mate wasn't keen for the police to be involved. But, of course, the nature of his injuries meant the police soon were. I told them we had been attacked, quite unprovoked, but as I was sitting waiting in the watch house, a door opened and a man came in. He did a double take when he saw me.

'That's one of them,' he said. 'That's one of the attackers.'

The cops dragged me back into the interview room, and tried to sort out the conflicting stories. Whether I managed to come across plausibly enough to cast doubt in their minds or whether I was so young they didn't quite know how to deal with me, I'm not sure, but I was let go without any charges being laid.

*

Wrights Hill was the focal point for all kinds of antisocial activity. Quite often, when we went up there, the tunnels would be echoing with bangs as people let off fireworks or (on occasion) fired real guns. There were some people who liked tinkering with explosives, making pipe bombs and flash-bangs and stuff. Once, I happened to be watching a guy carefully packing some potion he'd brewed up into a container when there was a sudden, shocking flash and bang. His hands were flayed like burst sausages, and he started screaming. His mates recovered from the ringing in their ears and bundled him out of there, bleeding and howling. My brother Jon gathered up the chemicals so that he could do his own experiments.

The stakes were being ratcheted higher all the time. And the ingredients for improvised explosive devices weren't the most dangerous chemicals I was dabbling with, either. By now, I'd discovered drugs.

CHAPTER TWO

Point of No Return

Anyone looking at me in my teenage years might have muttered to themselves that I was heading for prison. They were wrong only in the sense that I was already there.

When I was around 13, a family friend, who would play a crucial role in my eventual rehabilitation, once remarked to me that I was pretty antisocial. I remember scoffing at this pronouncement and being quite confused by it. I had lots of friends and I liked hanging out. What was he talking about?

What he was talking about was my inability to express points of view or indulge in behaviours calculated to promote the good of society. With me it was quite the contrary.

I was young. We're usually quite young when we start going off the rails, and we don't usually notice it. The world as we see it is our normal. And it's often impulses channelled in the wrong direction that are to blame. We're social animals. Everyone, young and old, needs to fit in, and it's this desire to be part of a tribe and to enjoy status within it that often drives us. Anthropologists call it a 'prestige economy'. To earn prestige within my peer group, to be valued and considered worthy of respect, I had to be tough, violent, uncompromising and up for anything. Parents would do well to ask what is it that their child regards as prestigious behaviour among their peers, what leads them to feel valued, worthy and that they belong?

Much of the psychological literature talks about 'self-defeating beliefs' and 'self-fulfilling prophecies' — our unexamined beliefs that condition what we consider to be our range of life choices. One of my favourite psychologists, Carol Dweck, became a leader in the study of this kind of disordered thinking. While examining why many people are capable of achieving far more than they do but don't attempt or even aspire to try to realise their potential, Dweck wondered whether teachers influence this kind of thinking. For example, if your teacher makes it clear to you they don't believe you can perform a task satisfactorily, does this colour your own perception of your abilities? In many cases, she found it did: a teacher signals to you you're no good at art and don't have a hope of passing the exam, so you lose any enthusiasm you may have had for art and fail the exam. The prophecy has fulfilled itself.

Nor are teachers or parents or sports coaches the only source of self-fulfilling prophecies. We're each capable of telling ourselves we're not up to any given task. When much later in life I read about this 'cognitive distortion' (disordered thought process), it rang true. The only valid career option I could see for myself was as a criminal or in the army, perhaps (one day) in the SAS. I'd even done the initial enlistment assessments. I didn't see much need for education in either line of work. But, beneath this was a deep-seated, corrosive fear, which was the underlying cognitive distortion. I was afraid — indeed, pretty convinced — that I might not be capable of achieving academically, so I assured myself that the criminal future or army career I imagined were the only possible futures. This belief sabotaged my academic performance.

It's this kind of disordered thinking — let's call it negative ideation — that puts bars on the windows and doors of what we consider to be possible. It's important to identify and understand the kinds of negative ideation you languish beneath. You're worthless, right? You're dumb, bad at maths, have no aptitude for sport. People of the opposite sex won't look at you ... Think the worst thing you can think about yourself that you believe or even fear to be true. Then try to work out where the idea came from and challenge it. None of us is born with a worldview. Ideation — literally, the formation of ideas — is what happens as we grow and develop.

Life isn't about finding yourself; it's about creating yourself. If we're lucky, we arrive at adulthood with a clear sense of our strengths and weaknesses and our possibilities. But most of us aren't this lucky. Along the way, we will have come to believe things about ourselves that will hold us back. It's these mistaken beliefs that are the building blocks of our mental prisons.

*

I was in third form (about 13 or 14), my first year at Wellington College, when I started selling drugs. I was given an ounce of dope 'on tick' (promise of payment) by an older guy I'd trained with at kempo. Fagan showed me how to measure it out and package it up in tinfoil. At this stage I wasn't into smoking dope as much as drinking, and I was drinking plenty. My sports were suffering. I wasn't enjoying kempo anymore, and when I competed my attitude was sometimes so bad I was disqualified for excessive aggression. I had been doing heaps of skateboarding and had become quite good — and it satisfied my thrill-seeking tendencies. I'd even attracted a sponsor, and my younger brother Chris was inspired by my example to take it up, too. But whereas he was driven, and went on to achieve great things — he competed on the professional circuit for over ten years, and won a number of international titles, including in the X Games — I preferred to hang out with my mates, drink, fight, and do crime, and I let skateboarding slide. Drinking and fighting and criminal ventures were ways to fit in, and they earned my new peers' respect. Dad tried to intervene, demanding I reinvolve myself in skateboarding or some other sport. He was right in his intuition that I needed a positive outlet for my energy and something to occupy my time. I half-heartedly tried picking skateboarding back up but lacked the motivation; I just got better at pretending to my parents I was spending my time productively.

By now, any interest I'd ever had in school had pretty much fallen away, too. I started wagging more and more, and increasingly when I bothered to go to school, which was usually on a Monday or a Friday, it was to sell tinnies — small amounts of marijuana wrapped in tinfoil — to my school mates. For the rest of the time, I became adept at forging my mother's signature on notes excusing my absences. When my form teacher occasionally raised my patchy attendance, I always shrugged, looked at my toes and said: 'Troubles at home, miss.' That shut the conversation down immediately. There was more than a grain of truth in what I was saying, even though Mum's prognosis was good, and the school was reluctant to challenge me.

The crowd I was hanging with were very much into crime. I'm not sure how much my parents suspected I was getting into deeper and deeper trouble. Dad would occasionally blow his stack at me when something obvious would occur — like the time I came stumbling home drunk at three in the morning. But, to be fair, they couldn't have known the full extent of my activities, as I was very deceptive, and would normally just tell them I was staying at a friend's house to give me free rein. Their focus was elsewhere. Mum was putting her energy into recovering, and Dad, who had never been a particularly interventionist parent anyway, was wholly focused on looking after her.

Jon knew I was going down a different road to him, however. While Jon had had a reputation for being a fearsome streetfighter, in many respects it was a role he had been drawn into by others' perceptions of him. He attended Scouts through his college years, was always involved in college sports, went straight from college to university to do a degree in psychology, and joined the army as an officer within a week of graduating. He also maintained a strong anti-drugs stance, which led me to hide those activities from him. Some years later, while he was on leave from the army, we were at a party together. He got in my face and started telling me I should pick up the nearby bottle and hit him if I thought I was such a tough guy. I knew he didn't want to look bad by giving me a hiding without provocation and was trying to get me to make the first move, but I wasn't going to make *that* mistake. Even then I think I recognised this was Jon attempting an intervention. He cared. He wanted to beat the shit out of me for the drugs I was doing and the crimes I was committing, but for reasons of honour, he needed me to throw the first punch.

I wasn't at all aware of my own feelings. There was stuff I wasn't dealing with. Not that long before, when I was about 13, I had been sexually abused, although I didn't recognise it as sexual abuse for many years. I had been downtown with Fagan, stealing from cars and generally making mischief. We were somewhere in the back alleys off Cuba Street, and I had gone off on my own. Someone called out to me. By the manner of her dress, it was clear she was a prostitute. She beckoned me over. I hesitated, but not for long. It was only when I got closer that I realised 'she' was a fa'afafine — a Samoan transsexual. By then she had her hands on me and was drawing me with practised ease into a doorway. I was confused, because I was aroused, but nothing about this scenario squared with my notions of my sexuality. She gave me a blowjob. It felt wrong — deeply wrong — but it also had me physically aroused. It was an extremely confusing experience for me and while I tried to bury all thoughts about it, it left the shadow of a worry about my masculinity on the periphery of my consciousness. I now recognise the role this experience had in my subsequent over-compensatory attempts to show I was a man and the niggling fears I had that there was something wrong with me.

It was only in the weeks and months afterwards that I felt the impact of this encounter. I didn't see myself as a victim — every fibre of my being was conditioned to avoid thinking of myself as weak or vulnerable — so I rationalised what had happened as some disgusting flaw in myself. Yet I didn't interrogate this notion too deeply, either. Homosexuality was a taboo subject for many New Zealanders, and it wasn't really discussed in our household: being British, Dad was pretty reticent about all matters sexual, let alone anything outside the norm. All of us knew that a sure way to spark Dad into taking disciplinary action was to call your brother a faggot or question his masculinity in some similar way. Even if I'd felt remotely inclined to tell anyone what had happened, my family culture would have precluded it. And of course, I wasn't accustomed to admitting to any kind of weakness or seeking help. Mum was always dispensing kindness and sympathy when she had the time or energy, but it would have seemed weird for me to go looking for it. The only appropriate outlet for pain and shame was rage.

*

I was going out with a Chilean girl named Carla at this time. We were keen on each other for a while. Even after I'd broken up with her and she started going out with a mate of mine, we stayed friends. Her family must have liked me and felt concerned about the way I was going. When they planned to return to Chile, her parents offered to take me with them, even though I was still just fifteen. On the morning of their day of departure, Carla's mother even came to court, where I was appearing on burglary charges relating to a string of break-ins my crew had carried out. My lawyer told the judge I had a ticket booked for Chile and Carla's mum stood up and told the judge they would take responsibility for me in Chile. The police prosecutor had no objection, so the court looked on this scheme favourably. The charges were dropped on condition I boarded the plane for Chile.

I walked out of court, went home, packed my bag, said my goodbyes, and that afternoon I was on my way to South America.

I was in Chile for about a year, and it was an interesting experience. Carla's family weren't wealthy, like the families who typically host exchange students. They had fled the repressive Pinochet regime in the 1970s, and were only now returning to try to rebuild their lives. We lived with some of Carla's relatives in a house on top of a steep hill in La Florida, a suburb of Valparaiso. Coming from a relatively wealthy country like New Zealand it was a real eye-opener for me. The family's standard of living wasn't flash and there were eight of us living in a four-bedroom house, but even so, it was a big step up from the shacks crowding the steep hillsides and some of the valley.

Carla's parents had told me in no uncertain terms that if I started fighting and carrying on the way I had in New Zealand, I would be on the next plane home. I stayed out of trouble, partly because of this ultimatum, but also because the scene was so different in Chile. There was lots of drinking and drugs — the weed wasn't as good as the Kiwi stuff but there was cocaine, which I'd never seen in New Zealand — but because some people carried guns, you didn't tend to get as many fights breaking out as you do when the stakes are lower. It's also probably an illustration of how your peer group determines your behaviour: my Chilean friends weren't into fighting when they were drunk the way my Kiwi friends were. They didn't seem to tell themselves the same unhelpful stories about what it means to be a man. As a result, I didn't feel the same need to prove myself.

Not that my time there was without incident. One night, after we'd been drinking down in the valley, a friend and I were faced with the walk home up the hill. Rather than take the direct route, which went virtually straight up, we decided we'd take a road that cut across the hillside. It led through a poor area, and it was dark and apparently deserted. We saw a car — it looked like one of the 'informal' taxis that abound in Chile — parked in an out-of-the-way spot, and we could dimly make out two figures inside it. The guy I was with decided it was likely a couple doing what couples do when they're parked in secluded spots, so he banged on the car and hooted and yelled a few smart-arse remarks as we passed.

The doors flew open and two men jumped out. One of them jerked his hand out of his jacket and what little light there was gleamed on gunmetal. We didn't hang around. We took off, expecting shots. None came. We kept running till we got home.

I was doing school by correspondence in Chile, but it was of as little interest to me as it had been in Wellington. I got quite good at Spanish, because it was the only way I could reasonably expect to talk to girls. I wasn't much use at anything else.

I should have done quite well in my school exams — not through innate ability and certainly not through hard work and dedication, but because the Chilean system was heavily weighted in your favour. A few of us were doing school by correspondence, and when it came to exam time, the supervising teacher told me quite openly that I could cheat if I wanted to. I did. In another room, a student was having a bit of difficulty with her paper. The teacher in charge of the room couldn't help her, but was happy to fetch another teacher who could. When our English exams were distributed, the examiner told us we were welcome to take them home to complete them in our own time and with our own resources. Needless to say, I should have smashed English, but I didn't. I managed to lose the booklet containing the questions on my way home. Not even the Chilean system could give me a pass on the basis of an imaginary exam script!

Around the end of that year, I got a call from New Zealand. It was my mum.

'You'd better come home,' she said. 'My cancer's back. The doctors say it's terminal.'

*

I arrived back in Wellington in early 1994, not long before I turned 17. It was amazing how quickly I was reabsorbed into the life I had left behind. One difference was that I returned with a strong political awareness and a much harder edge. During my time in Chile I had heard friends of the family I was staying with talk about their experiences of being tortured when they were captured by the Pinochet regime — matter-of-fact conversations about electrocuted genitals, discussed over afternoon tea. It made me realise how good life in New Zealand was and it led me to develop a strong affinity and orientation towards the underdog. Unfortunately, living in a country that was coming out of a military dictatorship probably contributed towards me assuming the worst of those in positions of authority and righteously being against the system. In different circumstances this could have led to a pursuit of social justice or other community-minded causes. In the environment I came back into, it lent itself to feeling justified in my criminality.

The only real change in Karori was how complicated things seemed to have become. Fagan found me pretty quickly, but it turned out he had fallen out with a kid we had both been friendly with. It had escalated into a full-scale feud, with some pretty scary stuff going on. One day, Fagan threw an axe through the windscreen of the other guy's car as he was driving by: it hit him in the head and he was lucky not to be seriously injured. Another time, Fagan planted a shotgun in a car belonging to one of his rival's crew and tipped off the police, apparently in a Machiavellian scheme to have him go to jail, where he would be easy meat for some of Fagan's gang associates. Fagan's own car got blown up, in apparent retaliation. I tried to stay clear of it all, but when I wouldn't take sides against my long-time childhood friend, Fagan took it badly. I was either with him or against him. He made it clear I was guilty of unforgivable disloyalty.

I finally got my driver's licence, and I met a girl I really liked. She was about a year older than me, but it didn't last. I was pretty cut up about the way things ended and, of course, the pain just made me angry at myself for being unworthy, which in turn left me angry at the world. I soon met another girl at a party, Tania, who was half Samoan and a bit older than me and had a daughter by a previous relationship. I liked Tania, and it didn't make any difference when I found out she was an intravenous drug user.

On the contrary: being an emotionally troubled risk-taker, I was up for trying it myself. When Tania moved into the council flat next to her mother, I basically moved in as well.

We ramped up our drug use. Lots of people use drugs, but only some people become addicts. The difference between social users who are in control of their use and those who become addicted is, commonly, that addicts are using drugs to deal with mental turmoil and lack life stability. This was me. With Mum slipping further day by day, and with me having no healthy sense of connection to the community or sense of greater purpose or meaning in my life, it wasn't long before I was fully hooked on opiates. My life dream of joining the army was now an unlikely prospect. Jon advised me it was better to join as an officer than as a simple grunt. To do this, I had to pass my University Entrance exam at the end of sixth form. Dad approached Wellington College to see if I could return there, but was told there were no places available. I managed to enrol at Onslow College in the northern Wellington suburb of Johnsonville. Unfortunately, this didn't last long. I still didn't connect with study and I'd been away from the school system too long to be able to make any kind of go of it. So I decided enlisting as a grunt would be fine, especially as it wouldn't impact on me trying to achieve my ultimate goal of getting into the SAS.

Although school didn't work out, I had joined a rugby league team put together to provide a positive outlet for wayward youth in my area. It basically comprised my crew. We were playing in a men's grade that included a couple of teams entirely made up of gang members. I wasn't the biggest guy, but I was hardworking and fearless on the field. I loved the physical, confrontational nature of the game, the collisions and the way you set out to dominate your opponent. I seemed well suited to it, both physically and mentally. It gave me an activity where I could feel a sense of pride and achievement for my efforts and progress. I had some natural talent and I got out of it what I put into it.

Drugs changed all that. I lost condition — a dozen kilograms, perhaps more — and I soon had little mental space for anything other than the wretched calculations a druggie is always performing with a view to securing their next fix. Morphine was readily available, but at a price. It was far easier to steal it. To my enduring shame, I wasn't above filching some of Mum's pain medication, but Tania and others put me on to other potential sources too. They alerted me to the fact that doctors on the after-hours roster kept supplies of opiates such as liquid morphine and pethidine. They would often leave their bags, drugs and all, in their cars parked outside their homes, and helpfully, there was a list of after-hours doctors in the phone book. I also learned that morphine came from opium, which came from poppies. I'd never been the slightest bit interested in gardening before, but suddenly I knew where every flower garden was within a ten-kilometre radius. I nearly got busted one day after raiding a garden. Seeing flashing red and blue lights in your rear-view mirror is bad enough at any time, but seeing them when you have the materials for the manufacture of class A drugs aboard is something you have to have lived through to grasp. I pulled over. The cop went through the rest of the car, then asked to see what was in the boot. We both stood looking at the load of poppies, me thinking I was screwed for sure. When he didn't immediately crow with satisfaction, I realised he had probably been expecting to find a boot-full of stereo gear and other hot goods. He didn't know what he was looking at.

'What's all this?' he asked.

'I've been doing some weeding,' I replied. 'Just taking it to the rubbish tip.'

He bought the story. He gave me a ticket for driving a vehicle without a valid registration and sent me on my way.

When I couldn't scrounge or steal drugs, I was forced to buy them. I had no real source of income, so I resorted to shoplifting and peddling dope to feed my habit. Another way to access cash was to break into coke machines. These machines could hold over $500 in coins if they were in popular locations and hadn't recently been emptied. Fagan had shown me how to prise the plastic off the bottom corner of the machine, then use a larger screwdriver to prise off the bottom of the bracket that housed the coin tray, which could then be removed. If you had time, you could use a $2 coin to buy a $1 can, which would give you the $1 change from a different compartment, plus the $2 coin back from the bottom of the machine. In this way you could gain an extra $100 or so from the change compartment.

One weekend I broke into the Karori mall and stole all the money from the coke machine. It ended up being many hundreds of dollars. After this success I decided to go back and burgle some of the stores in the mall the following week. My target would be cigarettes and scratch tickets. I went there about 10 pm and climbed on the roof to find a point of access. Meanwhile my mates were across the road from the front of the mall drinking. I had a hammer with me and decided to break a reinforced window, but before I could do that I noticed the beam from flashlights up on the roof. I had been spotted climbing onto the roof and the police had been called. The roof of the Karori mall has a number of different levels and features to accommodate skylights and vents. As soon as I saw the torch beams I knew I wouldn't be able to get back down the way I had come up. I was crouched on the other side of a slope and as the police approached I took my t-shirt off and wrapped it around my head to obscure my appearance.

I wasn't going to let them catch me without giving them a damn good run for their money, but even if I did manage to get away, which seemed improbable at this point, the t-shirt would allow for plausible denial if accused. As soon as they got closer, I bolted and the chase began. At first I ran to the edge of the roof at the front of the mall, but as I looked over to assess the prospect of escape I saw two police cars and police officers waiting down below. My friends let off hoots of encouragement as they saw me look over the side. I then ran to the other side of the roof, while the police followed and my friends enjoyed the show. Most of the roof was over two storeys above ground, so jumping down wasn't an option, but there were a number of projecting verandas below that formed steps down from the main roof to the carpark area. When the torch beams got close enough to ensure I couldn't be cut off, I went for it. I sprinted as fast as I could to that side of the roof with the police in hot pursuit, then leaped down from veranda to veranda.

Unfortunately, there were more police cars in the carpark on this side of the mall; they had obviously surrounded the mall before coming onto the roof. But there was no changing my course of action at this stage. The last veranda was a single storey above the concrete of the carpark. Below, a police officer waited. I ran and jumped off the end of the roof, sailing clear over the head of the officer and hitting the ground behind him then rolling and sprinting towards the corner of the carpark, where I knew there was a hole in the fence that led to an adjoining property. I launched myself through it, then jumped the neighbouring fence and raced across the property. I carried on in this manner for about twenty houses, knowing every fence I jumped was another fence between myself, the police and any police dog, which would need to be picked up and placed over the fence before carrying on the chase. I squeezed into a drainpipe that formed part of the system through which the local stream progressed through properties and under roads towards South Karori. I knew that getting in the water would be the most effective way to ensure any police dog on my trail would lose the scent. Approximately three kilometres later I was near my good friend Karl's house at Hazlewood Avenue. I had spent much of my adolescence at Karl's house drinking, listening to hip hop and yarning. Karl put my clothes in the dryer and gave me a place to crash. My friends at the mall couldn't believe I had managed to escape and it became something of a local legend among my crew. The t-shirt had clearly worked, too, as the last I heard from the incident, the police had completely failed to identify their suspect.

Tania and I tried to get onto a methadone programme — methadone is a non-addictive opiate offered by the public health system to addicts who want to wean themselves off the habit. We were told there was a six-month wait. I knew drugs were dragging me down; I was committing more and more crime to support my habit. I told the people at the clinic as much, but it would still be a six-month wait.

It was around this time I was walking along the street when a car pulled up alongside me.

'Hey, Paul. How's it going?'

It was Fagan, grinning at me as though we were still the best of mates.

'I've got some misties. Want some?'

A 'misty' was a morphine sulphate tablet, readily converted to a form that could be drawn into the barrel of a syringe and shot into your vein. I was keen, so I got into the car.

Fagan had recently declared war on the police. He had been taking every opportunity he could to stick it to them, and had even gone to the lengths of printing pamphlets denouncing the cops and their behaviour and distributing them around Karori.

I remember the police raiding our flat around this time in response to someone having burgled the local police station. I was on the phone when the police stormed in to execute the warrant and didn't even bother to end the call. One of the police snatched the phone out of my hand and threw it on the floor. The rest of the cops began tearing the house apart. As well as failing to find anything to link us to this crime or anything else that would warrant an arrest, my general cockiness was clearly getting up the nose of one of the constables.

'You know he's a police informant, don't you?' she said to one of my flatmates.

He just curled his lip. He knew both me and the police better than that.

Disappointed, she tried again.

'I think I might let Black Power know you're a nark, Wood. How do you think they would feel about that?'

I played it cool, but the comment rattled me. I knew Fagan had Black Power connections and could put them straight on this bullshit, but I was angry. Looking back on it now, I see that this is exactly what she was trying to achieve.

The cops packed up, and as they walked to their car, my flatmates and I walked to ours.

'Better watch where you walk alone at night, Wood,' the same officer said.

'You better watch where *you* walk alone at night,' I replied.

Big mistake.

'You hear that, guys?' she said to her fellow officers, grinning. 'I feel intimidated.'

They dragged me over to their car, and they weren't exactly

gentle about it. When I made a token show of resistance, they happily pinned me to the bonnet and laid into me with their fists. One of our neighbours paused in her pottering about in her garden and leaned over the fence to see what was going on.

'You can't do that,' she called.

The cops relented, apart from accidentally on purpose smashing me into the side of the car as they tried to bundle me in. After a few more blows, I was shoved inside. The constable who had baited me was driving; a male colleague sat in the back, hanging onto the chain that connected my handcuffs.

'We got you this time, Wood,' the female constable gloated from the front, catching my eye in the rear-view mirror. 'Lucky me. I'm the first person to have arrested you as an adult, so I get the satisfaction of seeing the charges stick.'

I mumbled some smart-arse comment in reply. The cop next to me jerked the chain of the cuffs.

'You think you're pretty clever, don't you?' she continued. 'Well, you're not. We'll have you in prison before you're twenty.'

'You're not smart enough to catch me for anything worth prison,' I shot back.

The cop jerked the handcuffs again.

Nonetheless, I was never tried for this offence. The police surveilled us and our flat for some time. They raided us again. I was pretty confident they wouldn't find anything, but my heart sank when an officer emerged from the bedroom with a tiny plastic-wrapped package in her hand. It was a morphine sulphate tablet I'd lost and had been looking for for ages.

'What's this?' she asked.

'It's ringworm medication,' I said.

I couldn't believe my luck when she handed the tablet back.

*

Mum's original cancer was in her left breast. Once the breast and a few lymph nodes had been removed and she'd finished a course of radiotherapy, the doctors were reasonably confident she was free of disease. But about a year after she finished her treatment, she started getting bad pain in her back. Scans showed the cancer had metastasised to her remaining lymph nodes and to her spine. It was inoperable. Dad had been caring for her at home, but towards the end of 1995, the job was beyond him and she was moved to Mary Potter Hospice. I went along occasionally to visit her, but not as often as I should have.

Tania and I were home one day. There was a knock on the door. I opened it to find Dad standing there.

'Mum's died,' he said, and stopped.

We hugged; one of the few times I had ever hugged him. I didn't know where to go with the feelings I had. Dad didn't recognise the signs at the time, but I was high. He insisted I go with him to the hospice to see Mum's body and say goodbye. As we sat at her bedside I felt the urge to tell Dad about my addiction issues, but couldn't think how to. The most loving, supportive person in my life was gone. And I didn't know how to ask Dad for help, so I went back home and set about getting obliterated.

*

In recent years, I have spoken and written many times about what happened three days after the death of my mother. I've tried to explain the events in academic terms, having learned how to analyse the ways human beings act and react. And whereas I spent much of my younger life trying to duck responsibility for what I did, regarding myself as a victim of circumstances, I have ceased shifting the blame.

I made a series of choices and I have been living with those choices ever since.

Being accountable for my actions and accepting responsibility for their consequences hasn't been a short journey. I spent much of my imprisonment feeling like a victim. Whatever else is said about the murder for which I was convicted, I made every choice that put me into the situation, and I made every choice that led to another's death. There were multiple moments at which I could have let him leave my house alive, multiple points at which self-defence was no longer the imperative; but instead of letting him leave, I chose to end his life.

*

Around midday on New Year's Eve 1995, the third day after Mum's death — the funeral hadn't even happened yet — the phone went. It was Fagan.

'Hey, Paul. Look, sorry to hear about your mum. Do you want some drugs? Misties? I'll bring some round in a couple of hours if you want.'

Of course I wanted drugs!

Just before Fagan was due to arrive, a friend of mine called Joe dropped around with a condolence card. He must have found me fidgety and distracted: I had little time for social niceties, fixated as I was on Fagan's arrival. I didn't want my friend to meet him because I thought he would guess the nature of our relationship. I had kept my drug habit a secret, or as secret as I could, given the ravages it had worked on my frame and appearance. My friend picked up on my discomfort and soon left. Shortly afterwards, there was a knock on the door. It was Fagan.

I had been expecting half a dozen pills, but instead Fagan gave me a single 60-milligram morphine sulphate tablet.

'This is on the house,' he said. 'I feel bad about your mum. We'll sort the rest of the gear later.'

I nodded, almost drooling at the pill in my hand.

It's difficult for people who have never used intravenous drugs to know how powerfully seductive they are, and it's not just the buzz you get from the drugs themselves. The ritual involved in preparing the hit is almost as addictive as the high itself. In the case of morphine, this ritual involves laying out one's metal spoon, glass of water, cigarette filter and syringe ready for use.

The morphine tablet would be delicately washed clean of its wax covering, heated in the spoon just enough to make it soft, and then crushed into powder. Enough water to cover the powder would then be added and heated until the morphine had liquified and the liquid turned a golden brown. You would then put a piece of cigarette filter in the liquid and draw the liquid up into the syringe through the filter. You'd do this over and over until all possible morphine had been extracted. Unlike the movies, where they squirt a little liquid from the tip of the needle to remove air bubbles, I would instead slowly squeeze any air out by moving the plunger up. No sense in wasting any of that liquid gold.

Next, you would place a tourniquet around your arm in order to optimise access to a vein. I always used my belt for this, and like most junkies I had veins I preferred. I was lucky enough to have good veins.

Then it would be the moment of truth. I knew people who didn't like inserting the needle themselves and would get other people to inject them while they averted their gaze. I actually enjoyed this part. The anticipation would be reaching its peak and yet considerable precision was required. The needle would go in and you'd jack back the plunger to ensure the needle was securely in a vein. A thread of blood mixing with the drug would indicate it was. If there was no blood, you'd missed the vein or gone through it, and if you weren't in the vein, you'd end up with a painful lump where the liquid was injected into the tissue. Far worse, you'd miss out on the rush.

Once I was sure the needle was where it should be, I'd release the pressure from my tourniquet and inject a good day into my veins. I would then sit back and enjoy the feeling, which is like a hot flush of warm pins and needles sweeping over your body and delivering a total sense of peace and euphoria.

Fagan gestured out to the road where his car was parked. 'I've got Boyd in the car. I've got to go to the money machine. Do you mind if he hangs with you while I'm gone?'

Boyd was a kingpin in the Wellington drug scene, and Fagan worked for him as a middleman. This should have immediately set alarm bells ringing because Boyd was noted for keeping well away from his customers. But I wasn't troubled. I was grateful to him. He was the man responsible for the sweet deal I was getting on my morphine purchases. Whereas the going rate was around $2 per milligram, Boyd was selling it to me for $1.30 per milligram.

'Absolutely,' I said.

Fagan went out to the car and returned with Boyd. He made the intros. Boyd was much older than me, around 42, and powerfully built. Apparently he had been a boxer back in the day. He would have weighed in at 95 kilograms, and while I had tipped the scales at around 88 when I was fighting fit, IV drug use had reduced this to around 67.

Fagan made his excuses and left us alone.

Tania was in the bedroom. This was our routine: I always tried to keep her away from the guys I associated with in that world.

After the initial rush of the drugs, I asked Boyd if he'd like a drink. He asked for a bourbon. I brought him one and sat down near him on the same three-seater couch.

We made a bit of small talk. It was hard for me to focus.

'You happy with the deals you've been getting, Paul?' he asked.

I nodded.

'Real happy. Yeah, real happy. I appreciate how cheap the gear is.'

'Good,' he said. 'Good. Always nice to know my customers are happy.'

He took a sip of his bourbon.

'You can always return the favour you know,' he said. 'I wouldn't mind watching while you get it on with your girlfriend. What d'you reckon? If you're cool with that. I could make it worth both your whiles with some more pills.'

I nodded slowly. Even with the drugs in my system, now the alarm bells were ringing like mad. I was conscious of the power he had over us. This wasn't anything I was into, but on the other hand, I didn't want to get offside with this guy. There was too much at stake. He had a pretty scary rep, but to be brutally honest, I was far more worried about what might happen to my drug supply if I pissed him off.

'I'll see what Tania reckons,' I said.

I went to the bedroom. I told Tania what had been suggested. She was as horrified as I was, and we tried to figure out a plan of action. She thought I should say she didn't want to do it. That would mean I didn't have to look like the one turning him down.

I went back out to the lounge and sat back down on the couch.

'Nah, she's not into it, eh.' I'm sure I appeared as weak as I felt.

He nodded.

He leaned over and grabbed me by the crotch.

I freaked out, and punched him square on the nose.

He grabbed me. I tried to shake him off, and yelled out for Tania. She came into the kitchen, saw what was happening, and disappeared back to the bedroom. This area of Karori wasn't the safest of areas, and Tania kept a baseball bat in the bedroom as a means of self-defence. She came back, carrying the bat.

I was doing my best to keep Boyd at bay by putting furniture between him and me, but it was only a matter of time before he got hold of me. And such was the difference in weight and condition that both of us knew he would easily overpower me. But the moment my hands closed around the handle of that bat Tania handed me, panic turned to rage. I hit him with the bat, and I didn't stop hitting him until the bat was broken.

After the event, it was easy to tell myself stories to justify having killed Boyd, to rationalise what I did and paint myself as the victim. One of the stories was that if I'd let him live I would have ended up with a 'hotshot', which is when someone is given a deliberate overdose to make their death look accidental. This would happen when a drug user got offside with someone and that person would show up with a syringe and a weapon and offer a choice: die slowly, in agony, or take the easy way out, rolling up a sleeve and slipping into oblivion at the end of the needle. Another rationalisation was to say he deserved it, but this was just a way to dehumanise him and to minimise the impact and seriousness of my actions. But all of this was just a way to make myself feel better about what I had done, to shift my focus and try to escape the reality of my actions. Had I been the person who had died that day, people would have said good riddance to bad rubbish. I wasn't someone making any kind of positive contribution in the world.

'We're going to have to clean the place up,' I said to Tania.

Tania grabbed a bucket and a sponge and started trying to sort out the blood-spattered floor boards. I dragged Boyd's body into the bathroom. I was suddenly overwhelmed with what I had done.

'Fuck,' I said.

We stopped trying to clean up. Instead, we turned all the lights off, with the intention of pretending there was no one home when Fagan returned. I don't know how long it was — it seemed like an eternity, but it could only have been a matter of half an hour or so — there was a loud knock on the door.

'Police,' said a voice. 'Open up.'

At the first sound of feet on the landing, Tania had taken off to the bedroom.

I just sat there, hardly registering.

There was another series of heavy blows on the door as it was kicked in. I came out into the corridor and two cops secured me against the wall.

'The neighbours reckon there's been a fight. What's been happening?'

I said, 'I had a bit of a fight with my girlfriend, a domestic. But it's all OK now.'

'Where is she? Is she here?'

'Nah, she's gone.'

The female cop stepped past me into the flat and went straight to the bathroom.

'Was anyone injured?' the other cop asked me, looking at the scrapes and bruises on my face.

'Nah, not really,' I replied.

'Where is your girlfriend now? Is she OK?' the cop asked.

I never got a chance to answer.

'Oh, Christ,' said the cop from the bathroom.

CHAPTER THREE

Four Walls

Contrary to what many in society think, our prisons are not predominantly populated by evil people. Sure, there are some genuinely bad bastards in there who you really need to lock up in order to protect society: psychopaths and those who have been so thoroughly brutalised it's hard to see where you might begin rehabilitating them. I met a few of them, as I'll go on to relate. But they are the exception rather than the rule.

The majority are those whose offending can be directly attributed to their background. Many come from socially deprived backgrounds, especially where education is concerned. They've grown up in situations where crime and violence are rife; the normal way of engaging with the rest of the world. The families of most offenders, where they have anything you could identify as a functional family, are often characterised by a lack of parenting skills, poor role modelling and, most fundamentally, an absence of any hope or aspiration that things might be different. To escape their reality, many become substance abusers and addicts, which is criminogenic in itself: to feed your habit you turn to petty or even serious crime. When you factor in the poor coping skills people in such circumstances have, together with a lack of neurodevelopment producing a general inability of adolescents to attach consequences to actions, most criminal offending is explicable in ways that don't rely on people being evil, or deliberately antisocial.

And this might come as the real shock to the hard-line, law and order, Sensible Sentencing types: there are very few strategic thinkers in prison. Contrary to one of the principles underpinning our entire approach to criminal justice, your average offender doesn't spend much time, if any, working out the probability that their actions will land them in jail. The truth is, most offenders, especially violent offenders, simply play what's in front of them. The life course of most of those in prison was changed in the heat of a few short moments. For many, many people, their entire view of the world, their expectations for their lives, the range of options presented to them are all set early, and once set, are very difficult to change.

Even among those from intergenerational crime families, who regard a stretch in prison as a normal and inevitable life event, they don't usually plan to go there. They are simply more accepting, less disturbed by the thought of ending up behind bars than those whose life prospects make it unimaginable to them. Not only is the normalisation of imprisonment a factor, so is the psychological, social and physical hurt people experience growing up in intergenerational crime families. For make no mistake, it's hurt people who hurt people.

None of this is intended to excuse crime or shift blame from the criminals. There are lots of people who get hurt and grow up in dysfunctional environments without going on to become criminals. But it is one explanation, and if we accept that it is deficiencies in the backgrounds of the majority of offenders that contribute to the conditions for their offending, then it is society that is seeking to shift the blame when it does nothing at all to address them.

And you only need to look at the statistics to see that deterrence doesn't work. If it did, the numbers of criminals would be steadily declining and prisons would be emptying out rather than bursting at the seams.

All of us have made bad decisions and live with the consequences. What is important is to identify what cognitive distortion or distortions led to making those bad choices. Knowing what it is about yourself that made the wrong thing to do seem like the right thing is the only way you'll avoid making similar bad decisions in the future.

*

The trip to the Wellington Central police station in the back of the cop car was surreal, both disturbingly clear and sort of blurry, as I was in shock and still high on morphine. As a habitual user, high had become my normal, so I was usually capable of thinking straight. But the drug had probably dulled the edges of my reality. My thinking was frozen, numb.

The cops had found Tania hiding under the bed. When we arrived at Central, the two of us were taken to separate interview rooms, small, windowless rooms, harshly lit by fluorescent light, empty apart from a plain wooden table and three chairs. I had been arrested on a charge of assault with a weapon, a charge to hold me until the police pieced together a clearer picture of events. I was allowed to phone a lawyer. My family didn't count many lawyers among our friends, so I asked the police to phone the duty solicitor. It took a while to get hold of one, because it was New Year's Eve. When eventually they found a man named Bill Johnson, they gave him a brief overview of the circumstances under which I was in custody. Then they put him on.

'Don't tell the police anything,' he said. 'They'll try to get you to talk by threatening to charge you with murder if you don't, but they'll charge you with murder whether you make a statement or not. Do yourself a favour and keep your mouth shut. Do you understand?'

I was in shock and could barely speak anyway. He had to ask me again before I could tell him yes, I understood.

He then asked to speak to the supervising policeman again, and told them that on his advice, I wasn't going to make a statement. They were to refrain from interviewing me.

Tania, in a different room, had more to lose, as the cops wasted no time in pointing out to her. They told her that she had been at the scene of what appeared to be a murder, and for all they knew she may have been an accessory either after the fact or to the crime itself. They threatened to charge her if she didn't cooperate, whereupon she would be locked up and her daughter would automatically be taken into care. She buckled at once, and of course, I don't blame her. She gave them a straight and honest account of what had taken place. Armed with her statement, the cops interviewing me wore triumphant looks on their faces when they came back in.

'Your girlfriend's told us all about it,' they said. 'We've got everything we need to charge you with murder.'

I was processed. I was told to undress and my clothes were bagged and taken, I was issued a paper boiler suit to wear, I was photographed, my fingerprints were taken and then I was led through to the cell area, a bleak, concrete corridor with a line of cells with heavy iron doors opening off it. There were pairs of tatty shoes outside several of the cells. The rattle of the keys in the lock echoed coldly. The door swung open onto a tiny space, concrete walls painted pink, a narrow concrete slab on the floor with a mattress on it with a pillow and a grey institutional blanket, a stainless steel toilet bowl and nothing else.

The door banged shut and the keys rattled again. All I wanted to do was go to sleep, in the hope that when I woke up, the nightmare would be over.

*

By the early hours of the morning after the murder, I was coming down from the drugs, and all I could really focus on was the craving for more, which was gathering momentum. Every time I lay down on the bench, a restlessness got me up again. Pacing around, I felt a trapped, claustrophobic terror building. I would lie down again to try to control the panic, but couldn't settle and would soon be up on my feet again.

The sweats, cramps, aches and chills that go with opiate withdrawal became more pronounced with each hour that passed. By morning, I was feeling nauseous, and refused the unappetising-looking breakfast that was offered. In a perverse kind of way, the withdrawal served as a distraction from my predicament: because of the New Year holidays, it was two days before my first hearing in court. On a couple of occasions during this time, a detective took me out of the cell and let me into an area where I could smoke. It was a pretext. On the way up, while I was there smoking and on the way back to the cell, he burbled away, trying to engage me in conversation, no doubt in the hope I would talk about what had happened. The cops would later earn themselves a reprimand from the magistrate for so blatantly going against my lawyer's explicit instructions not to interview me.

Early on 3 January, it was time to be handcuffed and move through to the cavernous, fluorescent-lit loading bay in the basement of the police station and climb into the van that takes prisoners from the police cells to court. I shared it with a small group of other miscreants who had started 1996 badly. It was a short drive. When the van doors opened, I was ushered into the concrete, garage-like reception space beneath the court building.

Inside the District Court building, I was led into a small interview room. Bill Johnson was due to meet me there, but he was late. When he arrived, bustling into the room, it was with the air of someone under severe harassment. He was in his fifties, I suppose, wore a rumpled suit and tie and was pretty tired and rumpled-looking himself. He asked if I had made a statement, and I shook my head.

'Good,' he nodded. 'They're going to charge you with murder.'

Then he told me what would happen. Given the seriousness of the charges I was going to face, bail was out of the question, so after today I would be sent to remand. After two weeks, I would reappear in the District Court, where it would be possible to ask for bail. I would then return to the court approximately every two weeks until a date for a depositions hearing was set to determine whether there was a prima facie case against me: that is, whether the police had enough in the way of evidence to send me to trial.

'It's a formality, really,' Bill Johnson said. 'You'll be sent for trial, all right.'

My plans for my future had always been pretty hazy, especially since I'd discovered Class A drugs. But the future my lawyer was sketching for me didn't fit with any of the scenarios I had imagined for myself. I was buffeted by alternating waves of unreality and cold, hard realisation.

When I was called, I was brought, still handcuffed, through a little door into the courtroom. There were dozens of people in the room, mostly members of the public awaiting the appearance of someone or another, not me. There were lawyers and court officials, and the police prosecutor in his uniform, studying a sheaf of papers. Across the way from him, Bill Johnson was sitting behind a stack of folders, presumably his workload for the day.

The hearing was brief. The police told the court I was facing charges that were too serious for bail to be considered.

In reply, Johnson tentatively submitted that since I was so young, bail might be an option.

'Bail's out of the question,' the judge replied, 'given the seriousness of the charge. Mr Wood, you are remanded in custody pending depositions. Stand down.'

*

I was escorted down into the bowels of the building again and locked in a cell for most of the day, until a van arrived to take me into custody. There were a couple of other people in it, young blokes, and they eyed me curiously.

'What you in for, bro?' one asked.

'Murder,' I mumbled, the word feeling ugly and unfamiliar in my mouth.

I saw wariness descend over their faces like a curtain falling.

We were in motion. From the street on which the court was situated, the van hung a right and drove along the waterfront. It could have been a glorious day, one of those rare still days when the sun glitters on the calm harbour, only a scrap of cloud hanging over the ranges beyond Hutt Valley to spoil the blue sky. Or it may have been blustery and overcast, threatening rain. Or it was fine but with clouds scudding across the sky. I had no way of knowing. In my new world, there was no sky, and no weather, only different kinds of cage.

We wound our way around several bends. I guessed we were driving around the shores of Evans Bay, heading for Miramar and Mount Crawford Prison, perched high on the backbone of the peninsula. Sure enough, after a brief run at higher speed, we slowed and the note of the engine lifted as the driver changed gears and we began to climb. After five minutes or so, the road levelled out, we came to a halt, the engine was cut and there was a rattle at the doors.

We had arrived.

*

Mount Crawford Prison was built in the 1920s using prison labour and locally sourced materials, mainly concrete blocks made sand from the south coast. Like most of the other prisons in the country, it's bleak. Inside, it's cold and draughty and sounds echo hard off the concrete and steel surfaces. Four prisoners were executed there, back when New Zealand still had the death penalty on its statute books. The place is haunted, although not (in my experience) by the souls of those four unfortunates. Instead, you are (or were — it closed in 2016) conscious as you walked in of despair and the sense of wasted human potential.

I was briskly and impersonally processed and my sorry, drug-ravaged body was weighed. Then I was taken into the prison itself. As I was led in, I was conscious of eyes on me from the cells on either side of the corridor. And there was the prison 'welcome': a kicking of steel doors, animal growls and shouted threats.

'Better hang yourself, you little shit!' was the one I remember best. ''Cause I'm gonna come and fuck you up in the morning!'

While I was being processed, I spent an hour or two in a holding cell, a tiny (2.5 metres square) concrete space with nothing in the way of furnishings but a wire-wove, steel-framed bunk and a toilet bowl. I had arrived after dinner, so the receiving officer, a Scotsman, went and got me some leftover sausages and bread from the kitchen. I didn't realise it then, but this was a real act of kindness, which went beyond what was required of him. I realise he must have felt compassion for this 18-year-old before him, whose life had just changed beyond what he could know, but I was too inexperienced and self-absorbed to be putting myself in anyone else's shoes or recognising what constituted generosity in my new world.

I was taken to cell 3 on the remand side of the wing. This was an observation cell. If you're on a serious charge, in drug withdrawal or considered to be a suicide risk, or, as in my case, all three, you're placed in what's known as 'PS', precautionary or preventive segregation. It's effectively solitary confinement while they suss out your attitude and demeanour and whether you're a suicide risk or not. For the first week, they come and have a peek at you every 15 minutes, to make sure you haven't died or killed yourself. The worst aspect of the observation cell was there was no internal light switch. If the observing officer forgot to turn the light off after peering in through the observation hole, you had to wait until another guard came along and ask him to turn it off. After a week or so, the observations were relaxed to once every half hour.

On PS, you're locked up for 23 hours a day, and allowed out for just one hour, when you're let into the exercise yard, alone. The yard is little better than your cell. It's a bit smaller than a tennis court, completely asphalted and surrounded on all four sides by high, concrete block walls with only a single, steel door giving onto it. There's an observation slot in the door, and an elevated walkway that the guards can stroll along and from which they can keep an eye on you. Above it all, there's a corrugated plastic roof, with maybe a block's-width gap between the top of the walls and the roofing. You can imagine how hot it gets when the sun is beating down into it.

For the first few days on remand, I was still in withdrawal from the drugs. I didn't have it as badly as some, but I had it pretty bad, sweating and retching and shivering and wracked by a fierce craving for a hit. I asked to see a medical officer about getting something to control the symptoms; she offered me Panadol, which I would soon learn was the prison panacea.

The symptoms probably peaked after three days. After that, they grew less acute, even if the craving didn't. I began to settle into a bit of a routine. Mostly, this revolved around my hour in the yard, where I would pace relentlessly backwards and forwards, from one wall to the other and back again. Every ten laps, I would do ten press-ups, or sit-ups or some other exercise, just to break up the monotony. Then I would resume pacing.

One day, while I was stalking up and down, sweating profusely in the heat of the yard, I heard the ring of steps on the walkway above. I looked up and saw a line of faces looking down at me. They must have been Criminology students, or something like that, and they were studying me as I walked. At last, after days of feeling nothing but nausea and misery, I felt something different: as though I were an animal in a zoo, I now felt exploited and powerless, and I was enraged.

*

67

After two weeks in PS, I was unlocked and allowed to mingle with other 'pre-seg' prisoners, while the prison authorities cautiously assessed how I would interact. We all sussed one another out diffidently. I was acutely aware that I didn't know the rules of social interaction. It was like the feeling you get on your first day in a country where you don't speak the language or know the customs. You'd think, given the hard cases I had mixed with growing up, that I'd be able to speak the same language as those in prison — violence — but there was a heavier dialect spoken in here. The threat of violence hung in the air, everywhere, lurking in every pause and inflecting every spoken word. Even the way people looked at each other was thick with it: there was a sense everyone was watching you and the way you carried yourself to see how capable you were of looking after yourself. Everyone was looking for weakness, as weakness could be exploited. Because I was known to be in on a murder charge, people were a bit wary of me. I was in terrible physical shape, but I still tried to carry myself with confidence, instinctively realising that any sign of weakness would be as good as an invitation to predators.

Good thing, too. Soon after I was unlocked, I went to use the phone at the end of the wing. From where I was standing, talking, I noticed a guy loitering outside my cell, checking it out. I excused myself from my conversation, let the receiver dangle and marched straight down to him.

'What the fuck do *you* want?' I said.

He initially puffed out his chest and tried to act tough, but when I pushed him into my cell and asked him if he wanted a 'go' he backed down. This was what it was like. It was the law of the jungle. If you showed weakness, they'd own you. If you responded aggressively, they'd move on to prey on the next potential weakling.

I was in pre-seg for three months. It's not easy being locked up for 23 hours a day, but it was made a little easier for me by my visitors. Dad and my brothers came. Tania came, and so did her mum and her sister, with whom I'd always got on really well. She gave me books, and even tried to give me a laptop: this wasn't passed on, as laptops were forbidden. These were acts of kindness I'll never forget: just to know there were people who hadn't given up on me or written me off, and who didn't think I was an unredeemable bastard … it's beyond words what it meant to me. And while Dad and I didn't talk about much — we had no real history of communicating about important stuff — it was great sitting in companionable silence, or hearing snippets of news from the outside.

It also meant I was able to get hold of some drugs. Visits were quite poorly supervised in those days. You were supposed to be strip-searched on your return from a visit, but with some guards, these were pretty once-over-lightly. My preferred method of getting drugs in was to slip capsules of pure cannabis oil into the little, hidden pouch-like pocket at the front of my Y-fronts. Even when I was required to strip, the drugs would remain concealed. Another popular method of smuggling was 'cheeking' — where you put contraband between your bum cheeks and clench to keep them in place. Staff were occasionally known to wrestle with prisoners holding drugs in this manner. Because the staff weren't particularly vigilant about these searches it wasn't necessary to use more determined methods, such as 'charging', which involves concealing drugs in your rectum.

Drugs were more readily available than they were on the outside, which makes sense when you consider that prison throws professional drug dealers together with people who are habitual drug users. In those circumstances, the dealers are hardly likely to *stop* dealing drugs.

Getting stuff into prisons is easy. Visitors smuggle in contraband, and 'trusted' prisoners in minimum security often get to go outside on work details and the like, and drugs are dropped at pre-arranged sites for them to collect. It was well known that certain prison officers would bring stuff in, for a price. And at some of the old-fashioned, high-walled prisons such as Mount Eden and Mount Crawford, drugs were regularly thrown over the wall packed into tennis balls.

In any prison of any size, most of the work outside actual administration is done by prisoners themselves. Those whom the authorities have come to trust ('trusties') are used to perform all manner of menial tasks such as collecting and delivering laundry and meals. This means there are lines of communication between different areas of the prison and across the different levels of security. Drugs pass back and forth and up and down these chains freely.

All sorts of currencies were good for obtaining drugs. Cigarettes, phone cards, gambling debts or meals — especially chicken dinners, which were particularly prized by prisoners — would do. If you had a good credit history, you could even get drugs on tick. Often a drug debt would be settled by making a phone call to someone on the outside. That person would deposit a sum of money to a TAB account belonging to the dealer, and the dealer would subsequently phone and check to make sure the funds had been paid in. The beauty of a TAB account is that it's pretty much anonymous and no records of deposits or withdrawals are kept. It was the perfect money-laundering set-up.

I was still on pre-segs when my drug use first came to the attention of the authorities. During yard time, all cells were routinely inspected. On one of these searches, an officer found a piece of burnt tinfoil — used over a lighter to vaporise the cannabis oil, which I then inhaled — taped to the underside of the bench in my cell. I came back from yard time to find the officer and the unit manager, or UM, waiting for me. The UM told me I was on a charge for having an article in my possession without the permission of an officer. I would soon learn that this was a catch-all charge that could be given to someone for almost anything they had in their possession without permission.

I shrugged.

'Is that all?' I asked. It didn't seem a big deal to me at all. I was on remand for murder.

I was taken by a couple of screws (prison guards) to the office of the custody manager (CM), where I was told to stand on a small mat in the middle of the floor. I was warned that if I so much as made to move off it, I would regret it. So I stood there, with one screw beside me and the other behind me. A senior officer stood by the custody manager, who sat on the other side of the desk in judgement.

After the senior officer had read the charge, the CM asked how I pleaded. I pleaded guilty.

'You're lucky we had a rough weekend,' the CM said. 'The pound's full.' 'The pound' was slang for solitary confinement. 'I suppose I'll have to sentence you to OPs instead.'

OPs or 'off-privileges' meant that any electricals (such as radio, stereo or TV) I had would be confiscated, and I would be locked up for the duration of the punishment period. That sucked. There are very few things you have any control over in prison and choosing what to watch on TV was one of those. It might seem like a small thing, but as a species, the sense that we have control over our world is a universal driver. This is why reducing people's options often prompts them to react in ways opposite to what you intend. This is also why feeling a lack of control in your job, for example, is one of the main causes of disengagement and workplace depression. You often see some people trying to regain a sense of control in the prison environment through obsessive cleanliness and tidying. TV is also a means to escape the reality of your situation in prison. Losing my TV left me staring at the walls with no sense of choice and no way to forget where I was.

*

While I was in pre-segs, my depositions hearing was held. It gave me a glimmer of hope because Bill Johnson had prepared some searching questions for the prosecution witnesses — mostly police — who were called. But it was a tactical error to use these in the depositions. All it served to do was highlight potential weaknesses in the Crown case, which would be thoroughly addressed by the time the actual trial rolled around. I didn't see this process as a way to establish the truth of what had happened and I had no interest in thinking about my responsibility for Boyd's death or what was right. I saw this process as a competition between my lawyer and the Crown, a competition to see who could win, rather than what was 'right' or 'just'. Some might argue that this is exactly the nature of our adversarial system of justice, but based on the way I saw the world and my own lack of moral maturity, I would have been doing everything I could to avoid accountability for my actions regardless of the system.

I was remanded back to Mount Crawford, and after three months on pre-segs, I was shifted from cell 3 to cell 8. This was a great move, as cell 8 was a 'normal' cell, by which I mean it had an internal light switch, a steel-framed bunk, a wooden bench and a cupboard. As part of the mainstream muster, I was allowed yard time every day from 8 to 11:30 am, and not only was the remand yard bigger and open to the sky but also I was allowed to mingle with other prisoners there, if I chose. I wasn't that keen on mingling, particularly after an older prisoner told me the only thing the yard was good for was getting into fights. Fortunately, because I was to be on remand for a long-ish time, the staff fixed me up with a job as a cleaner. There were five or six of us performing this role.

Three of the cleaners formed a vigilante group, which I will call the Gang of Three. Two of them were co-offenders on remand for dope cultivation and possession of firearms (they were later acquitted at their respective trials). Along with the third member of the Gang of Three, they had sworn to make life miserable for sex offenders.

It so happened that a particularly nasty offender — a young man who had murdered the father of his victim when the poor man had tried to get his son away from his influence — had arrived at Mount Crawford on his way north to the maximum security facility at Paremoremo and was being kept isolated from other prisoners for his own protection. Trouble was, the cleaners had access to the area in which he was housed, and the Gang of Three hatched a plan. They saved a couple of empty large fizzy drink bottles and urinated in them every day for a week or so, throwing in any other noxious substance they might happen to come across for good measure. On the day the child molester was to be transferred, the Gang of Three paid him a visit, spraying the foul contents of their bottles through the peephole of his cell and thoroughly drenching both him and his possessions, which were laid out on his bed ready for the move. The victim pushed his panic button and yelled in rage, but although his cell was right next to the staff room, the screws were mysteriously slow to appear and the perpetrators were nowhere to be seen by the time they did. The reeking inmate asked the screws if he could have a shower and change of clothes before the long bus-ride north. The screws had a good laugh and told him this wouldn't be possible.

Paedophiles were always fodder for prison violence and abuse, which is why they couldn't be housed with the general population. One reason for this is that a disproportionate number of people who end up in prison have experienced sexual abuse themselves. Also, finding someone you can judge to be a worse person than you can help you feel higher in the social hierarchy and avoid having to confront your own feelings of unworthiness.

*

There was always a high turnover of people in remand. I was there for ten months, and I met some interesting characters. I made friends of sorts with some, and I shared a cell with a few. Because I was in prison for a serious, violent offence and the staff were obliged to consider the safety of prisoners, they were reluctant to put anyone in with me I hadn't approved first, which gave me a kind of power of veto over my prospective cellmates. My main criterion was that they shared my enthusiasm for drugs. One of them was Fish, my friend from primary school who had taught me how to shoplift. He'd spent most of his adult life in prison. Another was a good friend of mine from both life and league, Koko. They, like several others, came and went over this period. Mostly I smoked dope with my cellmates, but we also shot morphine and methadone and one supplied me with some prescription pills. I'd never had much to do with pills before, and I found the experience freaky, especially when I experienced a bout of intense auditory hallucinations.

I got on well with some of the heavier inmates. Two were members of the Nomads gang. One I'll call Pace. He was in for violent offences, but I got along with him fine. Another was Manu and he was in for stabbing two people to death in a Horowhenua hotel. Then there was a Pākehā guy I'll call Mugshot. Mugshot was about my age and we became fast friends. He'd grown up in the system and had cottoned on very early to the necessity of using extreme violence to get by, first in borstal, then in prison. Because of his penchant for violence, he had been shifted to PS as a punishment. (Preventive Segregation wasn't supposed to be used in this way, but because it was much simpler than jumping through the proper procedural hoops necessary for disciplinary action, the authorities regularly did it anyway. All it took was for them to declare that you were a danger to yourself or others and you'd find yourself in PS, which was pronounced a 'management tool'.) If ever I seemed in danger of running out of drugs, all I had to do was ask Mugshot. He had no problem sourcing whatever I might happen to want.

It was Mugshot who told me of the 'charging' method of bringing contraband in, by inserting it in your rectum. I was horrified, and he enjoyed my reaction tremendously.

'Give it time, mate,' he chuckled. 'After you've been inside long enough, you'll find yourself doing all sorts of shit you never imagined doing out there.'

The gangs rule prison. Almost the first thing that happens when your cell is unlocked in the general prison area is you're paid a visit by the gang prospects. If you're a young Māori or Polynesian, they will look to recruit you or, failing that, beat the shit out of you and steal from you. If you are white, you'll probably just get beaten and robbed. It's my understanding that a similar cohesive situation exists for young white guys who come into South Island prisons because of the prominence there of white prison gangs such as the Fourth Reich. We know from the Dunedin Study, which is the most comprehensive longitudinal research (that is, a study that follows people from their birth and throughout their lives) in the world, that most teenagers will grow out of criminal offending by their early to mid-20s, but also that three things increase the likelihood young people will continue with their criminal offending: sending them to prison, gang membership, and alcohol or drug issues. The first two are often related, in my experience.

Because of my friendship with Manu he asked if I wanted to join the Nomads and prospect under him, which would in effect mean that he would be responsible for me and in charge of me.

'You won't even have to do anything,' he said.

I knew what he meant by this. If you were prospecting for the gangs, you frequently had to act as a kind of servant for a patched member, cleaning his cell, performing hits on other people on his orders, that kind of thing.

'Nah, I'm not really interested,' I told Manu. He was cool with that.

One day, I sauntered into the cell of another guy I got on with; I'll call him Stand. Manu was there, and they were standing there eyeballing each other. I was all: 'Hey, how you doing?' to both of them. They stopped talking, but there was tension in the air. Manu turned, and after a long hard look at me, walked out.

Stand breathed a deep sigh of relief.

'Thanks, mate. You saved me there.'

He and Manu or Manu's associates had had some kind of falling out and he was sure Manu was there to stab him.

On another occasion, Mugshot got into a big fight in the exercise yard. There were plenty of spectators. It finished in a stalemate, but of course, prison being prison, there would always be a sequel. Mugshot was attacked with a hard plastic knife later the same day as he was lining up to get his meal. This took place right in front of the screws — a fairly common tactic which ensures the attacker gets to maintain face and also that there will be no consequences if the attack fails because the attacker will immediately be transferred for his own protection and/or punishment. It doesn't always happen that way, though, especially if there's a full muster and nowhere to move the attacker, or, as was the case with Mugshot, the guards dislike the attacked inmate and don't have much of an interest in ensuring their protection.

Both protagonists were locked down after the mealtime attack. When they were unlocked again, Mugshot got me to watch his back while he had his shower. Attention then shifted to the next yard time, when the two would be at large together. Mugshot was on his way to the yard when two screws stopped him between the wing wall and the balustrade above the stairs to the shower. They wanted to search him. A brief standoff ensued. Then Mugshot pulled out a shank (a pointed stabbing weapon) made from a sharpened toothbrush.

'I suppose you'll be interested in this, then?' he called, and tossed it towards the guards.

He reached inside his jacket and pulled out a cosh made by slipping a few heavy batteries into a sock.

'And this?'

The guards just stood there as this thudded to the floor, too.

Then Mugshot swept a length of steel tube broken off a chair out of his pants and brandished it like a club.

'Are you interested in this, by any chance?'

After a moment, he stopped posing with it and threw it with a clatter to the floor. Then he went quietly.

He soon found himself in the segregation cell with the covered yard that I had occupied when I first arrived. He didn't fancy it, and after a few days, he decided he wanted a change of scene. He was in the yard one day when he started kicking the door and yelling for the screws. When a guard ventured in to see what the fuss was about, Mugshot set upon him.

Mugshot was a big, tough man who spent most of his time in prison either fighting or training to fight. It was lucky for all concerned that the guard he attacked was a man mountain too, standing about 6 foot 5 inches and weighing at least 120 kilograms. Mugshot was soon on his way to Paremoremo Maximum Security Prison in Auckland. When I spoke to the guard he'd attacked some time later, he told me he'd been impressed Mugshot had the balls to have a go at him. Not many did.

*

The criminal gangs weren't the only gangs operating in prison, either. There were also the guards. Most prison guards at the time (I entered Mount Crawford in early 1996) were ex-military types, hard bastards, some of whom had retired from units such as the SAS and who had taken on prison work as a relaxing career change before they put their feet up for good. Prison officers used to live in accommodation compounds provided by the government; effectively a small self-contained village populated entirely by like-minded individuals. They tended to be a very tight-knit bunch, and they most certainly didn't take any shit. If they took issue with something a prisoner said or did, many of them would simply take off their belt and radio and take the prisoner to the exercise yard and settle the matter with their fists. If it were more serious than that, a guard or group of guards would enter a prisoner's cell after lockup and beat the shit out of them. Official investigations into this style of 'goon squad' behaviour in the prison service were underway when I first went to Mount Crawford, but it didn't altogether deter the guards. I hadn't been there for long before I heard a door open and a scuffle start after everyone was supposed to have been locked up. I heard the same thing happen on several occasions. And I became aware — as everyone else was — that a particular guard paid regular after-hours visits to the cell occupied by a transvestite, where they presumably traded sexual favours for contraband or special treatment.

*

The most unusual prisoner I met on remand was John Barlow. Whereas most of my fellow inmates were young, dark-skinned and uneducated, John was older, Pākehā, and refined and well-spoken enough to suggest good schools and likely even university in his background. John was serving a life sentence for the murder of two Wellington businessmen whom he was alleged to have shot in their inner-city office for reasons that the police had never quite been able to explain. Like just about everyone else in prison, John claimed to be innocent, but in his case there were real grounds to believe him. He was on remand awaiting his third trial; the first two had ended in hung juries. You would have thought someone like him would be mincemeat in jail, but John had got by. For one thing, despite his age, he was quite tall and powerfully built. For another, he was a very astute manager of personalities and relationships. He'd managed to forge cordial ties with some of the KPs — the big gang guys, the King Pins — through sheer force of personality. Not only that, but he quickly recognised those guys for the intelligent men they usually were, and he had a surprising amount in common with them. Sure, he'd been attacked once or twice, but by the time I met him he was an accepted, even valued member of the prison community, if you can call it that.

He was kind to me from the outset, although I was probably standoffish. There were two reasons for this. First, he seemed so different from everyone else, including (by virtue of his age and education) me — he simply wasn't relevant to me at all. And second, I had by now learned that acts of kindness were to be treated with the most profound suspicion in prison. It was many years before I learned the proverb 'Beware of Greeks bearing gifts', but I saw plenty of evidence of its wisdom.

An example. Shortly before Mugshot's spectacular exit from the wing, I was hanging out with him and Stand, who was facing his second conviction for grievous bodily harm. He'd originally been moved to Mount Crawford from Rimutaka after being involved in a serious attack over there, and now he'd stabbed someone. Stand and Mugshot had been smoking pot with a Māori dude they vaguely knew, who had the distinction of having 'Trust No Cunt' tattooed on his neck. This guy — let's call him 'TNC' — was from the other side of the prison, the side for those who had been sentenced. Stand asked after some people he knew who had been shifted from remand to the sentence side. TNC started making derogatory racial remarks about the Pākehā inmates in question, and it pissed Stand and Mugshot off. After they'd gone their separate ways, Stand and Mugshot decided to take TNC out.

So they started hanging out more with TNC. They showed no animosity towards him. On the contrary: to all appearances, they were the best of mates.

The one thing people in jail aren't short of is time, so those planning revenge or pre-emptive violence are happy to play the long game. The kicker came when Mugshot casually suggested to TNC he join him and a few others smoking pot in the hobbies room. It was universally known that there was a spot in the hobbies room that wasn't covered by the CCTV surveillance cameras, and this was a popular spot to do drug deals and use drugs. It was also one of the best places in the prison to beat the shit out of people, which is what happened to TNC.

This kind of fake friendship is typical, so you learn fast to be wary of kindness. Nothing is free, or without strings attached or fishhooks embedded.

Trust No Cunt. I remember thinking at the time: he should have taken his own advice.

CHAPTER 4

Down for Life

Looking back at my time on remand, I see myself as an impressionable and easily influenced 18-year-old boy. At that age, it's easy to delude yourself into thinking you're your own man, when this is seldom the case. I had toxic ideas about what it meant to be a man, ideas that did nothing but create negativity and reduce my ability to lead a functioning and meaningful life. Some of these beliefs revolved around the idea that I shouldn't experience distressing emotions that made me feel out of control, vulnerable or weak. As a result, I tried to repress any such feelings rather than deal with them effectively. These days, I spend a lot of my time working helping people develop more realistic expectations of their emotions and giving them tools to more effectively manage them.

As a result of evolution, your brain is wired for you to worry and experience lots of other unpleasant emotions. There's nothing wrong with you when you feel scared, angry, frustrated or anxious. Nor is there anything that will stop you from feeling these emotions. If you want to be less affected by them, then the goal is acceptance of these emotions rather than avoidance. Society, however, tends to encourage us to believe we should always feel happy, so this idea of not avoiding emotions may appear disheartening. I have found it liberating. It has stopped me blaming myself or thinking there's something wrong with me when I have an unpleasant emotional response. This knowledge has enabled me to be more self-accepting and to focus my limited emotional and psychological resources on managing my unpleasant emotions instead of stressing out further about having them.

But of course, this realisation was a long way from where I was at 18. In the face of the turbulent emotions I was repressing at this point, I had two primary coping strategies. One was anger, which suited the prison environment and at least felt empowering rather than weak. The other was drug use. My days with Stand were devoted to the acquisition and consumption of drugs: pot, methadone, morphine, acid and pills. We would spend our days doing it all and discussing how we were going to get back at society, and how there was bugger all the prison could do about it. It was typical boob-talk, prison slang for the kind of tough stuff people in prison say in an effort to try to impress themselves and others, and to try to feel more powerful and in control than is the reality.

But I wasn't 100 per cent comfortable with the person I thought I was supposed to be. This is the little spark that lives within us all, that calls us to be better than we are, that recognises and fervently wishes to rise above our flaws. Even while I was wholly dedicated to living the life of the prison tough, there were pangs of conscience. It was like trying to wear a skin that doesn't quite fit. I remember one night when I had been on acid I dreamed that the ghost of my mother came and told me off. She told me that what I was doing was wrong and I was heading down the wrong track.

I woke in a cold sweat. This was some seriously scary shit — not least because deep down I knew it was true. But I had a means of coping with my subconscious, and it would get me through such crises of confidence for a number of years to come. I simply did drugs, and more drugs.

How do you deal with unpleasant emotions? Do you withdraw? Do you attack yourself? Or do you attack others? Quite often, people aren't even aware it is their emotions and their associated avoidant strategies that account for the behaviours they would, if they were being coldly rational, abhor in themselves. It's important, if you want to change the behaviours, to identify the chain of causation behind them. Sometimes, you can discover these for yourself. Quite often, it takes other people to point out the connections. Either way, a very great deal of self-honesty is required.

*

After just over ten months on remand, I went to trial. It lasted about a week, if I remember correctly, but that is a big if, as I was out of it for most of the time and for much of the time that followed my conviction for murder. There wasn't a great deal of media attention. There was a far more sensational trial underway at the time, that of an anaesthetist who was accused of being responsible for the death of a number of patients through professional negligence.

I had gone into my trial confident that I stood a chance of acquittal. At the very worst, I thought I might be convicted of manslaughter. Partly this was because the depositions hearing had gone so well. My lawyer had put some of the prosecution witnesses under some real pressure and they had not performed well. Fagan, for example, had appeared in the depositions hearing wearing lots of gold jewellery, which my lawyer pointed out. Wasn't it anomalous that someone who claimed to receive their income solely from unemployment benefit and to have nothing to do with selling hard drugs should be so blinged up? Well, when it came time to the actual trial, Fagan was dressed very conservatively, with not a glint of gold to be seen. Another example was the kids whose parents had rung the police. At depositions, it was apparent these kids had seen very little and that their testimony conflicted with forensic evidence and was of limited use to the prosecution. But by the time they got to the trial, their stories were different from those they had told at depositions: more damaging, and rock solid. I heard later that their mother and a policeman were giving them last-minute coaching in the foyer before they entered the witness box. My point isn't that this was wrong: it's all part of the way the adversarial justice system works. Nor am I trying to get at the kids. Quite apart from anything else, the constructive power of memory probably meant they believed what they were saying. But their performance at depositions had given me reason to hope the case put to my trial would be just as flimsy. To cut a long story short, it wasn't.

One interesting fact that came out in the prosecution's case was that Boyd was a police informant. I was naïve enough at this time to be gobsmacked to learn that Boyd had been using this position to maintain a monopoly on the supply of drugs in Wellington.

I don't remember much else about the trial. I remember feeling highly indignant at the way the prosecution conducted itself, at times. I thought the way the forensic photographer had represented the scene, for example, was just plain cynical. Yet, this focus on inconsistencies in other people's testimonies and my perception that evidence was misrepresented was just another way to avoid focusing on the far more pressing and important issue at hand: that I was in this courtroom because I had chosen to take Boyd's life, and that was fully on me. All these other points were just opportunities to avoid facing that reality and taking responsibility for my actions.

Years later I would reflect on this when reading about Socrates turning down an opportunity to escape his execution for the crime of corrupting young minds with his philosophy. His reasoning was that he had enjoyed all of the benefits and protections of Athens, so he was equally obliged to accept the penalties of its laws. My attitude couldn't have been further from such virtue and community mindedness.

Despite my focus on the prosecution's case, mostly, the trial passed me by, until the moment of truth arrived. It was a Friday night, and the jury had earlier come back into the courtroom and said it couldn't reach a unanimous verdict. The judge sent them back to deliberate further. When I was called back into the courtroom and they filed back in for a second time, it was to announce that they had reached a verdict, after all. The judge asked the forewoman what their verdict was.

'Guilty,' she said.

My counsel stood up and asked the judge to take the unusual step of polling the jury. The prosecution objected, but my lawyer argued that the earlier declaration by the jury that they couldn't agree raised questions about their unanimity. The judge agreed. He rather perfunctorily asked the jury if there was anyone who didn't agree with the verdict. A small, middle-aged woman in the front row of the jury tentatively raised her hand. The reporter from *The Evening Post* and my junior counsel both leapt to their feet, pointed to her and yelled: 'Her! She disagrees!'

But the judge missed the moment. Immediately after putting the question to the jury, he had gone back to reading his notes, and by the time he looked up again, she had dropped her hand.

'If anyone on the jury disagrees with the verdict, can they please raise their hand straight up so that everyone can see it,' the judge asked.

This time, everyone's hands stayed down. I'm not sure if it's true, but I was told later that the jurors were all holding hands by this point.

The judge then asked the prosecution if they wished to seek leave to apply for an extension to the minimum non-parole period of my sentence on the basis of any egregious factors. They didn't. The judge then informed me that the legislation left him no alternative but to sentence me to the mandatory term of life imprisonment, which meant a minimum non-parole period of ten years. I'm sure I didn't react. I was quite numb.

The two green-uniformed prison officers who had sat on either side of me in the dock then led me out the back door of the court and down the stairs to a holding cell. The escorting prison officers and court staff kindly let my father, Tania and Tania's mum come out the back to see me. I had held everything together to this point, but I'm not ashamed to say I shed more than a few tears then. After everyone had left and I was taken down to the lower holding cells, I took some of the pills Tania had slipped to me. They were coming on by the time I got back to the prison. Everyone was already locked up as I came back onto the wing. You're supposed to be put on observation when you're sentenced to life, but I told the officer on duty not to worry, that I wasn't suicidal. He looked at me thoughtfully and then agreed it wouldn't be necessary. I borrowed the wing's hair clippers and once locked up I shaved my head. It was an angry-looking haircut. This was the start of my new life. I could see my future in front of me, and I had no doubt that it would be an angry one.

*

For the next few days, people made an effort to stay away from me — not surprising, considering the chip I was carrying around on my shoulders. If anyone pissed me off, well, I had nothing to lose. Soon after I was sentenced, I was moved over from remand to the sentenced wing.

When you're on remand, you're still travelling hopefully because such is human nature that no matter how open and shut your case appears on the facts, you still imagine there's a chance you'll be acquitted, or that some mitigating circumstance will lead to a reduced sentence. Everything looks very different when you've been convicted. My lawyer sought leave to appeal. When legal aid was rejected, he asked Dad for a substantial fee to pursue the appeal. Dad paid it. The court wasted little time in denying leave, on the grounds of insufficient points of law on which to appeal. The judges asked if Bill Johnson's argument had been to show self-defence and provocation at the same time. They referred to this as 'an unusual line of defence' in my trial, and one which had 'stood little chance of succeeding'.

That was all in the background and in the future and had little significance for me just after my conviction. When you're not yet 20 years old and you're facing at least ten more years inside, it's pretty bleak. I'm naturally quite a positive person, but in the few days after the conclusion of my trial, I'll admit I had a few suicidal thoughts. This isn't uncommon, and nor is it rare for people newly faced with hopelessness to follow through on these impulses. I knew this for a fact, because while I was working as a wing cleaner on remand, I had cleaned out more than one cell after a suicide.

For me, drugs were still the answer, and I doubled-down on my consumption. As with the remand side, my drug buddy in the sentence wing was Stand. The Black Power gang, who had the numbers on the wing, were wary of Stand, and tried to stir up trouble for him. It didn't help that he had been buying dope from them on tick and meeting requests for payment with threats of violence. He looked a bit like a white supremacist on account of his very short haircut. I probably did, too. Truth be told, there weren't many hairstyle options in prison.

One day, I was playing pool with Stand when we were approached by a giant Samoan gang member.

'I got a question,' he said. 'Is it true you guys are White Power?'

I squared up to him, conscious that next to me Stand had changed his grip on the pool cue and was eyeing up potential strike points as I answered.

'Depends what you mean,' I said. 'If you mean am I white and proud of it, then yes. But if you mean are we members of a White Power gang who hates blacks, then no, we're not.' Even though we weren't White Power, it was important our response didn't communicate weakness. That would have been taken as an invitation to try and exploit or otherwise dominate us.

'Right,' the Samoan guy said. 'Makes sense to me. Didn't think you were White Power, but people were saying you were.'

Stand was celled up with another armed robber, and I had a motorcycle gang member for a cellmate. There was a small hole in the wall between our cells through which they would blow shotguns — exhaling the smoke from a lungful of cannabis for another person to inhale — after lockup. One day, my cellmate bragged that he did a nice tattoo, so I borrowed a boob gun (a home-made tattoo gun made out of a ballpoint pen, a toothbrush, a needle and a small electric motor running off a power adaptor). I got out of it on acid that night, and he got to work. When I woke in the morning and saw the finished product, a lame Celtic band, I was less than thrilled. I went next door and showed Stand.

'Wait there,' he said.

He disappeared for a few minutes. There were a few muffled shouts and dull thuds and he returned.

'Sorted,' he said.

He'd attacked my cellmate, broken some of his ribs and cracked his skull. He was carted off to hospital and not sighted on the wing again. It's a measure of my mentality in those days that I wasn't upset by this. On the contrary, I was pleased by the retribution taken on my behalf, and the message it sent: mess with Paul Wood at your peril.

*

The tensions between Stand (and by association, me) and Black Power were rising. But before they reached a flashpoint, another incident intervened. Drug dogs are a common presence at prison visits these days, but back in the mid-90s, their presence was relatively rare. So when Tania was stopped at a roadblock on her way to visit me and a drug dog was brought towards her car, she was caught completely unawares. The drug dog made a positive indication and in the subsequent search she was found to be carrying about 200 milligrams of methadone. This was bad enough, but when they looked in her bag, they found she was also carrying an assortment of knives. She was arrested and put into a cell. (Later, at her trial, however, the judge accepted that she had picked up the knives from the police station on the way to visit me — they had been confiscated during a raid on her house — and that she had been prescribed the methadone. She was acquitted.)

While she was being searched and arrested, I was in the wing awaiting her visit (and my drugs) with greater and greater agitation. After the roadblock packed up, a number of us were informed that our visitors had either been arrested or turned away. I was livid. Who the hell did these arseholes think they were to fuck with me like this? Stand and I got together for a meeting with a couple of the other hardcore guys in the wing. We decided there needed to be payback — a riot, or at least a 'prop' (an abbreviation of Protest for the Rights of Prisoners). We decided we would all get tooled up, go out into the exercise yard and refuse to come back in when time was up. I surreptitiously collected a number of pool balls, put them in socks, and hid them under my duvet. Others made similar preparations, and meanwhile, a young Black Power prospect who was in on the scheme went cell to cell telling people to get ready for what was going to go down. Looking back at this now, I have to shake my head at the outrageous sense of entitlement demonstrated by this whole incident, but I suppose such cringing at our adolescent behaviour is a good indicator of having grown up in the intervening years!

The screws had noticed these goings-on and had started to get worried. It didn't help that a couple of guys whose cells were near the office asked to be locked up early — a sure sign that something was going to happen, in which they wanted no part.

News of this great plan reached the cell of a respected old-school crim serving an armed robbery term (not his first), called Norm. He called the ringleaders together. He told us all exactly what would happen when our well thought-out plan was put into action. The screws wouldn't just come into the yard and fight us. They would call in a goon squad, put the fire hoses on us from the elevated guard walkway, drop in some tear gas, then come in with shields and batons and beat the hell out of us before rounding up the ringleaders and shipping us off to Paremoremo. After some debate, this old lag's cooler head prevailed and the riot was called off. Alternative action would be taken another day.

The prison staff seemed surprised and very relieved at 4.30 pm when lockup came and everyone stood by their cell. They had called in extra backup in case something happened and the tension was palpable.

It wasn't over though. A report to management named me as one of the ringleaders of the planned protest and someone they believed had made threats against a particular officer. A few days later, I was in the gym lifting weights when a screw told me the unit manager wanted to see me. I wandered over towards the administration section of the prison near the visiting room and remand wing. This should have struck me as odd, as his office was in the wing. I was still too green. I'd recently made an application to see him to talk about moving cells, and I assumed this was why I was being summoned. When I entered the visiting room area, about six screws were waiting for me. They grabbed me and placed me in wristlocks. I was then led into the custody manager's office. He was sitting behind his desk with the unit manager at his side. A line of officers stood between management and myself. The custody manager informed me I was being transferred.

I laughed. I was still ignorant enough to think they needed a reason for taking this kind of action. They looked unsettled by my laughter, but the custody manager repeated that I was being transferred out to another prison.

'Why? This is bullshit,' I said, but he nodded to the guards and they manhandled me out of the office and out to a waiting paddy wagon.

In the back of the paddy wagon was the Black Power prospect who had gone around letting everyone know the plan for our riot. He must have weighed about 105 kilograms, mainly muscle mass, and stood over 6 foot. He was one of the prisoners possibly responsible for the prohibition against beanies (woolly hats) in New Zealand prisons. One day, he and another guy had pulled beanies down over their faces and hidden behind another guy's door while he was off having a shower. When he came back, he was given a beating but was unable to identify his attackers because of the beanies; so, not long after this incident, beanies were banned. In subsequent years, people would just sling a t-shirt over their head, tying the sleeves behind their head and using the neck hole as an eye-slot.

'Where d'you think they're sending us?' the beanie guy asked me, sounding scared.

'Dunno,' I shrugged, feeling scared. The prospect of starting all over again in a new prison was daunting. This would be the first of many transfers I would experience during my imprisonment and they were always a source of anxiety and stress. You never knew who you would encounter who might have an issue with you and you would have to go through the whole process of being sussed out and potentially attacked by prospects of the dominant gang all over again.

'Wherever we end up, let's stick together, bro,' he suggested.

I readily agreed.

*

Our destination proved to be Rimutaka Men's Prison, east of Upper Hutt, around 50 kilometres north of Wellington. Upon arrival, we were taken to the receiving office. This is the area through which all inmates pass on their way to other areas. My companion was processed first while I was placed in a holding cell. That was the last I saw of him.

When it came to be my turn to be processed, I was determined to make things difficult for them. As far as I was concerned, the transfer was illegal. When I was directed to stand against a wall and have my photo taken, I refused. The processing officer calmly explained that a photo was necessary for their records. I again refused to comply.

'Well, we'll just put you back in the holding cell until you're ready,' he said.

'Why don't we just go out into the yard and have a fight about it?' I replied. I was expecting a beating from the staff sooner or later to show me who was boss, and it seemed like a reasonable suggestion to me that we settle it with a fist-fight, as often happened at Mount Crawford. Having a good, clean punch-up often avoided the need for the staff to send in the goon squad to sort you out after lockup.

The receiving officer looked genuinely surprised.

'I don't know how they do things in Wellington, but we're professionals here,' he said. 'We don't fight with the inmates. I suggest you just lose the attitude.'

After a bit, I calmed down and let them take my photo. I was put back into a paddy wagon and taken down to the unit 4 pound (solitary confinement punishment cells). This was my first real taste of the pound and it sucked. I was still in the clothes I had worn to the gym. My shoes were taken off me and I was placed in a small cinderblock cell without a window. It had a raised slab of concrete the size of a small single bed on one half of the floor. There was no mattress, only a grey blanket. The other side of the floor had a stainless steel toilet. I was furious, especially since I still hadn't been told why I was transferred. But the anger couldn't distract from the despair. I had nothing and no one.

When a screw came to do a muster later on, I asked where my clothes and things were. He told me they would be coming. It would be four days before they did, and when they eventually arrived, I found some of my property had either been binned or stolen.

The next day, the senior officer of the unit came to see me.

'Why was I transferred?' I asked.

'I don't know,' he said.

'But you must know why I'm in the pound. I haven't been convicted of any offence. Why am I being punished?'

'Oh, it's not a punishment,' he said. 'It's a management tool. You're on three months' pre-segs.'

This bullshit didn't improve my mood. The maximum term of solitary one can be sentenced to as a punishment by the prison was seven days, but simply by pronouncing the use of the pound as a management tool, you could find yourself in solitary for 14 days before the prison even had to apply to national office for permission to place you on preventative segregation. I didn't know all this at the time. But I thought I saw some light in the darkness.

'Hang on. If I'm not being punished, then I can have my electronics,' I said. 'Can't I?'

The senior screw shrugged.

'I suppose you can,' he said. He knew it was academic. There were no power outlets in the pound.

After three days, I was allowed to go to the kitchen area to make a phone call to tell Tania and my family I had been transferred. I remember that walk vividly, as on the way there, we passed a patch of grass. The colour was startling even after three days' sensory deprivation.

I found this stretch of pound psychologically very trying. It's never easy being on solitary, but it's nearly unbearable when you don't know how long it's going to last. To make things even worse, I was out of drugs. A drop had been planned for the day I was moved. I didn't even have cigarettes on me as I'd been at the gym. I was doing it real hard. I felt lost and desolate. I didn't take any responsibility for my situation at the time, and the reality was, I was finding ways to make my already bleak prison experience harder and harder for myself.

After about five days in the pound, the unit manager came to see me. She was a piece of work. She came into the yard I was allowed into, a tiny, concrete-walled space about half the size of a squash court, with a heavy grille over the roof. She had a cigarette, from which she took the occasional, luxurious drag. I have no doubt it wasn't lost on her I was hanging out for one.

I told her I wanted to know why I was in Rimutaka, and why I was in the pound.

'Don't try telling me you didn't do what you did,' she sneered. 'Don't even bother talking to me. I've met thousands of your kind before, and I've heard it all.'

I told her to fuck off. In her own time, she did. She went on to become Rimutaka Prison's site manager.

*

On 30 January 1997, after eight days in solitary, about six large screws came into the pound and told me I was off 'up top'.

'About time,' I said happily, thinking they meant I was being sent to the so-called capital cells, which were more like normal cells and at least had power points. I was confused and amused as to why they'd send so many screws to get me. I was handcuffed and put into a van to be moved up to the receiving office. Once back in the holding cell, I had a visit from the custody manager.

'So we're sending you to Paremoremo,' he said.

My stomach hit the floor and dread settled over me like a fog. I asked if I could call my father to let him know. I don't remember how my dad took it; I was too numb to pay much attention at the time. Then they took the phone away and left me to wait for my summons onto the bus.

Ten long minutes passed, as all of the horror stories I'd heard about Paremoremo played in my mind. But then the custody manager returned with another guy in civilian clothing, who introduced himself as the prison inspector. He told me he wasn't happy I was being sent to Paremoremo.

'I don't think you should go to Pare,' he said. 'You're young. You're not yet twenty. You're impressionable and easily influenced and I don't think Pare will do you any good at all.'

After a brief discussion, I was told I was to be given one more chance. I would be placed in preventative segregation in the capital cells, with a monthly review. If I behaved, I could come off isolation.

Later that day I was moved up to the capital cells. Each of the six cells was about 2.5 metres square and had access to a tiny yard, at the end of which there was a showerhead. You were on your own the whole time. The screws only needed to open your cell door twice a day, once in the morning when they would unlock the security door at the back of your cell so you could access the yard and shower, the other in the evening when they would lock this door up again. Your meals were passed through the slot in the door, and your access to the shower and yard meant you didn't need to be moved at all. It was good to be able to have more than one shower if you wished and to spend more than an hour outside — if you can ever really call a small concrete box with a security mesh roof 'outside' — but never going anywhere is unpleasant. It makes one stir-crazy. Still, at least after a few more days I was able to get my TV and radio again. I didn't understand personality differences between people at this time, but anyone who knows me well would describe me as highly extroverted. As such, I like to be around people, so I would find long spells of solitary confinement particularly challenging. I remember how I would sometimes start to feel a kind of rising panic in my chest, which I could only alleviate by walking tight laps back and forward in my cell or doing push-ups and star jumps.

The first visits I received at Rimutaka were non-contact visits, where the parties are separated by thick Perspex and communicate by a telephone-like intercom. Trouble was, these often didn't work, whereupon you would have to shout to make yourself heard through the Perspex and over the sound of inmates in other booths doing the same. I remember the first time my father visited me in these circumstances. I was very angry about how I had been treated by the system at this time and probably voiced such concerns. As was my pattern at this stage, I felt like the victim, disregarding the role I had played in my own circumstances. The fact I might in some way be accountable never occurred to me. My father was upset enough by this visit to write a letter of complaint, in which he described the experience as like visiting an animal in the zoo. Fortunately, I wasn't on booths for too long before my first pre-segs review came up and it was decided I could be placed back on mainstream.

*

I was moved from the capitals to unit 3, which was the classification wing of Rimutaka at this time. I was very happy to be around other people again. At this stage, unit 3 comprised two wings with interconnecting doors, which were open most of the day. The wing was dominated by the Mongrel Mob, which was fine: I had no real problems with the Mob.

It wasn't long before my visits and drug use were back into full swing. I also caught up with Mugshot again. He was transferred down from Pare not long after my own arrival. He'd had an interesting time up there. He'd run into TNC again, and TNC had seen the opportunity for revenge. He challenged Mugshot to a fight down in the gym. It was going Mugshot's way — no surprises there, given how hard of heart and strong of sinew Mugshot was — when TNC thought he'd alter the odds by whipping out a shiv (a homemade knife).

'Oh, you want a knife fight,' Mugshot grinned. 'I'm cool with that,' and casually produced his own shiv. TNC decided discretion was the better part of valour: plainly not much had changed with Mugshot.

During afternoon lockdown one day, I had my radio on loud and was trying to snap the weld on the seat in my cell, which was attached to the wall on a swinging arm, by pushing it back and forth. I'd been smoking gold cannabis oil all day and was smashed, so it didn't occur to me I was probably making a fair bit of noise.

I thought I heard some banging, so I turned off my radio and listened. My neighbour had been yelling out and thumping the wall. He was a Black Power guy in his late twenties who I think was in for armed robbery. I couldn't hear what he was saying and was too stoned to really care. I turned my radio back on and resumed trying to break the seat. After some more banging on the wall from my neighbour I stopped working on the seat. But I left the radio on so I could lie back and enjoy the music. I was 19, and concepts such as simple consideration were still beyond me.

The moment I stepped out of my cell at unlock at half past three, my neighbour smacked me in the face, sending me flying backwards onto the floor. The blow would turn into a nasty black eye. It happened right in front of the screws, so before I was even on my feet he was getting locked back up. At the time, I wasn't prepared to admit his anger at all the banging and loud music I'd been responsible for was justified. I was pretty pissed off, and disappointed he hadn't waited till we'd got to the gym so we could have a proper fight without the screws getting involved.

While he was locked in his cell, an older guy — he was probably about 35, but he seemed old to me — whom we both respected told him off for being a bully. I'll call him Harry. 'Yeah, you're probably right, Harry,' my neighbour said. He beckoned me over to share a joint with him, which was his way of making amends for attacking me. So I stood there and smoked a joint with him and Harry, passing it back and forth under the door.

Having bought into the prison ethos, it meant that despite smoking the peace pipe, I still felt I had a grievance against my neighbour, and I was reminded of it each time I felt the swelling around my eye or caught someone looking at it and smirking. It wasn't just the injury. I firmly believed that if I let the matter lie, it would be taken as a sign of weakness and everyone and anyone who wanted to punk me would have a go. I went and consulted Harry.

'He punched me for no reason,' I said. 'What d'you reckon I should do about it?'

He looked thoughtful.

'That's not an easy question to answer,' he said. 'If it was my brother, my brother would go and stab him up. But that doesn't mean you have to. You'll have to decide for yourself what the right thing to do is.'

I was in a quandary. I felt the correct thing to do was to have a one-out in the gym. But I knew I was on thin ice at Rimutaka, and was in danger of being sent to Paremoremo. That would spell the end of any thought I might have of escaping: escape was never far from my mind. That meant I couldn't risk getting in trouble for fighting.

I asked Mugshot what I should do.

'Easy,' he said. 'You take the fucker out suddenly so the screws never know.'

He suggested I await my moment to take my neighbour in a flying chokehold while I was walking past him, so that I could drag him into a cell and choke him unconscious without being noticed. It sounded like a good plan to me, and I spent quite a lot of time training for it with Mugshot. But prison being prison, my neighbour suspected I might not have let the matter drop. He never presented me with an opportunity. The one time I saw him approaching down the corridor, he was on his way to the carving room and had a chisel in his hand. He eyed me warily. And soon after that, he was re-classified and transferred to the low-to-medium security section of the prison. If I'm honest, I felt lucky he had gone as it let me off having to retaliate to retain my honour. Deep down, I knew it was my own lack of consideration that had led to the attack, but I was still too immature to take accountability for anything. And prison is the ultimate example of what is called an 'honour culture', which anthropologists define as a culture where people avoid intentionally offending others, and where cultivating a reputation for punishing improper conduct by others is paramount. Rights and wrongs aside, any perceived disrespect must be met with extreme consequences.

*

Not long after this, Mugshot got in a fight in the gym with a Mob associate who was using the piece of equipment that Mugshot wanted to use and refused to let him have it. Mugshot stepped him out, and he declared himself up for the fight. I was to stand lookout to warn them if the screws appeared. No sooner had the fight begun — I was watching the screws relaxing on the bench just outside the door — than other Mongrel Mob members barged past me to join in. I ran in, too, to try to break it up. The screws were close behind me, and everything was shut down before it turned into a full-scale brawl. Mugshot and I were escorted back to the wing and locked up for our own protection. I felt conflicted. When I'd first arrived in the wing, the Mob had invited me to sit at their table and had treated me very kindly. I liked Mugshot, but it wasn't the first time he had picked a fight with people I liked.

Fortunately, when I was unlocked, it was plain the Mob had no issue with me. Mugshot remained locked up until they moved him out of the wing. I will admit to more than a little relief when I saw him go.

*

During my time in the unit I spent quite a bit of time hanging out with a Mobster I will call Niccolò. Looking back on it now, I can see he was one of the most Machiavellian people I have ever come across. At the time, being impressionable and super-anxious to attach myself to people I admired, I just thought he was cool. He seemed like a smart guy: he knew how to make bombs and heaps of other cool stuff, and he had the best cannabis oil I had ever smoked. He had initially been sentenced to 19 years for armed robbery, and he had compounded matters by escaping and committing further armed robberies. He had also been involved in an incident in B Block at Paremoremo, where a member of a rival gang had pulled a knife on him. The mistake wasn't pulling the knife: it was not using it. Niccolò had beaten him with a weight bar and left him with a permanent brain injury. He was a dangerous man. But he seemed to take an interest in me, and was always very kind to me.

One day, late in 1997, Niccolò beckoned me over to a corner of the exercise yard. He looked all around us to make sure no one was paying too much attention or that we'd be overheard, then he leaned in conspiratorially.

'I've got a bro on the outside who's going to bust me out,' he said in a low voice. 'You should come too. We'll give you a gun. It's real sweet, it's a semi-auto that's been converted to auto. We'll give you a car and you can go your own way while we go ours.'

Niccolò outlined his plan to me. He had a mate — I actually knew the name, as he was often in the papers for his exploits as a Māori activist — who was going to snip his way through the perimeter fence and then climb onto the roof of the ablutions area of our block. The toilet had a small, plastic skylight which he (let's call him Trev) would cut through. During evening recreation time, Niccolò and I would climb out the window, let ourselves down to the ground and wriggle through the fence. Trev would be waiting with a car. Somewhere down the road, they'd give me the gun and the keys to another car. They'd roar off into the night and leave me to do the same.

I was stunned. I knew right away that Niccolò wasn't proposing to do me a favour. He wasn't offering to share his escape line — his safe house and ringbolt — with me. He was calculating that if not one but two serious offenders were on the loose, it would divide police resources and increase his chances of giving them the slip.

It seems crazy, but I seriously considered it. I gave it a lot of thought, but in the end, I declined the offer.

'Ah, pity. Pity,' he said. 'You can change your mind at any time.'

I had butterflies in my stomach on the evening the escape was planned. I lay in my cell during lockup thinking about Trev snipping his way through the fence. I decided I needed to try to remove any suspicion that I was involved, and after unlock I asked the screw if gym had been called. I figured if I was in the gym rather than in the wing when the escape happened, it would look better. Trouble was, the gym call had already been made and I'd missed it. I stayed in my cell.

Just before lockup, who should appear at the door of my cell but Niccolò.

'Didn't go down,' he said. 'Trev couldn't get through the roof.'

I went to sleep that night relieved I had made the right choice. I vowed that when I escaped, it would be on my terms and when I had everything in place on the outside to assist me. It was still years before I realised the only escape that would ever matter would be from my sense of entitlement and my inability to take responsibility for my actions. Any physical escape from prison would have only changed the superficial things that were holding me back. I would still have been carrying about all my self-defeating and distorted beliefs, which were far stronger chains.

The screw on night orderly duty woke me in the middle of the night for a muster. This was unusual. The night orderly would normally just shine his torch in your cell to make sure you were there. I guessed they had found the hole cut in the perimeter fence.

Next morning, we were unlocked at the usual time, but the wing was full of screws. We were all spread-eagled against the wall and patted down before we were led into the yard. Once everyone was in the yard the screws went through the cells. It was clear they weren't sure whether they were dealing with an escape attempt or a massive drop of contraband. I was patted down by a guard by the name of Scotty with whom I had a bit of a rapport.

'Surprised to see you're still here,' he said.

'What are you talking about?' I replied.

'Oh, I think you know,' Scotty grinned back.

It was probably no surprise I'd been identified as a potential escaper. Only Niccolò was serving a longer lag than me, and then there was my slightly unusual request to go to the gym the previous evening. Because the roof hadn't been cut, management probably assumed the escape would be attempted by people fleeing on their way to the gym or already there.

A couple of days later, I was brought in front of the visiting justice on a drug-related charge. I had been the subject of a number of incident reports and investigations, and this was just the latest. I had been rudely awoken in the middle of the night and my cell turned upside down and the barrel of a ballpoint pen had been found secreted in my cell. It was decided this had been used for drug abuse (it had) and I was sentenced to seven days in the pound and 28 days of OPs (off-privileges).

I appealed. I was guilty, of course, but that didn't change my determination to put my best foot forward on appeal. The system is adversarial. It's not set up to determine the truth of a situation, but instead your legal culpability. My experience was that, for either side, technical wiggle room, sleight of hand, or outright corruption determined such culpability — certainly not actual truth, or justice. And I still hadn't morally developed beyond the stage that judges right or wrong on the basis of whether or not one gets punished rather than whether or not one has done something wrong. As an interesting aside, we know from the research that the extent to which one will be punished does not significantly influence whether or not people criminally offend; what does figure in their calculations is the perceived likelihood they will be caught.

The way prison misconduct charges work is that you go up in front of the prison superintendent or their proxy. They find you guilty. If you disagree, you appeal your conviction and go up in front of a Visiting Justice of the Peace (VJ). The idea is that a VJ is independent of the prison authorities and will give you a fair and impartial hearing. What is supposed to happen is the prison lets the court registrar know when they need a VJ to come, the court registrar then consults the roster of local Justices of the Peace, who take turns to go to the prison. That's not the way it worked at Rimutaka, where they had a pet VJ they would contact directly, who, according to the stories, was firmly and unabashedly on the side of the authorities. It was this notorious woman who heard my appeal.

On the day I went up, I had all of my bush lawyer materials prepared. Niccolò had shown me the relevant legislation to quote and had otherwise helped me prepare. I presented my case, but I might as well have saved my breath. The VJ fixed me in a stern stare and said, in these very words: 'The law does not apply in the war against drugs.'

She then upheld the sentence of seven days in the pound and 28 days of OPs. I couldn't believe it. As I was placed in wristlocks by the guards and painfully dragged out of the hearing room, I made my eloquent, closing address.

'I'll have your fucking job for this!' I yelled.

Interestingly, this VJ did eventually lose her job, when one day a prisoner's advocate overheard her colluding with staff about the best penalty to impose on a prisoner *before* the hearing. Even so, the advocate had their work cut out to have her stood down. Rimutaka fought long and hard to prevent it.

*

My rage kept me warm in the pound. But I had a nagging feeling this would be my last stint of solitary at Rimutaka. I had avoided Pare by the skin of my teeth once already, and had been warned repeatedly since. Nevertheless, I still held on to the naïve belief that Rimutaka would need some reason to transfer me up to Pare. There was no way smoking a bit of pot was enough.

Normally, once your time was up in the pound you were taken straight back to the wing. So I knew something was amiss when, after my week was up, I was told to stay in the pound yard. A couple of hours later a whole heap of screws and the unit manager from three arrived. He informed me I was being moved to Paremoremo. Then I was told to turn around and back up to the yard gate so that I could be handcuffed through the bars without the screws having to enter the yard.

I had absolutely nothing to lose. I told the unit manager to get fucked. I told them to come and get me and that I sure as fuck wouldn't be going quietly. Negotiations were entered into. The unit manager told me to calm down, that no one wanted to fight with me. He told me I was moving and had no choice in the matter. I told him I would come quietly if they got me a packet of smokes and a lighter. They complied. Once someone had returned with some smokes they were passed through the bars to me. I had a smoke while they waited. I then backed up to the gate and let them handcuff me.

CHAPTER 5

Maximum Security

Many years after I got out of prison, a good friend would ask me why I had continued to engage in so much of the kind of behaviour that was guaranteed to make my life much harder. I've already discussed my inability then to be accountable for my actions and my sense of entitlement when it came to breaking rules I didn't agree with. On reflection, I also think that the fundamental human drive to feel you have control over your choices led me do the opposite of what I was being asked to do if I thought someone was trying to further limit my already limited choices. Perhaps the best way to understand this is to look at it from a less individual perspective. According to Erving Goffman, author of the 1961 work *Asylums: Essays on the social situation of mental patients and other inmates*, there are a number of ways in which an inmate can adapt to imprisonment, and they may adopt different strategies during different phases of their sentence or use a range of tactics at any one time. One form of adaptation is known as 'situational withdrawal'. When this occurs, the inmate apparently withdraws attention from everything except what is in their immediate vicinity, and will often interpret what's going on differently from others around them. This is sometimes referred to as 'prison psychosis' or going 'stir simple'. Another tactic is referred to as the 'intransigent line', whereby the inmate intentionally challenges the institution by flagrantly refusing to co-operate with staff. Rather than being dejected by their situation, the intransigent inmate's morale is often quite high. According to Goffman, intransigence is typically an early and temporary phase, with the inmate soon shifting to situational withdrawal or some other line of adaptation. I suppose it would be fair to say I had done a decent job of exemplifying intransigence in the first two years of my imprisonment.

These modes of adaptation are analogous to tactics we use to adapt to our mental prisons. We are often in denial of evidence that our thinking has become unhelpful or obstructive. You see it very clearly in alcoholics and drug addicts, whose perceptions of their own reality can be quite fantastic to an objective observer: an alcoholic 'can control' their drinking; a junkie 'can kick the habit any time'. Neither of them has a problem — it's everyone around them who has a problem.

But the self-deceptive thinking of the addict is just an extreme example of the kind of delusion that keeps us in our mental prisons. Most of us are resistant to change, even when we have a sneaking suspicion change is desirable, or even vital, if we're to improve our lives.

*

Every Thursday, a prison bus leaves Wellington Prison bound for Auckland, 660 kilometres away to the north. It carries custodial staff and prisoners, with the staff at the front separated from the prisoners in a caged-off area at the back. Its first stop after

Mount Crawford is Rimutaka Prison, which is where I boarded it in the early afternoon. Two other guys boarded at the same time. Both were off to the prison camps in the middle of the North Island, so they must have been sentenced to corrective training (CT), an army 'boot camp'–style alternative to prison. That made them young — to be eligible for CT, you have to be less than 20 years old — which meant they were probably only a couple of months younger than me. They were both white, and they looked scared and despondent, even though the maximum sentence for CT is three months. We didn't look that different from each other, but we inhabited very different worlds, and we were off to very different places.

The next stop was Linton Prison near Palmerston North. A couple more guys got on at this stop. We then moved on to Kaitoke Prison near Wanganui, where we were to stop for the night. This was the standard practice, and Kaitoke had special six- and eight-man cells set up to house overnighters. When we arrived, we found there weren't enough of these cells to go round, so the two CT guys and myself were housed in the remand wing for the night. This news brought me a sense of relief, as having to share a cell and try to sleep with multiple strangers was a high-risk situation. I instead found myself in a slot with one of the CT guys, while the other was taken off to be in a cell by himself. That seemed a bit odd to me, but I shrugged and prepared to settle in. But then the kid who had been mistaken for the lifer (me) pushed his panic button and drew the matter to the attention of the guards. We were soon swapped. That's how young I looked — young enough to be taken for a CT candidate. I remember eating, but not tasting, a cold meat and potato meal that night.

The following morning, it was back on the bus. Our first stop was at prison camps at Rangipo near Turangi, perched on the high, desolate volcanic plateau between Lake Taupō and Mount Ruapehu. The two CT boys were unloaded as I watched enviously. The three of us remaining aboard were given a packet of sandwiches for lunch, and we were soon joined by about six Māori guys. Three of them had been celebrating and were very drunk, from which it was plain they were heading back to Auckland to be released. They struck me as a bunch of loud fuckwits, and I was soon confirmed in this estimation. I was sitting towards the back of the bus with my cap pulled low over my eyes, minding my own business when one of the drunk guys lurched down the aisle in my direction.

'What you in for, bro?' he asked.

'Murder,' I replied.

His lip curled.

'What, you kill a granny or something?'

I could understand his thinking: a young white guy in for murder; it must be something dodgy. 'Nah,' I replied. 'I killed a police informant.'

That shut him up. He went back and joined his mates. I'd sized him up as a blowhard pussy the second I saw him, the type who would try and bully weaker inmates but would then piss his pants and run to the screws crying if anyone actually fronted him.

As it turned out, he puked about an hour after boarding the bus and went to sleep. I sat there trying to ignore the vomit smell and seething that the screws had allowed such obviously drunk inmates on the bus. But I knew the reality: they didn't give a shit. They were like the truckie who drives a stock truck to the works: the sheep in the back are just another load of meat.

After a long three hours, most of which I spent fantasising about smashing the drunk guy, our next stop was Waikeria

Prison, just out of Hamilton. We were all offloaded and put in holding cells while the screws cleaned the bus. By the time we got underway again, the bus was full. About seven of the guys who had joined at Waikeria were young Polynesian gangsters. I kept to myself with my cap down, as I had done all trip. But probably because the Māori and Polynesian contingent in the van well outnumbered the Pākehā, one of the more aggressive of the gangsters started making comments about the white people driving past the bus in their cars. Each time he made a racial slur of this kind, he looked at me, clearly looking for some kind of reaction. It cut me up having to listen to this shit. I felt a mix of fear and indignation building inside me. It sucks having to listen to people denigrate you and not be able to say anything in response. I would have loved to smash his face in. I half-wanted them to come and try to take me on, and I made plans for how I would fight them off if they did. Because they were all in seats in front of me, as long as I could get out of my seat quickly enough, I'd only have to take one or two of them on at a time and could make a good show of it. This is what I was thinking about to avoid admitting to myself I was scared and that not responding was really a sign of cowardice. But deep down I knew if I were a real man I wouldn't be putting up with this shit and the consequences wouldn't even enter into it. I guess that planning how I would deal with an attack helped me feel more powerful and repress this feeling of failure and unworthiness. Fortunately for both of us, he was just testing the waters. Or perhaps he just didn't smell the fear he was hoping to smell. Whichever it was, he soon picked someone further up the bus to hassle and left me to my own devices.

Inevitably, my thoughts returned to what lay ahead. Because of my lack of compliance, I had always known I'd end up in

Paremoremo, so while I was in Mount Crawford and Rimutaka, I'd asked some of the old hands what it was like. The most important thing, I was told, was to get into the right cell block.

The maximum security side of Paremoremo (now officially called Auckland Prison) was housed in the east wing in those days, a utilitarian set of concrete buildings surrounded by a fence topped with razor wire and studded with guard towers. The resemblance to the kind of jails you see on American television wasn't just coincidental: when Pare was being planned, New Zealand officials had flown to the USA to visit some of its maximum security facilities to get an idea of what worked. Paremoremo was modelled on the facility built at Marion, Illinois, to replace Alcatraz as America's most secure penitentiary. Pare was opened in 1968 and a medium security facility was added in 1981 to replace the ancient and no longer fit-for-purpose Mount Eden. As I write, a new maximum security facility is being built to replace the old east wing, and is nearing completion.

When you first arrived in those days, you were dumped in 'classification', where your behaviour and the level of threat you posed to yourself and others was assessed for up to three months. Depending on the outcome of this scrutiny, and according to a bunch of other considerations, including available space, you were then assigned to one of the three cell blocks. (There are actually four blocks, but the best-known, the notorious D Block, was not actually a regular cell block. It was for special cases: half was used for punishing prisoners, the other half was for so-called 'super-seg' offenders, those who posed too great a risk to other inmates or who were at too great a risk themselves to be allowed to mix with the general prison population. Because it was for the supposedly worst offenders, D Block was actually felt by prisoners to be a lot safer than the others, as everyone there was very closely supervised and behaviour was intensely constrained.) For a Pākehā like me, the best block was C Block, as it was relatively neutral, not being under the sway of any particular gang or ethnic group. Of A and B Blocks, B was by far the worse, being dominated, like most New Zealand prisons, by Māori and Polynesian gangs and well known for inter-gang violence and riots. As an old Pare bad-ass once told me back in Mount Crawford, I could expect to be 'eaten alive' in B Block. He wasn't trying to put the wind up me. I had asked, and he was just telling me the facts. I seriously didn't want to end up in B Block.

John Barlow had vanished from remand at Mount Crawford the day the jury in his third trial returned a guilty verdict. I had heard he'd ended up in C Block. I hoped one silver lining of my shift to Pare would be renewing my acquaintance with him — if I were to end up in C Block, too.

As we dropped down the northern slopes of the Bombay Hills and rode the motorway through Auckland's southern suburbs, I was thinking to myself that whatever happened, the only way to survive would be to try and do as much damage as possible to the first person who tried it on with me. This way I would at least send a message that I wasn't someone to be taken lightly.

Soon after the grim, volcanic stone walls of Mount Eden Prison hove into view on our left, the bus took the motorway off-ramp at Gillies Avenue. When we pulled up in the receiving area in the early evening, there was a paddy wagon waiting. I was called out to get off the bus. A hush fell. Everyone else knew what this meant. I climbed off the bus and was placed straight in the paddy wagon for the drive north over the Harbour Bridge to Paremoremo.

*

It was dark by the time I got to Pare — not that I would have been able to see anything out of the paddy wagon, anyway. I was initially placed in a holding cell. A little while later, I was brought out and briefly interviewed. I suppose this was to determine whether I was a risk to myself or suffered any obvious mental illness. Once this was out of the way, I was processed. Three screws made me strip and then provided me with prison kit. This was Y-front underwear, blue denim jeans, a white t-shirt, and a blue sweatshirt.

'What did you do to get sent up top?' one of the screws asked me.

I told him I didn't really know. All I had done was smoke a bit of pot. As far as I could tell, there had been a mistake.

'Oh,' he said, in tones of mock sympathy. 'My heart bleeds custard.'

I asked if I would be going to the classification block that night.

The screw laughed.

'No, sunshine. You're off to Butterfly Block, where they put all the lovely butterflies.'

'I thought I went to Class first?'

'Normally. But there's no room at the inn at Class, is there? It's B Block for you.'

My heart sank, and my anxiety increased. I was given my TV and other meagre possessions, which had been brought from Rimutaka, then led out of the receiving office and towards B Block. The screw and I walked in silence down the long, harshly lit corridor off which the cell blocks opened, accompanied by the noise of the steel doors sliding shut and locking with a clang. This corridor was known as 'the airstrip', presumably because it was long and straight. I was scared and my stomach was churning.

My only consideration was *how* bad it would be. That it would be bad wasn't even a question.

Each cell block was three storeys high. The bottom floor housed the mess room, a recreation room and hobbies rooms. On the bottom floor, there was a 'sally port' that led out into the yard. A sally port is an enclosed space between two security gates. If you wished to go to the yard, you would have to be let through the grille comprising the internal gate, whereupon you would find yourself in a holding area. This grille would then close behind you. Then the outer grille would open and walking through this, you would find yourself in the yard. All movements in Pare were controlled by sally ports, and all sally ports were opened and shut electronically — meaning guards didn't carry keys. The idea was that this made guards safer, as they were less likely to be assaulted or taken hostage by prisoners. In the middle of Pare, at the end of the landing strip, was an area with bullet-proof, mirrored glass windows from which all movements out of the blocks and around the prison were monitored. This control room was known as 'the fishbowl'. You passed it every time you went anywhere from the cell blocks to visits, the medical centre or the pound.

The second and third floors of each of Pare's cell blocks were where the prisoners were held, 48 to a block, 24 on each floor. Access to each of these levels was by a set of stairs at the front. The cells were arranged in a U-shape with 12 cells on each side (each side being called a 'landing'). The third-floor landing on the left as viewed from the front of the block was known as 'top-left'. The right-hand side landing on the second floor was known as 'bottom-right', and so on and so forth. At the entrance to each landing was another barred gate that could be locked off to separate one or all landings from the rest of the block if the need arose. From the top-floor stairwell, you could look all the way down to the concrete of the bottom floor, and yes, people were occasionally thrown down from the third floor. In fact, I would hear some years later that the guy who had punched me in the head at Rimutaka Prison experienced just this fate.

In keeping with the jail's American design, the cells didn't have doors. Instead, they had bars that opened onto the landing and an electronically operated sliding grille door. The space between the blank rear walls of the cells was accessible by another stairwell, from which repairs and maintenance to services could be done, and from which the riot squad could gain access to each landing if, for any reason, the main stairs were inaccessible.

Everyone was already locked up as I arrived, so I was paraded past the curious and hostile glares of the residents of bottom-right as the screws took me to my cell at the back. The only thing I was pleased about was that bottom-right was the landing closest to the block's guardroom.

As I neared my cell, an ugly little white guy with lots of crude tattoos on his neck peered out at me.

'Good,' he said in a loud voice. 'Another white boy.'

I immediately felt a wave of worry hit me. Fuck off, I thought. Don't tar me with your brush, you little fuck. The last thing I needed was to step into someone else's bullshit.

The screws placed me in my slot and the bars slid across and closed with a squeal and a clang. I did a recce, which didn't take long. The slot was furnished with a toilet against the back wall, a solid iron bed frame bolted to the side wall, and a metal bench bolted to the other wall. There was a power point for the TV above the bench, but I noted with disgust that the aerial jack was located right at the other end of the cell. I guessed (correctly) this meant you couldn't watch TV until you'd got hold of an especially long coaxial cable. I later found out you could buy one of these through the prison.

As soon as the screws' footsteps had faded away along the landing, I hunted around in my gear for a paperclip, which I bent to fashion a small, flathead screwdriver. I used this to open the transformer housing of an electric wood burner tool I had been allowed to bring with me, where back in Rimutaka I had sellotaped about four big, fat roaches (as the butt of marijuana joints are known) for a rainy day. It had been a hell of a week and tomorrow wasn't promising to be any better. This, I thought, was about as rainy as it could get. I sparked up and lay back on my bed, dreading the morning's unlock.

*

The doors unlocked with a bang at eight the following morning. The cell doors could be operated individually or, as now, en masse. I joined the straggle of prisoners slouching their way down the stairs to the mess room to get breakfast. I tried not to meet anyone's eye.

All of the kitchen staff at Pare were drawn from C Block. Each block had a mess man, whose job it was to receive meals through a metal hatch in the far wall of the mess room and place them on the tables, while the block inmates waited behind the Perspex and steel entrance door. Meals at Pare were served on disposable plates, and as in all moderate-to-high security institutions, you were issued with plastic cutlery. When the mess man was finished, the servery door would close and the entrance door would slide open. Everyone would come in and find a place at the tables where their meals were already waiting. This was the bit I hated: looking for a seat. Luckily for me, one of the guys who was sitting at the table closest to the door told me there was a seat at that table. I was so grateful to him.

All the same, I grabbed my breakfast and went back to my cell, as you were allowed to do. As I was walking back up to the second floor, head down, eyes averted, someone moved to intercept me.

'Bro.'

I glanced up at a heavily tattooed face — not the kind of face you'd be pleased to see in the normal run of things, but one which I was positively delighted to recognise. It was Pace, whom I had last seen as he was escorted, wrapped in nothing but a sheet, from the remand wing in Mount Crawford after a stabbing in the showers. He was convicted for his involvement in that incident, and I had heard he was soon moved out of the wing altogether after a late-night raid prompted by a tip-off that an escape was imminent.

'Good to see you,' he said. 'Where they got you?'

I told him where my cell was and he came up to visit after breakfast. He had done quite a lot of work on his facial tattoos since I had last seen him. He was a member of the Nomads, and he told me the Nomads had the numbers in B Block. This was like music to my ears. As long as I was in with Pace, I was in with the Nomads and relatively safe. He also told me Manu was in the pound and would soon be back. I was pleased to hear that, too.

I spent quite some time chatting with Pace down in the hobby room. There were three separate carving rooms in B Block. They were basically separated along gang lines. One belonged to the Mongrel Mob, one belonged to the Nomads and the few Black Power members who were on the block, and there was a little bone carving room that was shared by a couple of lifers without affiliation to either group.

'You right for dak, brother?' Pace asked. When I told him I had run out, he gave me a few joints to tide me over until I could sort out my own supply.

Pace told me what I could expect in Pare. He told me about the food. I'd already had breakfast, and we would soon have lunch — three sandwiches of questionable nutritional value and zero taste. They were wrapped in greaseproof paper. (The other prisons I had been to wrapped their sandwiches in Gladwrap, but Gladwrap can easily be turned into an edged weapon — all you need to do to make a stabbing implement with plastic wrap is wrap it tightly around a toothbrush or pen and then melt it and shape it until it is a hard plastic blade. You then sharpen its edges by rubbing it back and forward against a concrete surface — and there is no shortage of suitable concrete surfaces in prison.) Pace told me not to get my hopes up about dinner, and when later that day I went down to meal parade, it was to receive some truly horrendous slop on a plate that would turn out to be representative of most Pare meals. I wasn't impressed, although I will admit to having been pretty fussy in my early years. Still, I remember reading a newspaper report about how good our meals were at Pare. The accompanying picture didn't look like anything I saw during my stay there.

The other prisoners I was to share the table with were there by the time I arrived. There were eight people to a table: three on each side and one at either end. The only person who really made an impression on me when I first sat at this table was a member of the King Cobras, a Samoan gang. This guy was a real arsehole. He ate with his fingers and regularly tried to provoke me. I just ignored him, swallowed my indignation like a hard lump, and went to sleep each night dreaming about cutting his throat. That sounds terrible, and it's abhorrent to me now, but violent fantasies such as this served a purpose throughout my time in prison. I'm aware of some psychological theories that contend that such fantasies predispose you to commit actual violence. But my personal experience is that they helped me avoid dwelling on the people I would willingly have hurt for the grief they caused me. Later on during my term, I would attain great satisfaction by imagining I was dropping each of those on my shit list down a well, one by one. After doing so, I found I would then stop thinking about them. Interestingly, in later years, I became familiar with the work of David Buss, an evolutionary psychologist from the University of Texas, who asked his students to state whether they had ever seriously considered murdering someone, and if they had, to write their homicidal fantasy out in detail in an essay. He was astonished to find that 91 per cent of men and 84 per cent of women had detailed homicidal fantasies. Since only a small number of people ever acted on these, he concluded that such fantasies were part of the 'normal' suite of psychological coping strategies.

While Pace helped me to acclimatise to life in B Block, there were some things I had to find out for myself. In the other prisons, you wore mufti. Pare was the first I'd been in where you wore a uniform, which was issued to you when you first arrived: so many t-shirts, jeans, pairs of socks, undies and so on. At the end of the week, you put your laundry out for collection. I hadn't really thought it through, but of course, there's no way of distinguishing one person's clothes from the next. Everything arrives back in a great, big, anonymous pile, and you help yourself to what you need. I didn't mind wearing someone else's socks or t-shirts, but I wasn't too bloody thrilled about wearing second-hand undies.

When I complained about this to Pace, he just laughed.

'You don't put your undies out, man,' he said. 'You wash them in the sink!'

*

Soon after I had settled in, I heard there was a game of Crash going in the gym. Crash is a bit like rugby league, in that the object is nominally to carry a ball from one end of the pitch to the other, but its main purpose is to provide an excuse to smash people. It's always rough, but games at Pare were ruthless and brutal. It wasn't uncommon for people to break bones. This was partly due to the fact the games were generally recorded on a video camera and then the tapes were played on the prison video system. This meant every block in the prison could watch the games of other blocks. Of course, prison machismo being what it is, there was no way people from one block would leave themselves open to accusations of weakness from other blocks, so games were never friendly.

Crash at Pare was played on the wooden gymnasium floor, which wasn't too bad compared to the usual concrete of a yard. People used to rip pieces of foam off their mattresses and bind these to their elbows and knees to minimise wood burn and other injuries. On one side of the 'field' was a stage, on the other side a wooden rail at about waist height. This rail separated the spectators' seats from the court.

I wasn't fazed by any of this, but what I found disconcerting about the first game I played at Pare was that about ten minutes into the game one of the gang members was tackled and there was a glint of steel as something flew from the waistband of his pants and clattered on the floor. A shiv spun lazily on the boards. The owner nonchalantly bent down, retrieved it and replaced it in his pants. There were times when half the field were probably playing while carrying weapons.

As a relatively light white guy, I was initially the target of many concerted runs down the field. Fortunately, this didn't last long. I just went low, as always, and put a few big guys on the floor. Then my opponents changed tactics, and I was given the ball on attack. I got hammered, over and over again, colliding heavily with tacklers, the stage, the handrail and the ground. No matter how much it hurt, I always bounced back up and carried on as though I hadn't felt a thing. I always considered Crash an important way to demonstrate I wasn't scared and an excellent way to signal to those on the lookout to victimise and exploit others that I wouldn't be easy prey.

In my time at Pare, I was an enthusiastic player of Crash. My performances didn't go unnoticed. Years later, I would catch up with one of the craziest guys you could ever meet. He'd been in A Block and remembered me as one of the only white guys who would play Crash, and one who wasn't afraid to put his body on the line during the game.

*

Although the Nomads ran the block in terms of muscle, the money and drugs behind the muscle at this time was a notorious New Zealand criminal I'll call The Builder. The Builder was a huge man, who was serving the longest prison sentence ever handed down at the time for cannabis cultivation. His had been a highly sophisticated operation that had produced thousands of pounds of high-quality cannabis over the years, and he had amassed millions of dollars, both from drug dealing and from other gangster-ish behaviour. He had houses, cars, boats and even his own racing car, into which he had poured over a million dollars. His empire crumbled when he brought his illegitimate son into the family business. His son was pulled over by the police while driving around with enough pot in his car to warrant a possession for supply charge. Unfortunately for The Builder, his son wasn't sufficiently conditioned in the criminal code to take the charge and keep his mouth shut. Instead, he spilled his guts about The Builder's multimillion-dollar growing operation. The police raided The Builder and found a number of 44-gallon drums stuffed with cannabis. Fortunately for The Builder and much to the annoyance of the police, this pot was only poor-quality leaf awaiting conversion into commercial-grade cannabis resin. All the really good quality bud was buried in 44-gallon drums elsewhere. This stash would continue to serve him well during his years of imprisonment.

The Builder must have stood about 6 foot 3. He had a chest like a barrel and a huge gut to boot. When I first saw him, he had the remnants of a black eye inflicted by a guy who had attacked him while he was in bed sleeping. The Builder enjoyed ribbing people, and if you didn't know how to take it, it could be difficult to handle. This guy didn't know how to take it. After the attack, he arranged to be spirited out of the block in a move that almost certainly saved his life. I think his sense of humour is one of the reasons I always got on with The Builder. I used to give as good as I got. I remember one evening he had been giving me some stick after lockup. A couple of hours later, he called out to ask if anyone had a roll of toilet paper he could have.

'You need a roll?' I called back.

'Yeah,' he replied.

'Use your hand,' I told him.

There was wild laughter at this, and The Builder joined in.

I would do lots of business with The Builder during my stay in B Block. He was the man who controlled the drug flow. He would bring in ounces of pot every week and Manu and his crew would then distribute it. When I knew The Builder, he was hooked on methadone and painkillers. He had suffered from serious back pain and other medical problems for years and this was how he got his relief. It wasn't long before I brokered a deal with The Builder to supply him with methadone in exchange for pot. I arranged for Tania to supply an associate of his with between 300 and 500 milligrams of methadone every week. He would then provide me with pot to the equivalent value. The deal valued the methadone at $1 per milligram; ounces of good quality marijuana were about $300 at the time. So I was the happy recipient of about an ounce of pot a week. A vital condition placed on this arrangement, and one I clearly understood, was a restraint of trade, whereby I wasn't to attempt to sell any of the pot I was given. It was for personal use, not to undercut The Builder's business in the block. I was more than happy to comply, as pot runs out surprisingly quickly when all you do with your time is smoke it.

The Builder's pot came in distinctive, cylindrical tubes about an inch in diameter and four inches in length. It was so tightly compressed that the most efficient way to extract a piece to smoke was by slicing it off with a razor blade. The block — and the rest of Pare, for that matter — was awash with this pot. Because of strip searches, cell searches and dog raids, it was always necessary to have a good place to stash your drugs. The Builder had the business-end of the type of screwdriver needed to undo the special, tamper-proof screws with which the light and electrical fittings in the cells were fastened. He loaned it out, and all you needed to do was fashion a handle for it by melting and moulding plastic cutlery. It was possible to hide about four of The Builder's cylindrical ounces in each cell's light fitting. Because there was only one light in each cell and The Builder had so much pot to hide, a lot of cells were needed. Manu, who was The Builder's right-hand man, took care of the logistics, and most of the Nomad cells in B Block had pot stashed in their light fittings. Even then, there were periods when the block was so flush with pot that non-Nomads ended up with ounces stashed in their cells. I had some in mine on more than one occasion, including once when the drug dogs were brought through the cells. So good was the light-fitting stash that not a single one was identified, and so successful was The Builder's operation in B Block that he later hatched a plan to turn the whole jail into a production line for bone carvings. It would be set up as an assembly line, where people would be assigned positions according to their skill set and paid in joints according to their output. The Builder went as far as having a block meeting about this idea. But before it could be put into action, he was moved to a lower-security institution.

The Builder used two primary methods to get his drugs into the prison. The first method was pretty straightforward: he'd pay a particular prison officer $500 per drop. The screw would bring in drugs, cellphones and whatever else The Builder required and drop them during the night shift, when only he and a handful of other officers were on duty. The cage-like frontages of the cells at Pare actually facilitated the shifting of contraband, as no one needed to open any doors to do it; you simply handed stuff through the bars.

The second method was more novel. When out at visits, The Builder would heft his gut and place a number of cylindrical ounces in the fold before letting his belly sag into place to secure them. The screws never thought to ask him to lift his belly during a strip search.

*

After I had been at Pare for a few months, I was shifted to the upper-right cells (on the third floor, on the right-hand side as viewed from the front). My new next-door neighbour was another Pākehā whom I'll call Bull. Like me, Bull was serving a life sentence for murder. He told me he had already spent eight years in B Block. I hadn't yet done one, and I could only imagine what doing eight would do to your head.

Bull showed me how to make an ice pick shank, one of the range of improvised weapons most prisoners carried. The fronts of our cells had once been closed in with a sturdy steel mesh, but this had been mostly broken and removed. Only pieces remained, and by working a length of this back and forth, back and forth, it could be snapped off. One end of this was inserted at right angles into a piece of broomstick about three inches long, while the other was sharpened on the concrete to a lethal point. You held the piece of wood in your hand with the point projecting between your knuckles, ready to do damage: it made for a scary-looking weapon.

Another guy I got friendly with was an expert safecracker whom I'll call Samson. Like his biblical namesake, Samson's fortunes had taken a dive on account of his hair. He was a member of the Hole in the Wall gang, a highly effective group of burglars who specialised in large-scale heists from commercial premises in New Zealand and Australia. Their modus operandi was to break into a business next door to their target and then knock a hole through an adjoining wall: hence the name. Or they would peel back a piece of roofing, drop into the ceiling and then disable alarm sensors from above. Their primary targets were jewellery stores, and they travelled the country ripping them off, but they also pulled off some spectacular raids on automatic teller machines, using heavy machinery to pull them bodily out of the walls into which they were anchored. Samson's downfall came when he was arrested in connection with one of these burglaries. He knew the police didn't have any evidence, but the police got around that by holding him down in the cells and extracting a few hairs from his head. These turned up as Exhibit A in his trial, supposedly hair found at the scene and obviously an exact DNA match. 'Who were the jury going to believe?' Samson asked as he told me this story. 'The accused criminal or the buttoned-up, scrubbed cop who swears he found the hair at the scene?' I spent hours in Samson's company, smoking dope and listening to his amazing yarns. Besides the ballsy burglaries and the booty he and his gang scored — caskets of jewels worthy of any pirate — he also recounted his escape from custody, his recapture and his extradition from Australia back to New Zealand.

Around this time, I caught up again with John Barlow. Only a set of bars separates the of C Block yard and B Block, and you can talk with prisoners from the other wing during yard time. I spotted John, and we shook hands through the bars. He seemed genuinely pleased to see me. I knew I was pleased to see him!

'How're you keeping?' he asked me.

'OK,' I nodded. 'You?'

'I'm well,' he replied. It turned out he was as adept at managing relationships in Pare as he had been back in Mount Crawford.

We spoke a few times subsequently, but then I heard he had been transferred back to Rimutaka.

*

One day soon after I had shifted cells, I was approached by my former neighbour, The Weed, the ferrety little skinhead who had hailed me as a white supremacist brother when I first arrived on the block. He told me that The Builder had put out a hit on a particular screw he was having difficulty with, and that he had accepted it. He'd been paid half an ounce of pot in advance, with another half-ounce payable on completion. This wasn't particularly handsome remuneration, so the hit wasn't to be that serious. What The Weed planned to do was pour a bucket of boiling water on the screw as he was coming up the stairs. He wanted me to wait about on the second floor as the screw started his muster, and then walk ahead of him as he came up the stairs to the third floor, so that my appearance would indicate to The Weed that his target was in position for the attack. I told him to get lost, and good thing I did. After smoking his advance and before carrying out the hit, The Weed fled the block, and as is the way with scumbags, ratted out everyone he could think of as a parting gift. If I'd got involved in the plot, I'm sure I would have been fingered.

The Weed was from Christchurch. He had told me early on that he'd been sent to Pare after stabbing his brother in the neck in the mess room of Paparoa Prison; he'd done that because his brother had been convicted of child molestation. He was heavily tattooed on his hands, neck, and throat, and he received pot in return for doing tattoos on others. He was a neighbour when I first came into B Block, and in the first few days I was there, he passed me pot after lockup, sliding it along the ground under the bars. After he'd been giving me pot over a couple of days, The Weed asked if I could place my TV on an angle on the floor so he could place a mirror out on the landing and watch. I still got a good view of my own TV, but it was on an awkward angle and very uncomfortable to watch. Still, I thought, he did me a good turn, so ... It was a classic example of what psychologists call the 'foot in the door' tactic — taking advantage of 'the reciprocity effect', the natural tendency people have to feel obliged to return a favour done to them. Sales people often use it, making a display of generosity towards you in order to engender a sense of obligation in return. So do psychopaths.

Looking back, I can see The Weed for the textbook psychopath he was. Such people are adept at bending your will to theirs, and needless to say, you often come across them in a maximum security prison. As I got to know him better, The Weed told me about some of the shit he got up to before his imprisonment, such as torturing cats and other small animals. It was repulsive to hear, but just as disturbing was his apparent inability to recognise the effect his stories were having on me. Some time later, I heard that The Weed had got off to a rough start at Pare. He'd been placed in a holding cell on arrival with a guy who had been convicted and sentenced to eight years for rape. The Weed was his next victim. Despite the fact I despised The Weed and pretty much everything about him, I cringed for him when I learned this. It wasn't until much later that Tania confided in me that The Weed had propositioned her during a Family Day at Pare, when I'd gone off to the toilet. That was pretty bad. But far worse, he had phoned her at home. In order to get her number, he had to have searched my cell. It made my blood boil when I learned this. Lucky for him Tania kept this information to herself until I had left Pare, otherwise I may well have had his blood on my hands.

*

I had been at Pare for nearly a year when there was a shift in the political landscape of B Block. There had been a PROP, and the authorities had taken it as an opportunity to weed out those whom they regarded as problem prisoners, whether they were involved in the protest or not. Several were manhandled and beaten and their stuff trashed. The Builder was moved, as was Pace. Just like that, the Nomads were no longer in charge.

Around the same time, four young Black Power members arrived, who had been convicted of murdering a police witness whom they had shot through the front door of his house when he came to answer their knock. They were all facing life sentences with a minimum non-parole period of 17 years, so they came into B Block angry and with nothing whatsoever to lose. Suddenly there was a palpable rise in tension. Because the Nomads were originally a splinter group of Black Power (established in 1977 when the Nomads' founder, Dennis Hines, a patched member of Black Power, decided they weren't hardcore enough), there was some affinity, and with their rivals, the Mongrel Mob, having a solid support base, it was expedient for Black Power to unite with the Nomads against the common enemy. But as soon as Black Power had the numbers on their own, they cut the Nomads loose. This wasn't good news for me or for my mates Bull and Samson, all three of us white. Strange as it may seem to mainstream New Zealand society, which at least pretends to be colour blind, race matters in prison. For me, Bull and Samson, the 'prison tan' just accentuated the pallor of our skin. You could just about feel the hostility in the stares we were getting from the Black Power guys. My day-to-day anxiety levels increased accordingly.

One day, I was allowed to see a prison doctor because I was having trouble sleeping. I knew it was pretty much futile going to see the medics, because most of them saw themselves as members of the custodial staff. Generally speaking, the only medication you were ever going to get was Panadol. The exception was when management saw the opportunity to deal with problem prisoners and had the doctors administer a psych-bin med such as Largactil, which was known as 'liquid handcuffs' in the penal setting for its effectiveness in controlling people by turning them into drooling, shuffling zombies.

Sure enough, after a cursory consultation, the doctor gave me a couple of Panadol and told me to try to relax before I went to bed. I was being escorted back to my cell past A Block along the landing strip when a physically massive Black Power member with full facial tattoos thrust his face up to the bars of his cell and spat at me, eyes rolling:

'I'm gonna kill you, you fucken white cunt!'

He sounded like he meant it. Never has a doctor's advice seemed so completely inadequate.

With the change in the political landscape, old scores were beginning to be settled, and a number of hits went down. A Nomad decided to stand over another inmate to try to get him to hand over the Playstation that he owned. Trouble was, this neutral was in favour with Black Power, and they weren't happy. Rather than start an all-out gang war for the sake of an associate, they decided to stand over a tall white guy who had recently arrived in B Block in the wake of a riot at unit 3 of Rimutaka Prison. I'll call him Stretch. Stretch had a computer and was friendly with some of the Nomads, which made him a perfect target for payback. He was sitting on the toilet when one of the young Black Power prospects was sent in to attack him and take his computer. Stretch didn't know that it's best, if you need to use the toilet during the day, to take one leg out of your trousers, so he was a bit hobbled at first. But even so, he managed to fight off his attacker and throw him out of his cell. The prospect had to go back to his masters empty-handed.

Of course, it was never going to end there. Black Power couldn't afford to let one of their own get some treatment from a neutral white guy without retaliating, but nor could they risk a pack attack, as that might draw in the Nomads. So Stretch was told he would have to fight a one-out with the prospect after dinner. Everyone who was sick of the way the Black Power guys were swaggering around the block offered him advice and encouragement, and he spent the day getting tips from seasoned combatants on how to approach the fight and what tactics to adopt. This advice paid off. After tea, most of the block went down to the area in which the weights had previously been housed, before one too many inmates had their head stoved in with a weight plate. A circle was formed and the fight began. Stretch was on top from the start. It was obvious the prospect didn't want to fight. He was knocked down repeatedly, but the patched Black Power members kept making him get up and keep fighting. Stretch was wasting him, but there was no admission of defeat. The fight eventually ended, but Stretch was soon told by the Nomads and Black Power alike that he had to leave the block. There was a general fear that if there was any violence on his account, it would stuff up the Family Day, scheduled for a week's time. If that happened, he was told, he would be stabbed up.

It wouldn't be long at all before I was drawn into the politics of B Block.

CHAPTER 6

Institutionalised

In the previous chapter, I referred to some strategies, identified by the eminent psychologist Erving Goffman, that help prisoners adapt to their incarceration. He mentions a couple more, which you might broadly consider to be forms of 'institutionalisation' — an acceptance of the reality in which prisoners find themselves. One of these he calls 'colonisation', and it occurs where a prisoner decides that life in prison is representative of life in the outside world, and that the maximum satisfactions procurable within the prison are the be-all and end-all. The 'colonising' inmate will seize on any evidence that suggests life on the outside is sub-optimal, which reduces the desire to be free and which in turn reduces any desire to reform one's attitudes or behaviour. A typical coloniser will still claim to loathe prison, but this is generally to maintain an esprit de corps with fellow prisoners.

Another tactic Goffman describes is 'conversion', whereby the prisoner appears to take on the official or staff view of themselves and tries their utmost to conform to the ideal of the model inmate. Whereas the colonising inmate builds as much of a free community for himself as possible by using the limited facilities available, the convert takes a more disciplined, moralistic, black-and-white line, presenting himself as someone whose institutional enthusiasm is always at the disposal of the staff.

And of course, there are those who employ both tactics, presenting themselves to staff as model prisoners while also cultivating fellow-feeling with other inmates.

Institutionalised prisoners will often find it necessary to mess up just prior to their slated release or to reoffend immediately on release. In much the same way, those of us who are too afraid or unmotivated to escape our mental prisons will indulge in self-sabotage, finding excuses to preserve the status quo and avoid change. We are, by nature, designed to maximise pleasure and minimise pain and discomfort. We are compelled by our nature to make a virtue of necessity, to feather our nest no matter how precarious the perch. After all, as any well-adapted prisoner will attest, even a bad situation can be turned into a comfort zone.

What untruths do you tell yourself to convince yourself that the better future you could have is not all it's cracked up to be?

*

A day after Stretch's fight with the Black Power prospect, Bull, Samson and I were in the exercise yard between A and B Blocks. We were smoking the last of my stash of dope. There was a Black Power guy in the yard, too, a short, muscular guy none of us knew, whom I'll call Squat. He was talking to a bunch of other Black Power members through bars on the window of A Block. Tensions with Black Power had been high in B Block, and Samson didn't like the look of things. We decided to re-enter the block as soon as we could, but the sally port was closed. We thought we would walk up and down a bit to kill time.

As we passed the joint back and forth, Squat sauntered past us to the window of B Block. Even in my impaired state — I was stoned as — I saw there was something furtive about the way he was moving. There was nothing out of the ordinary about this: because of its reputation for violence, B Block was treated differently to other blocks in that you were searched for weapons on your return from the yard. This meant people were always ferrying drugs, information and weapons between the windows of the blocks.

Squat stood at the window for a minute or two with his back to us, apparently doing some deal or another. Then he suddenly spun round and swung an object at Bull, who was standing closer to him than I was. Luckily, Bull had been keeping half an eye on Squat and got an arm up and deflected what turned out to be a short, steel dumbbell bar. Bull and Samson took off. It took me a moment to work out what was going on, but by the time Squat swung the bar at me, I was off, too. We legged it down the yard to get into the guards' line of sight, and stood there debating what to do.

The adrenaline was pumping through my system and my heart was racing in my chest. 'Let's take him out,' I said. 'I've fought guys with weapons before. With three of us, we can take him easily.'

'Nah,' said Samson. 'It's not that fucker I'm worried about. It's the other guys inside tooling up for us.'

He nodded towards the B Block window.

My heart sank and my mouth went dry as it dawned on me what he meant. For whatever reason, war had been declared on us. There was no running and no hiding.

As soon as we could — around half an hour after the attack — Bull, Samson and I went inside. We were fully expecting a welcoming committee of B Block Black Power, but nothing happened. We made straight for our cells, where we set about tooling up. I taped newspapers and magazines around my midriff as protection against shanks, and dropped a couple of heavy batteries into a sock to use as a cosh. Bull and Samson arrived, both armed with Bull's home-made ice picks. I unplugged my TV and put it under my bunk so it wouldn't get damaged in whatever happened next.

'They're on their way,' Samson said.

'What do we do?' I asked.

'Play it cool,' Samson replied. 'Follow my lead.'

We heard footsteps, and Squat appeared in the doorway of my cell. Samson stood facing him. I assumed a side-on position, slightly to one side and behind Samson. That meant I presented less of a target, and could conceal the cosh, although I was ready at the slightest signal to swing it and bury it in Squat's brain. I was hyper-aware and everything slowed down and became very focused.

That signal never came. Samson managed to talk Squat down, and he left without doing anything more than offering a few threats.

'What are we doing, letting him go?' I said. 'We shouldn't have just let him walk out of here.' The calm focus I had been feeling was replaced with worry and distress.

All of us knew this wasn't going to be the end of it. But a message came through from A Block. Someone who had witnessed the yard incident had brought it to the attention of a notorious hard man I'll call Boy. Boy was an armed robber with links to the Hole in the Wall gang. He told the A Block Black

Power contingent that if Samson or his mates were harmed, he would personally take the lot of them out. Coming from Boy, this was no idle threat. Even in maxi, he was regarded as dangerous, and he held the record for having knocked more prison guards unconscious — no fewer than 36 of them — than any other prisoner.

The day after this message came through, when Bull and I crossed paths with Squat, he put on a convincing show of murderous rage. 'You cunts are fucken lucky,' he yelled. 'You ever smoke weed in front of me again and I'll fucken waste you!' But he visited Samson in his cell and apologised.

Bull, Samson and I convened a council of war. The situation was complex. I'd never read William Shakespeare's *Hamlet*. It was years before I came to read it, but when I did, I recognised Hamlet's dilemma right away. His father has been murdered, and while Hamlet's personal inclination is to let it slide, his duty to seek vengeance is clear. He's torn between his instincts and his duty. This was exactly the situation we found ourselves in.

When I recently came to re-tell the story of the debate we had over our course of action, I stated it was Samson who argued forcefully that we couldn't let the situation fester and we had to take Squat out. According to this version of the story, I said 'Nah, nah, nah,' even though I knew he was right. It was the unwritten law, the law of the jungle.

But when I re-read the manuscript I'd written just before my release from prison, when I was much closer to events and they were far fresher in my mind, I found that in fact it was *me* who was calling for a swift, decisive and violent response, and Samson who was arguing to let it go, as we were safe under Boy's protection. How's that for the constructive power of memory? As I have put psychic distance between myself and the world I lived in while in prison, I have acquired a more conventional view of right and wrong. I remember myself as a moral agent in the sense that I am one now, one who abhors violence. While I wasn't consciously setting out to paint my past self in a kinder light, that's what I did. I find this fascinating. It turns out you can be as self-aware as you like, but none of us is immune to the tricks our minds and memories play.

*

Samson rightly pointed out that it was Bull who had to decide whether or not to exact utu. We told him we would back him with whatever he decided.

Bull didn't have to think about it for long. He hadn't lasted eight years in B Block letting this sort of shit slide.

'We take him out,' he declared.

We cooked up a plan. Squat's cell was on upper-right not far from ours, and he had to walk past the showers and end space to get to his slot. I would wait in the showers until he was approaching and then step out. While Squat was thus distracted, Bull would step up behind him and stab him in the throat. Bull was never one for half measures.

The only trouble we could see with our plan was the scheduled Family Day in a week's time. We were comfortable with having the entire B Block contingent of Black Power after us once we'd taken Squat out. We accepted that. But if we did anything to jeopardise the Family Day, we'd have the whole block on our case, even those we considered our friends and allies. Bull decided the hit would go down after the Family Day.

We were all jumpy over the next few days. Squat's expression whenever he saw us was a mixture of aggression, caution and confusion: he was probably wondering why none of us had fled the block for protection, and would likely have concluded we meant to even the score. But the longer we took to try something, the weirder the situation must have felt to him. I remember those few days as some of the most stressful in my life. On one analysis, it was from Bull rather than me that Squat and his gang cronies would have been expecting attack. But this was academic, really. Bull had merely been the closest target of the three of us. And while Samson could probably rest easy under the mantle of Boy's threat of retaliation if he were attacked, I couldn't be assured the same level of protection would apply to me. So I spent every day after the attack and before the Family Day lying on my bed tooled up and facing the cell door. I would lie on my side with my hand gripping the cosh under my pillow, and with the ice pick close to hand. The only time I could really relax was when we were locked up at night. I gave up smoking dope during the day in order to keep my wits about me, and I longed for evening lockup when I could relax and light up. But even the ritual of smoking dope had become a source of stress because I didn't want everyone on the landing to smell my weed and start thinking murderously jealous thoughts. So I made a small bong — small enough that any smoke it produced could be drawn into my lungs with none left over — and I would exhale the smoke into a wet towel. It seemed to work well.

Like Hamlet, I fretted. It was as though I had been caught in a riptide that was dragging me further out into a place I didn't want to be. But every time I tried to think of alternatives, I drew a blank. There was nothing to do but go through with the plan. The prison code demanded it, but my emotions weren't in support. These days I would interpret such emotions as pangs of conscience.

*

A few times a year, the prisoners in each block would have the opportunity to invite three or four adults and however many children to see them and have a meal. Some of these visits were simple Family Days; others included a little concert with a band coming in from outside. In my experience — I was there for one of each — they were bedlam. They were held in the gymnasium, a maximum-security enclosure within the prison. Visitors would come in and sit down with those they had come to see, and once they were seated, the screws would simply stand at the end of the gym by the door. The prisoners and their visitors would then have a feed, smoke drugs and pop pills, or slip away to the toilets to have sex. I even knew one guy whose girlfriend had a baby son they named Gym in honour of the location of his conception. The screws, meanwhile, must have known what was going on, but they turned a blind eye. After all, what was the alternative? Creating a hostage situation for the sake of a little substance abuse?

The Family Day I attended was supposed to begin at 10 am, but it was 10.30 before everyone was in and seated. I was really looking forward to seeing Tania, but by the time the doors were closed, she hadn't arrived. It turned out that history was repeating itself; she had been picked out by a drug dog as the visitors were screened and was found to be carrying methadone. She was placed in a holding cell until the police arrived — the only woman, so far as I know, to have been locked up at Pare. She later managed to beat this possession charge in court, too.

I didn't know anything about this at the time. I spent the day with Samson and his family, all of us smoking the highest quality skunk marijuana you'll ever strike. Everyone was grumpy about the half-hour delay to the beginning of the day, and by the time we were supposed to return to our cells at 3 pm, word had got around there was going to be a PROP. Sure enough, when time for lockup came at 4.30, people were milling about outside their cells and refusing to go in to be locked up. If we thought we were creating a problem for the prison authorities, we were wrong. They simply locked off the landings, and by 9.30 pm everyone had taken lots of the drugs they had got from their visitors and were lying zonked in their cells. That's what they were waiting for. The doors were locked.

The next day, payback began. The doors weren't unlocked at 8 am as usual, and we were told we were in lockdown for a week. Meals would be slid under the doors of cells.

During this week, the goon squad was brought in to remove a number of people from the block and to search the cells. It was an unnerving experience. The goon squad comprised a bunch of very fit screws sporting military haircuts and wearing black fatigues and boots. They lined up on either side of the landing as officers went cell to cell. Each inmate was told to stand at the back of their cell. The door was then opened and the inmate was held securely on either side. They were then required to proceed down the gauntlet formed by the screws. Once they reached the end of the landing, they were strip searched while their cell was literally torn apart in the search for weapons and other contraband. Ironically, the only item they confiscated from my cell was my copy of the prison legislation, which was duly taken away — in contravention of that very legislation! (I did get it back, but not until some time had passed, an indication of the scorn in which the whole notion of prisoners' rights was held.) I was then led back down the gauntlet and placed in my recently renovated slot.

It was then my neighbour's turn. I heard them tell Bull they were moving him out of the block. He told them he didn't want to go and refused to come out. The goon squad went into his cell to get him. He gave them as good a fight as he could, but these guys didn't just swan into these things. They use well-rehearsed procedures, to hem you in and control you with their shields. Then they put you down on the ground and place you in wrist, ankle or head locks. Depending upon their mood and the risk you are perceived to pose, you are either led away under your own power with your wrists and arms twisted up behind your back or, as in the case of Bull, you are carried away with a screw on each arm and leg, and a screw leading the way holding you around the neck. So ended Bull's eight-year stint on B Block. Samson was gone, too, moved to the medium-security units to make way for new arrivals. It was the end of our conspiracy to murder Squat. I was left on my own in B Block with Squat and Black Power and could no longer hope I was under Boy's protection. My existence would be defined by fear of attack.

*

I found myself torn during this period in Pare. I was at war with myself. On the one hand, what I now recognise as the 'real' me, submerged for much of the early part of my imprisonment, was relieved Bull was gone and no one else would be getting hurt. But there was another part of me, the carapace I had grown in order to survive and which made it feel as though I belonged in the milieu I inhabited. This part of me felt that letting Squat go unpunished was bad form.

I received feedback from a couple of older, and as I saw it, wiser heads. I ran into Manu, who had been shifted to A Block.

He told me he'd heard a bunch of white boys had run away from a Black Power member who was waving an iron bar. Was I one of them? he asked. When I confirmed I was, he expressed surprise.

'The Paul I knew on remand wouldn't have run away from shit like that,' he said. 'He'd have fucken got even.'

I sucked up his criticism. I didn't have much choice. The calloused, institutionalised part of me believed what Manu said to be true. But a couple of days later, I was back in the exercise yard and talking to another Nomad whom I'll call The Bird. I had first met The Bird when he was on remand awaiting trial for armed robbery. He was acquitted of that charge, but now he was serving a nine-year sentence on another charge. I told him about the iron bar incident and about Manu's disappointment.

'That's bullshit,' The Bird said. 'You're a neutral. You've got no one to back you up. Squat's a gangsta with the numbers. If you'd tried to take him out then and there or since, they'd have come for you. They would have killed you or cabbaged you. Man, your only job while you're in here is to stay alive, and fuck what Manu or anyone else thinks of you.'

I was incredibly grateful for this advice. It spoke to the better part of me. The Bird was a man who had done many awful things in his life, but at that time he was a positive influence on me. I was only just beginning to wonder if there might be a different and better way when we had this conversation. To hear someone else tell me it wasn't madness to be thinking this way was like being told, when you're locked up in darkness, that there is a door.

*

All the same, I wasn't anywhere ready to set the carapace aside, as those who visited me at the time assure me. They found me cold, cynical and negative. I was lucky enough to have a few visitors while I was in Auckland. Besides Tania, my father came up on a number of occasions. It must have been bloody hard for my father during these years, especially after losing Mum. And now his son was in prison, and not showing any signs of amending and treading the path of the righteous. Many times he came to see me, I had cuts and bruises on my face. I must have been the cause of much concern.

It wasn't just that I was in prison. It was that I had chosen to project to everyone that I belonged there, even to those who loved me. Talking and thinking tough becomes a habit in prison, so much so that it's hard to switch it off. Hindsight is, of course, 20/20, and I now realise that there were alternatives to the course I adopted, but we can only operate on the basis of the options we're aware of at any given stage of life. Unfortunately for those who were attempting to support me, I didn't have the emotional or psychological maturity to give the heartless cynicism a rest during visits.

One day, my younger brother visited, bringing with him a mate and his mate's mum, Mary, who had been an incredibly kind and supportive person to me. She had lit a candle for me at my mother's funeral, and she visited me repeatedly while I was in prison in Wellington. When Mary made the effort to accompany her son and my brother to Paremoremo, she found the environment in maximum security particularly disturbing. I think they all did, but while my brother and his mate stayed for the duration of the visit, she abruptly got up and left them to it. She was so visibly upset as she left that one of the prison officers asked her if she was all right. I understood why she was upset. The coping strategy I employed on a day-to-day basis was to normalise the negativity of my situation, but this environment could be a real shock to those who weren't used to it.

Poor Tania had a pretty crap time of it visiting me in Pare. One day when she flew up to Auckland to visit me on a Family Day, she was running a bit late. She presented herself to the screw who was on duty, only to be told there was no Family Day. She was an approved visitor whose name was down to visit, so he had no grounds to exclude her, but this is the kind of shit screws pulled at Pare, especially the screws who didn't work in the blocks and who didn't need to worry about reprisals. Then, of course, she was busted bringing in drugs, and although she beat the charge, she was removed from the approved visitors list.

*

After I'd been in the block a few months, one of the screws took me aside.

'Hey, Wood. Would you be interested in shifting to C Block? It can be arranged, if you do.'

C Block was the block I had originally wanted to be assigned to, as it was the most laid-back area of the prison, and the place where all the kitchen staff were housed.

'Nah,' I told him. 'C Block's full of fucken narks. If youse shift me over there, I'll fuck someone up.'

This is what I had learned in Pare. If the screws wanted you to do something you didn't want to do, you threatened violence. This would normally stop them; they would get in too much shit later if you proved true to your word and it came out they'd been warned.

'No problem,' the screw shrugged. 'Stay where you are. No skin off my nose.'

A couple of years earlier, this screw had nearly died after being stabbed multiple times in the chest by a Mongrel Mob prospect with a shank. Apparently this mobster was about to be released, but the gang had given him the order to go and stab this screw, so that's what he did. I remember the person telling me this story said this screw was a whole lot less of an arsehole after the stabbing.

'Nothing like getting shanked to wake the cunts up,' the inmate said. 'He's scared of getting stabbed again if he keeps on being an arsehole.'

At the time the screw in question offered to move me out of B Block, I had a different impression. It didn't seem like he was offering me a kindness because he was scared. It seemed more like the real thing: genuine kindness. As he walked away after I'd given him and his offer the bum's rush, I had a nagging feeling I'd let him down. I think I dimly perceived he was a man who'd confronted his own mortality and it had changed his perspective. He had seen me as someone who might perhaps be saved from succumbing to the Pare mentality, but he'd either been wrong or he'd got to me too late.

As quickly as those doubts surfaced, though, they were crushed under a kind of vainglorious pride. Fuck him. I liked B Block, I told myself. I knew the guys who ran it. I had a certain amount of prestige in the scheme of things. I could get all the drugs I wanted in there. I knew all the threats, and fuck them, too. I could deal with every single one of them, I told myself with false bravado.

Another screw was stabbed while I was in B Block, and I was right there to witness it. A guy — let's call him Kurt — had just come back into B Block from D Block, and he was angry and hell-bent on vengeance. I don't know what he was seeking to avenge and I didn't know him well enough to speculate on his motives. From what I heard, he was pretty much just set on violence towards the screws — he was the real-deal A.S.L. (Anti-

Screw League). His preferred target was a female officer who had got a bad reputation for herself on the block for trying to stir shit among people. I had seen her in action first-hand when, while engaged in searching the landing one day, she took a pair of jeans from a cell belonging to a Nomad and stowed them under the bunk in my mate Moppy's cell. Moppy was about my age, and had been a member of a gang that specialised in armed robbery. Lucky for him, he had been arrested and convicted on a violence rap that was unrelated to the gang's activities. I say lucky, because he was sentenced to only seven years, whereas the rest of the gang all received sentences approaching the 20-year-mark when they were rounded up. Sometimes you never know what worse luck your bad luck saves you from; sometimes you do. Moppy was a good sort, quite smart and keen on improving himself. I used to kick out with him. Anyway, it was just lucky that Moppy happened to look under his bed when he came back in after the search, otherwise he would have been branded with a bulls-eye for being a tea-leaf (thief). As soon as he spotted the jeans he pulled them out, identified whose they were, and returned them to their owner. This was the sort of thing she was known for.

Who knows whether it was because he couldn't get at her, or whether another screw just happened to be at the wrong place at the wrong time, but it was a male officer against whom he had no known grudge that Kurt took action.

I was there when it went down. The screw was on his way into the third-floor staff area where the screws would go to have lunch or a coffee. My cell was only a few doors along from it. As the screw paused at the door, Kurt came at him with a shiv. Pare used to have blue plastic mop buckets with handles made of inch-wide metal strips. The handles were forever going missing, and reappearing as nasty weapons, typically a shiv three millimetres thick, an inch wide, and ten inches long. That's what Kurt was holding as the screw went to put his key into the door. He saw Kurt coming at him from the side and turned his hand holding the key towards the shiv. Kurt had been aiming at the screw's stomach, but the blade went through the palm of the screw's outstretched hand instead. The screw yelled and the next thrust entered his stomach. The screw grabbed hold of Kurt and they fell to the ground, wrestling, the screw yelling in fear and panic. Kurt managed to stab him once more, this time in the thigh, before they became deadlocked.

I witnessed all this from Moppy's side of the block, upper-left. One minute we were standing there watching the attack, the next we were literally swamped by a sea of screws in their green uniforms. Kurt was on the ground and those nearest to him were giving him a good kicking. Luckily for him, there were too many screws and not enough room. None of them could land a decent shot. Meanwhile, they quickly locked everyone down. It didn't matter where you were or where your cell was, you were poked into the closest cell and locked up. I ended up locked up with Moppy. A couple of hours later, I was escorted to my own cell and the entire block was locked down for what ended up being two weeks. That night, the end of my landing was thronged by police and ESR scientists doing a scene examination and gathering forensic evidence. The landing was a cacophony of abuse. Prisoners were yelling out 'You're next, pig,' and making squealing noises.

During lockdown, meals were slid into the cells and the dirty plates retrieved the same way. The screws were stony-faced and jumpy: they never reacted well to one of their own being attacked, and we heard threats had been received that another screw was going to be stabbed.

After a week of lockdown, we were taken down to the mess room for a meeting with the unit manager. He was relatively new in the job, and he struck me as a bit of an egg. He laid down the law about who were the prisoners and who were the staff and reminded us who ran the place. But he had clearly heard the same rumours we had heard because he asked anyone who had a problem with the female officer in question to stand up and identify themselves. Like that was going to happen! The room remained silent. He nodded as though he'd proven a point, but we all noted that he'd known about the activity that had supposedly caused the problem but had done nothing to change his officer's behaviour. There was such a strong 'us versus them' mentality on both sides that this unit manager would rather risk his officers' safety than admit to himself that his staff were capable of doing wrong. I suppose you could argue that admitting as much would be the equivalent of giving into terrorists' demands, but his approach certainly didn't model anything that would encourage rehabilitation or reduce the likelihood of reoffending from anyone present.

We spent about another week in lockdown. The only softening of the line was that we were released two at a time for showers. After this, our privileges were restored. Normality gradually resumed, but for all the tough talk about who was running the joint, we noticed that the officer whose behaviour was at the bottom of it all wasn't back on day shift for a while, and when she did reappear, she was never walking around alone.

This was my world. I had adapted to it and it had become normal for me. I had no hope for a better or even a different future. Hope just seemed a mockery. It was easier to do without it. This was rock bottom. The only way forward was up.

PART TWO

Five Steps to Freedom

A journey of a thousand miles begins with
a single step.

—Lao Tzu (604–531 BCE)

CHAPTER SEVEN

Born Free

'Man is born free,' the French philosopher Jean-Jacques Rousseau once wrote, 'and is everywhere in chains.' Rousseau was talking about the tension between individual liberty and the obligations imposed by civil society, but his words have always resonated with me.

The first of my Five Steps to Freedom is what I call 'Born Free'. It's the reminder I give to people who are languishing in a mental prison that they were not born this way. Infants begin with a blank slate. Infants don't get depressed contemplating their own limits because it never occurs to them they have limits. Children are great dreamers. It's only later in life we become convinced that dreams and reality are diametrically opposed. We come to accept and wear our limitations, as if we are putting on our own chains, shackle by shackle.

You were born free. Reminding yourself of the limitless potential you are born with is the first step in refusing to settle for the limits you have come to believe you have.

For me, the first glimmer of daylight I saw, through the bars of the mental prison I had been living in since I was a young teenager, was when I began to contemplate pursuing education as a useful way of spending my time while I was locked up. It's not as though the walls immediately came tumbling down — far from it. But without that first thought, that 'let-there-be-light' moment, the walls would never have come down at all.

The moment came about because I was exposed to a perspective that collided with my own. I became sociable enough to mix with people who thought differently to me. As soon as you become aware that there are alternative ways of seeing things, it calls your own thinking style into question. You begin to perceive the crucial truth that you have a choice in the way you think. There's a line in *Hamlet* I have always loved: 'There is neither good nor bad, but thinking makes it so.' You could put it another way, and use one of the kinds of slogans that abound in social media memes and the speeches and books of self-help gurus: 'Life doesn't happen to you. It happens for you.' The way you view your situation, your potential and your life choices is dependent upon the way you are accustomed to think. If you are inclined to focus upon everything that gets in the way of your goals, then it's quite likely you will feel victimised by circumstance. If, on the other hand, you suffer all of the same constraints but can focus upon every available way of working towards your goals anyway, you are more likely to feel empowered. Nothing about your circumstances is different. It's just the mindset from which you view them. And perhaps the most potent realisation is that everything you dreamed of when you were a free-born child is still within your grasp, no matter how the walls have closed in around you since.

So the first step in gaining your freedom is to contrast your present situation, your sense of what is possible for you, with what you might have hoped for yourself when you were younger or if circumstances were different. Ask yourself: what kind of person would I be in five years from now if I started to play to my strengths and strive towards my potential? What kind of person would I be and how would I feel if I started focusing my attention on living a meaningful life? On the other hand, what fears, beliefs and behaviours are preventing me from striving towards my potential and having a meaningful life? What will the cost be five years from now if I continue to allow myself to be governed by these influences that diminish me? Then ask yourself: am I a victim in all of this who only blames others and the situation as I am swept along by fate, or am I a participant in life who is responsible for the choices I made that led me here? Am I empowered to affect my future through the choices I make now?

The effect of these questions — especially the last — is to shift the locus of control from outside yourself to inside yourself. After all, if there is nothing objectively good or bad about your situation, then it must be the way you perceive it that colours it good or bad. Changing the ways you perceive your circumstances can be as simple as asking: is this happening to me, or for me? There is a quote I like in a book by Carlos Castaneda that encapsulates the difference between the victim mentality and the participant mentality: 'The basic difference between a warrior and an ordinary man is that a warrior takes everything as a challenge, whereas an ordinary man takes everything as a curse.' Once again, the question becomes: do you treat life's adversities as a challenge to be embraced or as a threat to be avoided?

Everyone with a normally functioning brain has self-defeating and distorted beliefs. The only real question is which ones most apply to you. The most common of these are listed below. I highly recommend you go through the list and based on how much you relate to them mark each as V, Q, N (Very like me, Quite like me, or Not so like me).

Self-defeating beliefs

	V	Q	N
Emotional perfectionism: I should always feel happy, confident, and in control of my emotions.			
Performance perfectionism: I must never fail or make a mistake.			
Perceived perfectionism: People will not love and accept me as a flawed and vulnerable human being.			
Fear of disapproval or criticism: I need everybody's approval to be worthwhile.			
Fear of rejection: If I'm not loved, then life is not worth living.			
Fear of being alone: If I'm alone, then I'm bound to feel miserable and unfulfilled.			
Fear of failure: My worthwhileness depends on my achievements.			
Conflict phobia: People who love each other shouldn't fight.			
Emotophobia: I should not feel angry, anxious, inadequate, jealous or vulnerable.			
Entitlement: People should always be the way I expect them to be, and I expect them to give me special treatment and consideration.			
All or nothing thinking: I judge myself in black and white terms.			
Overgeneralisation: I may have made a mistake or had some bad luck, but I generalise this to my entire being.			
Mental filter: I dwell on a bad event and let it discolour my entire view of life, a little like a drop of ink that discolours a glass of water.			
Discount the positives: I overlook my many good qualities.			
Jumping to conclusions: I generalise based on one or two qualities or events to form a negative overall judgement; if I have one bad interaction with someone from an organisation, ethnicity, nationality or religion, I tend to regard the whole group negatively.			

	V	Q	N
Magnification: I blow events out of proportion.			
Emotional reasoning: I feel like a born loser, so I believe I really am one.			
Shoulds: I have a list of ironclad rules about how I and other people should act; people who break the rules make me angry and I feel guilty if I violate those rules. I may, for example, have the belief that I should always be successful at things and never fail; I may also believe that if I am good and try hard, then life should always go smoothly.			
Labelling: I label myself as a born loser instead of trying to learn from the situation or think about the best way to overcome it.			
Blame: I automatically hold other people responsible for my pain, so that nothing that goes wrong is my fault. Alternatively, I take the blame myself entirely for every problem or reversal, when the event (such as a redundancy or relationship breakup) might be happening to many others.			
Mindreading: Without their saying so, I know what people are feeling and why they act the way they do; in particular, I am able to divine how people are feeling towards me; I think my assumptions about what others are thinking are true.			
Catastrophising: I expect disaster. I notice or hear about a problem and start 'what-ifs'. What if tragedy strikes? What if it happens to me? I immediately assume the worst possible outcome.			
Personalising: I think that everything people do or say is some kind of reaction to me; I compare myself to others, try to determine who's smarter or better looking; I tend to relate everything to me.			

Arguably the most common self-defeating belief is 'I'm not good enough.' For some people, this self-doubt comes out in their work. In fact, it is so common for people to get promoted to positions of seniority or leadership and then think they are not as good or talented as they are supposed to be that this condition has its own title: the Impostor Syndrome. The other common areas of self-doubt relate to your identity in respect of who you should be as an individual or who you should be in relationships.

Self-doubt about my identity as a man was one of my biggest and most derailing distortions. I didn't think I was enough of a man; I felt I needed to be tougher, less scared and anxious, and that I should be able to stand on my own two feet, when the reality was I was spiralling out of control. As a result, I was always overcompensating, always trying to prove what a man I was, that I wasn't afraid, that I wasn't scared of anyone, and that I could assert control over the world through violence and aggression. For other people, their doubts around identity might be about not being smart enough, or pretty enough, or thin enough, or muscly enough, or young enough. The other focus of doubt I mentioned was relationships. It is the norm to feel you're not worthy in your relationship, whether because you perceive yourself not to be accepting, caring, considerate, supportive, warm, attentive, available or present enough. It is also normal to doubt the worthiness of the person you are in a relationship with. I recently heard about a survey that suggested if you go to bed two nights a week wondering what the hell you are doing with this person, then you are in a normal relationship!

One of the most effective ways to figure out which self-defeating beliefs and cognitive distortions apply to you is by asking people who know you well what it is that they see. All of us have blind spots: outsiders can perceive mental habits that are so engrained we are unaware of them. And, crucially, outsiders can often provide a far more realistic appraisal of our potential than we can ourselves, so root-bound does our thinking become with self-doubt and cognitive distortions and biases.

Self-honesty can be a frightening thing, but it usually pales by comparison with how scary it can be to seek honest feedback about ourselves from others. The fear most commonly arises from shame, which is the feeling associated with the previously discussed fear of not being good or worthy enough. It's in our nature to seek pleasure, after all, and to avoid pain. Not surprisingly, given we are a social species that longs to belong, shame is one of the more uncomfortable feelings we routinely experience, and it's usually the desire to avoid feeling ashamed that leads us to deploy our coping strategies.

According to the literature (and you can see it all around you), there are four common coping styles for dealing with the unpleasant emotions associated with our feelings of shame. One is to avoid any situation that might cast you in a bad light. This is often why you'll see people with high potential not even trying to realise it: it's the fear they will try then fail and feel ashamed as a consequence. Another is to withdraw. Some people are happy to engage but only to the point where they feel threatened, whereupon they will abruptly become remote. Another is to attack yourself, subjecting yourself to an internal diatribe to the effect that any failure is your fault, that you should have done something differently or better, and that you were never worthy of aspiring to any given goal in the first place. And another common one, the one to which I am most prone, is to attack others, which delivers a sense of empowerment that deflects attention from yourself and your failure to live up to your own expectations of yourself.

In every case, there are reasons why you adopt the coping strategy that you do. And as noted, a strategy will sometimes have served its purpose at one time or another in your life. But when they cease to serve, they must be confronted. You must remind yourself that you were born free, and that the thoughts and beliefs that hold you back can be challenged, tamed and replaced, no matter how hard it seems to remember this at times. You must also remind yourself that uncovering and discovering the beliefs and thoughts you need to change will be an ongoing, probably life-long, process. No matter how much work you have done in this area, there will be new barriers to discover, accept and manage. To live the most fulfilling and meaningful life you can, the goal is not to be good or perfect but to get better. And the goal of getting better never stops.

*

I was hanging with Samson one day in his cell, smoking dope, when he scrunched up a ball of paper.

'What d'you reckon, Paul? You're a smart guy. If I drop this ball of paper and this tennis ball from the same height at the same time, which one will hit the ground first?'

I stared at him. It had to be a trick question. I might have been stoned, but I knew the answer was obvious. Of course the heavier object, the tennis ball, would hit the ground first. I told him as much.

'Want to bet on it?' he grinned.

'Go on then. Drop them,' I said.

He held up the tennis ball and the scrunched-up paper and paused for effect, so I could see for myself they were at the same height. Then he dropped them.

They hit the ground at exactly the same time.

My head was spinning. There had to be a trick.

'Gimme those,' I said. I was expecting there to be a concealed weight in the balled-up paper, but I could feel there was a significant difference in mass: the tennis ball was heavy, the paper was light. When I tried the experiment for myself, the result was exactly the same.

'Wow,' drawled Samson, enjoying my bewilderment. 'Nearly four hundred years after its first demonstration, inmate Paul Wood discovers the Galilean principle of gravity.'

It seems a little thing, but in the scheme of things, it was huge. It was the first time I could remember one of my unshakeable convictions about the world and how it worked being proven false. And I kid you not when I tell you that this was like a magic trick to me! It literally blew my mind and I spent considerable time that day trying to find heavier and heavier things to drop in place of that tennis ball, in case it was some kind of trick. That first shake was followed by significant aftershocks. If I was wrong about something I had accepted without question, how many other things might I be wrong about?

One of the things that distinguished the Hole in the Wall gang from other criminals was that they were all highly intelligent. The ring-leader, Simon Allen Kerr, could have been a professional artist, or just about anything else he chose. Samson could have done anything, too: he scored at Mensa Club levels in intelligence tests. Unfortunately for society, both became addicted to the adrenaline, the lifestyle and the drugs that their criminal activity entailed.

Samson occasionally told me I should try to get some education. He wasn't the first. Back in Rimutaka, the man who I am calling Niccolò had one day seen me in the exercise yard, pen in hand, frowning at a newspaper.

'What you doing there, Paul?' he said.

I showed him the Word Find I was doing.

He made an impatient noise.

'What you want to waste your time on shit like that for? Do something that gives you useful knowledge.'

John Barlow, too, had often told me I should use my time in prison wisely and try to better myself. Trouble was, these seeds of wisdom fell on barren ground at the time. I simply wasn't ready to listen to pro-social advice.

Coming from Samson, however, who at this stage in my life was one of the coolest people I knew, the suggestion was food for thought. He would set riddles for me, things like: what is lighter than a feather but the world's strongest man can't hold for long? Answer: His breath. Sometimes I could figure them out for myself. Sometimes I would need help. He also recommended books for me to read, and some of these had a profound influence on me at that time. One was Jack Henry Abbott's *In the Belly of the Beast*, an autobiographical account of the author's time in America's hardest maximum security institutions. Abbott was doing it way harder than me, but he found time to read philosophy and to write his own book. He quoted philosophy — by Friedrich Nietzsche and others — and what he quoted struck a chord. I realised with a shock that there were philosophies and philosophers I might be interested in. Even if I couldn't entirely follow the arguments, I could definitely relate to the big questions they were grappling with, and see their relevance not only to Abbott's situation but also to my own. They didn't change my life overnight, but exposure to these questions changed it in the end.

I spent a bit of time with Moppy in his cell going through the dictionary, quizzing one another as to the meaning of this apparently obscure word and that. And in the meantime, acting on Samson's suggestion, I eventually made an appointment to see the prison's education provider — an underworked man, if ever there was one. He had been a screw, but he seemed all right, and genuinely supportive of my desire to improve myself, at least in principle. He got me to sit a test, presumably to work out whether it was a waste of time giving me permission to study. My literacy was pretty average, but he was satisfied with the results.

I was interested in enrolling in a legal executive course. While I'd like to pretend I was, at that stage, keen on education as a means to self-improvement and rehabilitation, my main motivation was to become more effective in my battles within the prison system. I had decided quite early on in my sentence — and other capable bush lawyers such as Niccolò had encouraged me in this belief — that one way to bring pressure to bear on the prison authorities was to engage them in a paper war. Prison complaint forms were in triplicate in those days. One copy was retained by the inmate, one went to the prison and the other to the national office of the Department of Corrections. It was this last one that caused headaches for prison authorities, because while they could (and did) ignore prisoners, they often received a 'please explain' from national office upon receipt of complaint. By law, a reasonable response to any and every complaint had to be made within two weeks of being lodged. Little surprise, then, that prison officers tried everything they could think of to avoid supplying you with a complaint form, preferring to fob you off by giving you an interview request form, which could be dealt with within prison walls and with no need to involve them nationally.

One of the first things I did when I was transferred to Pare was to ask my father to buy me copies of the Penal Institutions and Regulations Act, the New Zealand Bill of Rights and the United Nations Charter on the Treatment of Prisoners. I ramped up my litigation in the wake of my transfer, and my father maintained relentless pressure from the outside, too, to have the transfer reconsidered, to restore his ability to visit weekly as he lived in Wellington. Within two weeks of my arrival at Pare my father had become well known to the Department of Corrections, the administrations of Rimutaka and Paremoremo prisons, the prison inspector and the ombudsman. And I hadn't been there many more weeks before I landed myself an interview with the unit manager. He seemed quite a reasonable man, and although I was causing him headaches, he didn't seem to resent me personally. He had my file on the desk in front of him, a folder about three inches thick.

'If you want to get a transfer back to Wellington,' he said, patting the fat file, 'the first thing you're going to have to do is stop this file growing.'

I was convinced the path to getting a transfer lay in the opposite direction. If I caused the staff enough grief with paperwork, they would be more than happy to see the back of me. So I carried on complaining. I put in complaints about the food. When we heard that a temporary transit landing received new pillows and we didn't, I put in a complaint alleging I had suffered discrimination. I submitted a request under the Official Information Act to see the paperwork relating to the reasons for my transfer and to have access to my file. I eventually hit the jackpot with the results of this last initiative.

*

One afternoon, around three weeks after I had lodged my OIA request, I was summoned to the unit manager's office, where my file was lying on the desk in front of a chair. As well as the unit manager, there was a screw, and both kept a close eye on how I handled the material. I sat down and eagerly opened the folder.

I leafed through the thick sheaf of complaint forms and the occasional incident report (an incident report is written up by prison officers and ends up on your file if it provides evidence of your misconduct) until I found the inmate transfer form completed by the Rimutaka Prison custody manager. My eye lit on the field headed: Reason for Transfer.

'Prisoner to be moved back to his regional prison,' it read.

What the fuck? I mouthed.

The custody manager at Rimutaka had personally warned me I would be moved out if my behaviour didn't improve. My behaviour hadn't improved in respect of my attitude and drug use, but he and I both knew this didn't warrant a move to maximum security. So he had plainly decided the easiest course of action was to lie. Corrections policy stated that unless there was a valid and compelling reason for it to be otherwise, inmates serving life sentences should be housed in a prison in their own region. He knew perfectly well that Wellington was my regional prison.

'Can I get a photocopy of this?' I asked the unit manager. 'I've got a right to it under the Freedom of Information Act.'

He didn't argue. I immediately wrote to the ombudsman and made an appointment to see the prison inspector when he visited on his monthly round. I'd met him before, when he had reported to me on my earlier request to look into my transfer. He'd been unable to get a response from Rimutaka when he'd asked for an explanation. I'd met the ombudsman too, but he'd had no more luck than the inspector on that occasion.

I'm not sure my hopes were high when I finally sat down with the inspector. I had a pretty jaundiced view of the system and was convinced they'd find some way or another to keep me where they wanted me. But I was encouraged by his response when he saw the copy of the transfer document.

'And Wellington's your regional prison? There's no mistake about that?'

'No,' I replied. 'I've lived in Wellington all my life. My dad and my partner live there.'

'Right,' he said. 'We'll sort this out. They can't just make stuff up to get you moved.'

I kept a lid on my excitement at the prospect of Pare drawing to an end, partly to avoid disappointment, but mostly because if people suspected I might be shifted, they could well bring forward plans to settle scores. I was thinking of Squat in particular. My anxiety was constant during unlock hours at this stage, as I was just waiting to be attacked by him. My hackles rose every time I saw him, and my heart rate spiked every time I walked into a room and saw him deep in conversation with his Black Power henchmen. On more than one occasion they paused their conversation to look at me.

Three weeks after my meeting with the inspector, I received a letter. I opened it with trepidation, and then I had to read it a couple of times to make sure I had understood it correctly: '[I] direct that Prisoner Wood be transferred to Rimutaka Men's Prison, Wellington.' I was to board the bus in the morning.

I knew I couldn't tell anyone I would be leaving in case it got back to Squat. I felt so happy, but knew that the threat wasn't over until I was physically out of the block. The last thing I wanted was to give Squat a heads-up that his opportunity to attack was about to pass.

After lockup, I packed up my cell. When the screws came to escort me to the bus after unlock the next day, I unplugged my TV and picked it up. As I carried it down to the office on my way out of the block, I saw Squat. You could see from the expression on his mean, tattooed face that he knew what the little procession he was witnessing signified. His eyes fastened on the TV, which had been tucked under the bunk when he came into my cell on the day of the altercation in the yard.

'Aw,' he said, his voice heavy with regret. 'I didn't know you had a TV.'

We both knew what he meant. He'd missed the opportunity to try to take it off me. I was very glad about this. Only one of us would have ended up with the TV. The other one would probably have ended up dead.

*

The bus ride down the North Island from Paremoremo to Wellington was so much more pleasant than the journey up, almost a year earlier. I could feel the stress of the last few months ebbing from my body. I don't think I had even realised how stressed I'd been. I could readily believe what they say: that stress takes years off your life. We're designed to handle short bursts of it. In fact, stress isn't a negative thing in and of itself. Without stress we aren't appropriately stimulated to reach peak performance in any area. Furthermore, there's a wealth of biological evidence that the experience of mild stress prompts our genes to code for new proteins, which build new neural and nervous system structures — in other words, stress literally unlocks our genetic potential and enables us to become more than we would have been otherwise. In psychology, we differentiate between this kind of positive stress called 'eu-stress' and the more harmful stress we often think of when we hear this word, called 'dys-stress' (distress). A big difference between them is whether you have voluntarily put yourself into a situation or not. Another difference is the length of time you experience it. The kind of non-voluntary and unrelenting stress I had endured in Pare was definitely the type of distress that does you real, physical harm.

As before, we stopped at all the prisons along the way and then spent the night in the eight-man holding cells at Kaitoke. By the afternoon of the next day, I was back at Rimutaka. By the time I was processed, the rest of the muster was on evening recreation. I carried in my boxes of property and was locked in my cell. The policy in unit 3 back in those days was that for the first week, you were kept locked up during evening recreation.

Hardly had the echoes of the screws' footsteps faded away when there was a heavy bang on my door. Two gang members — from their facial tattoos, I could see they were Mongrel Mob members — were kicking it and screaming and yelling.

'Hey, you! White cunt! Wait for unlock. We're gonna fuck you up in the morning!'

So much for escaping stress! I didn't get a really good look at them through the safety glass, and I didn't want to study them too closely, anyway, but I was pretty sure I'd never seen either of them before; having had no beef whatsoever with the Mob, I didn't know what any of this was about.

My heart, which had been positively buoyant, sank again as I made preparations for the morning. I needed to keep my anxiety at bay and increase my odds of survival by focusing on what I could control and what might help me deal with this situation. I looked around to see what tools I could fashion. I settled for a humble ballpoint pen. I could have put together a cosh with the batteries and socks I had, but braining someone on my first day back would be a bad look. Much better to be able to argue I was holding an innocent pen when called upon to defend myself. I decided I would stab whomsoever was first through the door in the morning. Hopefully I would get them in the eye or somewhere equally vital.

I can't say I slept that well, and I was awake an hour before unlock. As 7.30 am came around, I was waiting. I was hyper-aware, my mouth was dry and my heart was pounding in anticipation of what was to come. I had moved all my gear to the back of my cell where it would be out of the way. I had tied the laces of my shoes up tight, a trick I had learnt from my elder brother, Jon: the tighter your shoes in a fight, the less they're likely to be an impediment or fly off when delivering kicks. The practicalities of combat.

The moment my cell door was unlocked, I gripped my pen tightly and assumed a sideways posture right inside the doorway. The key in this type of situation is to stop one's assailants getting into the cell in numbers. In a narrow doorway, a bunch of people will find their numbers count against them, whereas numbers are to their advantage once inside the cell. I was pumped with cortisol and adrenaline, and tensed every time I heard a noise outside in the corridor. But after a couple of minutes, no one had come. Five minutes passed, and still no one came. My respect for the pair who had hammered on my door faded with the adrenaline. Nothing is ever going to happen through a closed door: threats yelled from one side of a locked door amount to nothing.

It had plainly just been a couple of blowhards saying, 'Welcome to the wing.'

*

Soon after unlock, a screw came and found me and took me to the unit manager's office.

'You were a bit of a problem for us when you were last here, Wood,' he said. 'But if you can keep your nose clean for three months, we'll move you to the units.'

The units were like Shangri-La, some mythical place of unknown wonder. They were for people whose security risk was graded low to medium, and they were rumoured to comprise wooden cells with windows to the outside that had no bars on them. It was hard to know how much of this fairy tale to believe. Wooden cells, maybe, but bar-less windows? I wasn't *that* gullible! Still, there wouldn't have to be much truth to the rumour for the units to be a big improvement.

After returning from the unit manager's office, I was placed back on the wing. Unit 3 had changed since the last time I was there. As a result of a riot in 1997, the connecting door between the two wings had been sealed and the wings now ran as separate units. Those in my part of the wing were, for the most part, long-term inmates awaiting a lowering of their security classification so they could get down to the units. Those housed in the other wing were still awaiting their initial classification, were likely to receive a low classification straightaway, or had been chased out of the wing I was in and were there for their own protection.

I saw the pair of mobsters who had been booting my door the night before. One of them was a patched member of the Mob. The other was a prospect. They were a pair of eggs, as far as I was concerned, so I'll call them Big Egg and Little Egg respectively. Later that day, Big Egg wandered into my cell. The moment he was through the door, his eyes were darting this way and that, scoping the place out, seeing what I had that might be worth stealing. I say 'stealing' rather than 'taking', as my estimation of him was a big-mouth without the balls to back up all the tough talk.

'Where'd you come from?' he asked.

'Pare,' I replied.

'No shit?' he said. 'Didn't think they'd let you keep a flash pair of shoes like those.' He gestured at my Nike sneakers. 'We're not that generous here.'

It's not often I hated someone so soon after meeting them.

I was tensed up, waiting for him to demand my shoes. When he did, I told myself, I would lay into him without mercy.

Instead, he had another desultory look around and then sauntered out to be a fuckwit somewhere else. This, I was to learn, was typical of Big Egg: he was fond of talking tough and taking things to the brink, but he always stopped short of stepping over the line, unless someone showed weakness. As far as I was concerned, he was the worst kind of prison parasite.

Luckily, not everyone in unit 3, or the Mongrel Mob, for that matter, was an egg. I got to know a guy I'll call Rick, who was typical of lots of the gang members you meet who are just really likeable people. By the time I landed on unit 3, Rick had been in a few years on a 12-spot sentence for being party to a murder. He had supplied the firearm for an armed robbery during which a bank teller was killed. I liked Rick and used to smoke a bit of pot with him. One day, we were smoking and Big Egg came in and started talking shit to me. I could see that Rick was in a fix. Being a gang member, especially a patched one, Rick was obliged to have automatic and unquestioning loyalty to another patched dog, whether or not Rick liked that dog or that dog was an idiot. That's just the way it was. Big Egg was a patched member, and being a neutral and not a mobster, I had no status. I thanked Rick for his hospitality and left. The look I saw on his face said it all.

*

As one heavy drug user to another, Rick warned me about one of the unit 3 screws, a real stickler for the drug regs who was generally known as Cowboy. As if to prove his point, Rick was soon busted with a number of caps of cannabis and was transferred to Paremoremo. And it wasn't long before I was in trouble, too.

One morning, I had been smoking cannabis oil before breakfast and was so wasted that I hadn't cleaned up the oily fingerprints I'd left all over my cell by the time I went out into the yard. Cowboy did the usual inspection and spotted the prints for what they were right away. You could say I was caught green-handed. But although Cowboy had found fingerprints, he couldn't find any actual drugs.

I was in the yard with a close smoking buddy, a Nomad from Otaki whom I'll call Majestic. As everyone made their way back inside, Majestic and I were held back to be searched. Even though I had two caps of cannabis in the pen slot of my shirt pocket and about half an ounce of pot in a large pill container in the hidden pocket in my Y-fronts, I wasn't too worried, as the screw who stopped us was OK. We knew he wouldn't be too thorough in his search. But then Cowboy came out and I knew I was in trouble.

I needed to get rid of the pot. Majestic was the first taken for a search. He was led across the yard to the searching area while I was locked in a vestibule between the kitchen and the wing. It was a tiny, sterile area without windows, drains, or anywhere else I could potentially stash the weed. Not only that, but I had a screw with me to keep an eye on me. I figured I would have to take my chance while I was being led across the yard. There was a patch of grass in the yard with a picnic table on it, right near the door. I hit upon a plan. I undid one of my shoelaces, and as surreptitiously as I could, I reached into my undies, fished out the pill container and stashed it in my side pocket for easy access. Cowboy and the other screw came to get me. Cowboy walked at my side while the other screw walked in front. As we neared the bench, I stopped and put my foot on the picnic table and proceeded to tie my shoelace. I had already palmed the pill container and as I reached to do up the shoe, I flicked the container into the grass under the bench. It was a good plan, or at any rate, the best I could come up with under the circumstances. If it worked, I'd make sure I was first out at afternoon yard to retrieve my pot.

Cowboy was onto me. He wandered over to the grass and picked the pill container up. A big grin spread across his face. I was gutted — at first. But Cowboy's first mistake was he neglected to get the other officer to witness his find.

Cowboy kept grinning at me as I was searched, turning the pill container over and over in his hand.

'That's right,' I thought to myself. 'Keep right on doing that. Rub off all my fingerprints.' At Cowboy's insistence, they fully stripped me, but they managed to miss the two caps in my pocket. I would still be able to get my buzz on that night. And still Cowboy hadn't told the other screws he had found a pill container full of pot.

Later that day, I was told by the head screw I was on charge for having an article in my possession without the permission of an officer, namely an oil-stained sugar bag. Once a week, you were issued a small, brown-paper bag of sugar for your tea or Weet-Bix. I must have been handling mine while I was smoking, or shortly afterwards. He also said it was likely I'd be facing an external charge laid by the police for the large amount of pot I'd been caught with.

'Good,' I said. 'Bring it on.' As far as I was concerned, I stood a much better chance of beating the charge in a real court than I did in the kind of kangaroo court I'd be fronting inside. I already had a defence in mind.

It's interesting to me now that the rights or wrongs of the matter didn't enter my head. I had fully bought into the adversarial nature of the justice system, and much less so into the justice aspect of it. I was able to rationalise this approach by telling myself I had been poorly served by the system in my murder trial. I believed the prosecution had played dirty in order to secure a conviction, and if it was good enough for them, then it was good enough for me to do the same to beat the rap on a crime of which I knew full well I was guilty. I'd also been shafted by the visiting justice last time I was at Rimutaka, and by the prison authorities. As far as I could tell, morality didn't come into it.

A few days later, I pleaded guilty to having an article in my possession without the permission of an officer, namely the sugar bag, for which they had me cold. I was sentenced to three days in the pound and 14 days' loss of privileges. I just shrugged. This was the shortest sentence to solitary I had ever received.

Shortly after coming out of the pound, I was taken over to a secure room where two police officers waited to formally charge me with possession of cannabis. There'd been less than an ounce in the pill container — lucky I'd smoked as much as I had — so they could only charge me with possession for personal use, not supply. They invited me to make a statement about what had happened. I told them I'd love to, but would have to consult my lawyer first. My preferred lawyer was unavailable at the time, so the police would have to wait until court to hear what I would say.

The reality of my situation was that I had nothing to lose. As a lifer, even if I was convicted, I wouldn't face any extra penalty. Consequently, I was looking forward to a day out of prison. I was taken to the District Court at Lower Hutt to enter a plea, and I enjoyed seeing a bit of the city and a few glimpses of the river out of the rear window of the paddy wagon. I waited in the court holding-cell for a while, then was taken up into the courtroom. Even this was a welcome change of scene for me, and the civilians in the public area of the court were the first 'normal' people, besides visitors, I had shared a room with since my imprisonment.

The charge was read.

'How do you plead?' the presiding justice of the peace asked.

'Not guilty,' I replied.

'The matter will go to depositions,' the justice said, and named a date. 'Stand down.'

I was taken back down to the holding cell, where there was another guy being held pending his hearing for some minor matter. He didn't look ecstatic to hear I was a convicted murderer. Nor did his comfort level increase when one of the duty policemen told me to put out the cigarette I was smoking and I told him to get fucked. When he insisted and I still refused, he threatened to pepper spray me. This would have been a new experience, so I told them to go and fetch their pepper spray.

As they stalked off, the other miscreant in the cell watched in bemusement as I tore the striker off my matchbox and wrapped it up in some toilet paper with most of my tobacco and some matches and shoved the parcel in my undies. I was ready. But in the event, I didn't get sprayed. A more senior cop arrived to negotiate a deal, whereby I would hand over my smokes and I would be taken to the police station cells, where they would be given back and I would be allowed to smoke. I agreed. It was all pretty much academic, anyway. I didn't have time to smoke more than a cigarette or two before leaving for Rimutaka.

Meanwhile, I had a conversation with the prosecuting sergeant, who seemed genuinely interested to know why I was pleading not guilty to possession, especially since we both knew there would be no consequences if I pleaded guilty.

'It's the principle,' I replied loftily.

I pointed out that I had pleaded guilty to the charge relating to the oil-stained sugar bag, but wasn't going to roll over on the possession charge because the drugs Cowboy had found weren't mine. I told him he could have the pill container fingerprinted if he wanted, because I knew they wouldn't find my prints on it.

A few weeks later, I was taken back to court, this time for depositions. Before the hearing, the prosecutor came and saw me in the police cells.

'We're not going to proceed with the prosecution,' he said. 'I think you're innocent, and we don't prosecute innocent people.'

My surprise must have registered on my face.

'I believe [Cowboy] planted the drugs,' he continued. 'Would you be willing to assist an investigation into this officer's actions?'

This was exactly what I had wanted all along, to cast aspersions on Cowboy and his honesty, but when push came to shove, I couldn't follow through. As much of a rascal as I was and as much as I disliked the man, I just couldn't do it. I told the prosecutor I didn't feel comfortable taking part in such an investigation. It makes me cringe to think back on my behaviour and intentions in this situation, but the decision of the prosecution to drop this case was another piece of contradictory evidence that countered my cynical view of the system and those involved in it.

*

It was just my luck that the regulations relating to drugs and drug abuse in prisons had been changed. Under the new regime, you could be ordered to supply a urine test if they suspected drug use, or merely at random, and gone were the days when a positive urine test couldn't be used as grounds for imposing punishment. Now, those who returned a positive test would be declared IDUS (Identified Drug User Status). You were IDUS for six months, unless you stated you were clean after three months, whereupon you would have to submit to two tests within eight weeks. If they came back negative, your punishment would be remitted. The punishments didn't change: using drugs was punishable with solitary confinement, loss of privileges, loss of remission (the official name for what is commonly referred to as 'time off for good behaviour') and the very rarely used loss of earnings. But the Department of Corrections found ways to impose other punishments, too. If you were IDUS, you were placed on mandatory non-contact visits, where you would sit in a booth on either side of a Perspex screen, with an ineffective intercom system. The prison authorities claimed non-contact visits were a 'management tool', not a punishment, a feat of sophistry of which the Soviet authorities, as depicted in Solzhenitsyn's *The Gulag Archipelago*, would have been proud. As far as I was concerned, if it hurt and it was meant to hurt, it was a punishment.

The first IDUS would earn you three months' booth visits, three days of solitary, 14 days of off-privileges, and three days of loss of remission. If you returned another positive result while IDUS, you became IDUS2, and received six months' booth visits, five days' solitary confinement, 21 days' off-privileges, and five days' loss of remission. If you returned yet another positive result within six months of your last positive, you became IDUS3. For your third and every subsequent IDUS, you received 12 months' non-contact visits, seven days' solitary confinement, 28 days' off-privileges, and seven days' loss of remission. If you returned a positive for drugs other than cannabis you would start at the same management tool structure as for cannabis, but at the highest tier in terms of solitary confinement and the other legitimate punishments.

As a result of my conviction for the oil stain charges, I was declared IDUS and placed on booth visits for three months. These visits sucked. They sucked to the point where even the prison officer who supervised one of my visits became distressed watching Tania, her daughter and me trying to communicate. He didn't tell me this, but he filed a report indicating how unsatisfactory the booths were to prison management. I came across this report some years later when looking through my file. I was quite taken aback: I hadn't credited prison officers with this degree of humanity.

*

Not long after my court appearance, I was playing pool with Majestic at a table that was positioned alongside the screws' office. I saw Cowboy come into the wing, and I knew he was on his way to the office. I turned my back to him and pretended I hadn't seen him. I began casually swinging my pool cue from side to side at about waist height, for all the world as though I was just waiting for my turn. I knew full well Cowboy couldn't get past without getting hit. I kept it up for about ten seconds. As soon as I stopped, Cowboy stormed past to the office. Majestic and I had a good laugh and continued our game.

When I saw Cowboy getting ready to come back out of the office, I turned the other way and started swinging the cue as before. Cowboy came out of the office and, rather than wait, this time he gave me a shove in the back, which I allowed to send me sprawling on the table. By the time I got up spewing invective, Cowboy was exiting the wing. He didn't look back. Majestic and I had a good laugh at his loss of control.

I didn't think much more of the incident. Majestic and I spent the rest of the afternoon being the rascals we were. We went and got stoned (again). When I came back in from the yard, the senior screw on duty called me into his office. He told me Cowboy had written up the incident, claiming that I had been blocking his way and threatening him with a pool cue, so he had pushed me aside and exited the wing. I spotted it for arse-covering right away.

'This is bullshit,' I told the senior screw. 'Remember what happened last week? Do you think [Cowboy] would walk away if someone threatened him with a pool cue?'

Only a couple of days beforehand, an inmate had muttered something under his breath in Cowboy's hearing, so Cowboy, who had represented New Zealand in wrestling, had wrestled him to the floor and taken him down to the pound on charges of threatening an officer. Management had deemed this conduct to be excessive.

I told him I didn't care about being 'brushed aside' by Cowboy, but I couldn't allow a report like that to be entered on my file. If he persisted with it, then I would have no choice but to complain about being assaulted. I told him I was prepared to forget about the whole incident if Cowboy withdrew the report.

An hour later, I was summoned back to his office and told that Cowboy stood by his account. I told him I was left with no choice but to respond officially in order to protect myself. I handed him an interview form requesting a meeting with the unit manager.

That was Saturday. On Monday morning, I was unlocked and asked to accompany the screws. I had been expecting this, as I knew the unit manager would want to see me about the interview form I had filled in. But, instead, the senior screw I had been dealing with on the Saturday was there.

'Pack your bags, Wood,' he said. 'We're sending you to unit 6.'

I had been back from Pare for two and a half months. I had been told that if I behaved, I would be down in the units after three months. I had been nothing but trouble and here I was off to the units two weeks earlier than promised if I had behaved myself! Undeserving as I was, I was pretty happy with this turn of events.

CHAPTER EIGHT

Break Out

The second step on the Five Steps to Freedom is what I call 'Break Out'.

This is about choosing to break out of your mental prison, and not only believing it is possible to do so, but having the courage to try, the courage to get out of your comfort zone. When my brother Jon visited me early in my time in prison, he brought me an SAS cap badge with its iconic motto: Who Dares Wins. At the time, it seemed more of a reminder of the career ambitions I had once had and lost. But as I came to understand the need to take risks in order to reap the rewards of transformational change, the truth of those words kept resonating with me. To win, you must dare.

Having recognised that what's holding you back are your thoughts and beliefs about the world, the next step is to choose to do something about those inner bars and try to regain all the opportunity you are denying yourself.

One of the reasons making this choice is so hard for people is that some of the things that constrain us are the defence mechanisms we've used to make our reality palatable to ourselves — the things that make us comfortable. As already noted, these defences may even have served us well at different times of our lives, but we may have reached a point where they are no longer constructive. Setting them aside is like asking a child to throw away a comforter. The way forward is unfamiliar and unpredictable, and if there's one thing the human species dislikes, it's uncertainty. In a recent piece of research, participants were given two options — a low-intensity electric shock delivered at random, or a significantly stronger electric shock delivered right now. People's aversion for uncertainty and ambiguity means the subjects preferred the instant, stronger shock.

In my case, breaking out was a slow and incremental process. This is the norm. To avoid emotional and psychological discomfort, I had steadfastly averted my eyes from much of what I would need to comprehend in order to achieve real change and growth. But fortunately I didn't need to engage with it all at once; to start with, I only needed to see the way ahead. And the first step in breaking out is simply believing it is possible to do so.

Once I discovered reading, I began to read voraciously. At first I chose books that seemed relevant to my own situation. In the early days, I would read these with a dictionary next to me to make sense of some of the more difficult words I'd come across. Perhaps the one that had the most impact upon me at this time was *The Gulag Archipelago* by Aleksandr Solzhenitsyn. This was a book about the prison — or rather, death camp — system in the Soviet Union under Stalin. It, along with Viktor Frankl's *Man's Search for Meaning* (set in the Nazi death camps) taught me the value of 'comparing down'. Whereas human beings are much given to envy (comparing your own situation unfavourably with those who are better off than you), it's far more constructive to compare yourself and your situation with those who are worse off than you. It's a kind of 'worse things happen at sea' mentality: I read about the abuse and deprivation others had suffered and, as a result, found my own situation to be not quite so bleak as it had seemed.

Later in my sentence I would be deeply impacted by reading Vice-Admiral James Bond Stockdale's account of his experience of using Stoic philosophy as a prisoner of war in Vietnam. Like the late Senator John McCain, Stockdale was a navy pilot who was shot down over North Vietnam. Like McCain, he survived a long period of imprisonment and endured hideous torture: if I thought my situation was bad, I didn't know I was alive by comparison! Before being sent on active duty, Stockdale had studied philosophy, and was particularly attracted to the ancient Greek philosophical school known as the Stoics. Stoicism has had a significant influence down the ages — some of the greatest Roman thinkers and statesmen such as Cato and Seneca were avowedly Stoics, as was Marcus Aurelius, whose great work *Meditations* was a huge influence on me. One of the principal proponents of the movement was Epictetus, who lived between AD 55 and 135 and who was, at one time, a slave belonging to the notoriously musical Roman emperor Nero. He was also a teacher and philosopher, and after being granted his freedom, he founded his own philosophical school.

In the surviving volume of his thinking, the *Enchiridion*, Epictetus divided everything that bore upon us and our actions into two categories: prohairetic (within our control) and apohairetic (outside our control). It is useless, he argued, to concern ourselves with the apohairetic. Our opinions are within our control: everything else is irrelevant. We have already seen the power of this belief: there is neither good nor bad, remember, but thinking makes it so. Whether our circumstances are good or bad is a matter of opinion, and we can choose what to think. As his chute opened after he had bailed out of his aircraft, James Bond

Stockdale apparently told himself that he had just left the world of technology and was entering the world of Epictetus. Rigorously differentiating between what was within his control and what was entirely out of it enabled him to endure what most of us would regard as the unendurable.

Once you decide it is within your power to change the way you view yourself and your future, it is possible to grasp the fact that you can influence your future. John McCain perceived this, and one of his favourite quotes was from Ernest Hemingway's *For Whom the Bell Tolls*: 'Today is only one day in all the days that will ever be. But what will happen in all the other days that ever come can depend on what you do today.'

Deciding to seize the day and work to make yourself better has a lot to do with the difference between what psychologists call a 'fixed mindset' and a 'growth mindset'. One of the more common cognitive distortions that holds people back from working to better themselves is the belief that everyone is born with a fixed and limited potential. This mindset says things like: I'll never achieve at school, because I'm not smart. I can't take up the piano, because I have no musical talent. Or the reason I achieve at school is that I have more of this fixed attribute called intelligence. But if I find something hard or fail then I have overstretched. Someone with a growth mindset, by contrast, will acknowledge the fact that none of us are born good at anything very much: we learn as we grow, and the results we achieve in any field of endeavour tend to combine our natural talents and the amount of effort we put in. You can do a self-assessment quiz on Carol Dweck's website (https://mindsetonline.com/) to find out what kind of mindset you have. Once you have decided which cap best fits, you can decide what to do about it — whether to change your fixed mindset or harness your growth mindset — in order to have the future that you want for yourself. I was someone with a fixed mindset. I believed I was a certain type of person with certain limitations. I didn't believe I was academically capable enough to study at university level — I had been held back a year at primary school and never felt any connection with education. Yet in 1998 I would enrol at Massey University, the only university to offer psychology as a distance learning subject, and not only achieve but, after a time, excel. The process of education and the small successes I experienced gave me the confidence to believe it was possible to change. Small successes build confidence, but taking those small steps requires the courage not only to try something new, but also to risk failure. You don't wait until you feel confident before you start something: you get confident from taking action, and taking action requires courage. Fortunately, one of the things I would discover was that courage was like a muscle, and the more you exercised it, the stronger it became and the easier it was to use.

Once you believe it is possible to change and you have the courage to try and do so, you still need to find the motivation to do so. It wasn't hard for me to want to change: my life to this point had led me to a maximum security prison. And I had lots of examples around me of what my future would look like if I didn't take action. Yet even if you are driving a late-model car to your perfect house in your perfect neighbourhood, motivation to strive towards your potential and have the most meaningful life possible comes readily when you focus on the reality of your own mortality. If you live to 70, you only live 840 months, or 25,550 days, or 613,200 hours. Be sobered by that fact and allow it to motivate you to break out of your mental prison and build a more meaningful future for yourself, before your short life is at an end.

What do you want your future to look like, anyway? The best way to answer this question is to ask yourself another set of questions.

The first is, what are your values: that is, what is most important to you? You can make a list of values, and rank them from one to ten.

And if you need help in deciding how to rank what is most important to you, you can ask yourself further, self-reflective questions. Suppose you were able to attend your own funeral, what would you most like to hear said about yourself? Another, less confronting way to think about that is to consider what would you most like to hear (or dread to hear) about yourself if you sought honest feedback from your loved ones? Or: suppose you were diagnosed with a terminal illness and told you had five years to live, during which time you would retain your full health and faculties, what would you do with them? Or: if you identified the moments in your life that you regard as your peak experiences — when you felt happiest, most satisfied, most fulfilled — what were they, and what did they have in common?

The reason I like the question that imagines you attending your own funeral is that it chimes with another of my favourite quotes, from the German philosopher Martin Heidegger. 'Every man is born as many men,' he says, 'and dies a single one.' Right up to the moment we die, we have a choice as to who we will have been — a choice among our possible selves. There is no time like the present.

*

Just before my transfer to unit 6, I received two visitors. The first was Steve, an investigator hired by Dr Donald Stevens, a lawyer who had taken a keen interest in my case. He had been collating information on a group of people who were serially molesting teenage boys in Wellington, and my victim, Boyd, was one of the persons of interest in this enquiry. This much Steve told me, but no more, and the meeting was pretty informal and didn't seem to have much point to it. But he asked whether he could come back and talk to me again, and even though the topic of the conversation made me quite uncomfortable, I shrugged.

'Why not?' I said.

If nothing else, it was a break from the routine. Having visitors was a welcome distraction; the only exception to this was when it was *too* good to see people. This sometimes left you sensing your isolation and imprisonment more than before the visit. This would lead some people to ask their loved ones not to visit them. It was an impulse I understood, but never indulged.

The other visitor was Mary, the kindly woman who had visited me in Pare and found the experience so distressing. The weather was cold, and she had brought me some thermal underwear, which I much appreciated. Aware that my twenty-first birthday was approaching, she asked whether I would like her to bring me a birthday cake. I laughed scornfully at this suggestion. The kind of life I was living didn't include birthday cakes! I was too immature and lacking in empathy to spare her the bleakness of my own outlook. This was the last visit she made, and it served me right.

As it turned out, my birthday present was the transfer to the units, which happened on the day itself. On the night I nominally came of age, I was in a wooden cell looking out the bar-less window and smoking gold cannabis oil and thinking it was all way too good to be true. True to my mentality at the time, I suspected a trap: they were surely giving me all this rope so I could hang myself.

It wasn't until much later that I learned I had arrived in unit 6 with quite a reputation for recalcitrance. The manager called a meeting of the staff to decide what their approach should be.

They believed two courses of action were available to them. They could let me know who was boss and crack down on every conceivable infringement of the unit's rules. Or they could cut me some slack and let me find my feet and settle in. Showing a degree of humanity I simply did not credit them with, they decided the latter option was worth a crack.

There were 60 prisoners in unit 6, who worked around the prison; I was soon given a job cleaning the showers on the side of the unit in which I was housed. The reward was that conditions were much better than in the wings. As soon as I stepped out my door in the morning, I was in the fresh air — an unimaginable luxury. And it got better when, after a couple of months, I was moved from the northern side of the unit to the southern side, which meant I got the sun in the morning.

Before 1997, those serving seven years or longer were allowed more personal effects in their cells than those doing shorter stretches, and while the rules had supposedly changed, in unit 6 people like me still got a fair bit of leeway. I had my own duvet and a couple of potted plants in my cell. My favourite was a creeper that eventually reached right across the ceiling.

Visits were on Saturday and Sunday mornings and afternoons, and they were heaps better in the units than anywhere else I had been housed. You could even sit outside and have a cigarette with your visitors. The strip searches when visits were over were a lot more relaxed, probably because the staff were a lot more laid-back down there than in higher security and they were, for the most part, not interested in looking at other naked men.

I couldn't believe the amount of liberty I was given. Unit 6 gave me my first inkling that prison officers could be people rather than just screw enemies. There appeared to be an unspoken agreement in unit 6 whereby if I didn't smoke dope in their face then the screws wouldn't go out of their way to find ways to bust me. One of the senior staff members in the unit got me a job mowing lawns — not just the lawns within the compound, but even those surrounding it, outside the fence. I couldn't believe my luck every time I walked out the gate. I was supposed to be supervised by an officer, but after a while the more relaxed staff members would leave me to it. On these occasions, I would sometimes go down the scrubby bank and sit and smoke next to the little creek that ran by. One time when I did this, a senior officer panicked that she couldn't see where I was. I heard her hurried footsteps crossing the road and I climbed back up as nonchalantly as I could.

'What have you been doing?' she asked.

On a sudden inspiration, I held up the drink bottle I was carrying.

'Getting water for the mower,' I replied.

'Phew!' she said. 'You had me worried there for a moment.'

Lucky for me she wasn't clued up about the workings of two-stroke motors.

*

Thoughts of escape had never been far from my mind from the moment I was first sentenced. I used to plan escapes in great detail, and now that I was in unit 6, the opportunity to put all that planning into practice had never been more within reach.

Three things served to ensure I never put these dreams and schemes into effect, however. One was that I had decided to give studying a go again. After my transfer back from Paremoremo, I had asked the authorities at Rimutaka about the process, but received no satisfactory reply. The staff on the floor told me I needed to speak to someone from education, and when I did that

I was told I needed to see the on-the-floor staff. I hadn't read Joseph Heller's *Catch 22* at that stage, but I knew a bureaucratic regressive loop when I saw one. In the end, I asked my father to make enquiries about enrolling at a university. Massey offered a legal executive course by distance learning, but when it proved problematic to sign up for that, I decided to have a look at psychology and chose to enrol in two double-semester psychology papers — a degree seemed too big a goal for me at this stage. Part of my interest was in better understanding what made people tick so I could more effectively and safely navigate the prison environment. Yet with psychology it was more about studying something that seemed inherently interesting for its own sake. This would be the most important decision I would make in rehabilitating: becoming someone who could effectively reintegrate into society and live a better life than I had ever imagined for myself. It was the beginning of the journey that would make me aware of all the options available to me in life and lead me out of the darkness of my own ignorance.

The second thing that dampened my enthusiasm for attempting to break out of prison was that Steve the investigator was visiting me on a regular basis. When he returned soon after my transfer to unit 6, he told me I had come to the attention of Dr Donald Stevens because in the course of their investigation into the paedophile ring of which Boyd was a part, they had been told by an informant about a number of people who had been victimised by Boyd and his associates. One of those nameless victims sounded very much like me.

Steve pretty much left it at that. He left and I went straight to my cell to get stoned, in an effort to numb the feelings that the conversation had evoked. I had spent years trying not to think about what had happened to me in that back alley in Cuba Street.

When he returned about a week later, Steve told me about his own experience of sexual victimisation and the self-destructive path it had launched him upon. I listened, aghast. My own feeling, which I had never dared interrogate, was that being abused raised questions about one's masculinity. I had grown up believing that being a man meant being able to look after oneself both emotionally and physically, and being abused was a failure to live up to this ideal. It was something my entire upbringing, both before prison and in prison, had encouraged me not to talk about. Yet here was Steve talking openly about what happened to him and how he felt about it. It was as though he had stood there in front of me and dropped two objects of different weights and they had, against my expectations, struck the floor at the same time. Reality was not necessarily as I had conceived it to be.

In the face of his candour, when Steve asked if I had experienced anything similar, I didn't deny it. It would be a long time before I would feel as certain as Steve told me I should feel, or feel that what I had experienced was not my own fault, or consider it something I could talk about as openly as Steve. But even though I didn't recognise it at the time, hearing his story was a big step in my eventual road to recovery. Steve suggested I ask to speak to a psychologist. After an intense internal struggle, I made an appointment with a prison psychologist. I didn't tell him what I wanted to discuss, and in the event, I cut the consultation short. At the time I reasoned to myself I couldn't possibly talk to an effeminate homosexual, which is what I judged the psychologist to be. But if I'm honest, this was just avoiding looking into the abyss of my own feelings of shame and unworthiness.

Steve said Dr Stevens took the view that my conviction for murder rather than manslaughter might possibly amount to a miscarriage of justice, in light of my history of sexual abuse and the nature of the advance that Boyd had made towards me. My counsel had never thought to ask me if I had ever suffered abuse, and of course, I had never volunteered the information. And crucially, counsel had resisted the idea of submitting me for a psychological assessment. Who knows what might have been the outcome if I had been assessed, although I highly doubt I would have been open and brave enough to have revealed anything relevant.

But as a consequence of learning that Dr Stevens was interested in looking into the possibility of a petition to have my conviction overturned, I became less interested in escape. Why risk everything trying to bust out if I could walk through the door early? These days, I'm glad this didn't progress further, as the full length of time I served was the least I owed Boyd and his family. Boyd didn't have to die, and I chose to kill him. I didn't have to end his life and I chose to do so. Attempts to re-litigate and claim a lesser degree of culpability now just sound to me like whining and a lack of gratitude for being able to move on with my life when I took away any chance of reform and redemption Boyd could have had.

Of course, the third reason my escape plans never came to fruition was that I was still a prolific drug user. This both reduced any chances that I could take effective action on pretty much anything, and it meant I was constantly broke. I knew that breaking out of prison itself was the easy part. The second, and far more difficult, part was what came next. Most successful escapers had a ringbolt organised — some means of leaving the country — and this meant having willing assistants to help with the logistics and securing a false identity. None of this came cheap, and if you're spending all your money on drugs, it is unlikely to amount to anything more than a pipe dream.

My routine was that I would mow the lawns in the morning and in the afternoons I would study. I would be stoned most of the time, while mowing and studying, and on the weekends I would see Tania and shoot either morphine or methadone. The syringes smuggled into prison would generally be reduced in size by cutting down their barrel, and while hypodermic needles are supposed to be used only once before they are disposed of, they are repeatedly used in prison. When they become blunt and painful to use, they are simply sharpened by scraping them gently against the striker of a matchbox.

When I had morphine tablets to use, I shot morphine. Most often, however, Tania would bring methadone, which is usually supplied by pharmacies diluted with water so it can be taken orally. Tania would cook it down to concentrate the opiate and remove the water, which made it not only easier to smuggle but also more effective to inject. Even so, it would still require several injections to deliver the whole dose. While the effects were not as intense as those of morphine, they lasted longer — a couple of days instead of a few hours. It was only when I was high on opiates, leaning back enjoying the buzz and listening to music, that I could bear prison.

*

Under the circumstances, it's a miracle I managed to produce anything resembling academic work at all. It wasn't just the drugs. At first, I had to try to settle down and work in my cell, and I had no appreciation whatsoever of what was required of a university essay. I still smile (and cringe) to recall my first assignment, which I handwrote in capitals because I imagined it would be easier to read. I had little grasp of grammar, and even less of punctuation. I also wrote the whole thing as a single block of text because I didn't really understand what constituted a sentence or paragraph. The marker would have known from the return address to which they sent the marked assignment where I was, even if they likely had little or no idea what it was like in prison. Bless them if they didn't restrict themselves to the gentlest of constructive criticism and display sufficient generosity to give me a pass (50 per cent exactly).

After a while, the authorities allowed me to go to the Programmes facility — a block where inmates undertook non-violence and drug rehabilitation courses — to work. Here, I was given access to a little room with a computer on which I could write my essays. There wasn't any internet access, but as I'd never seen the internet, it wasn't missed. A very nice civilian lady named Catherine was in charge of Programmes at this time, and she was very supportive and encouraging. There was also a Catholic nun who was usually about. Sister Marie Roche was part of the prison chaplaincy. I wasn't in the slightest bit religious, and I was narrow-minded enough back then to doubt the motives and mental stability of such people. Sister Marie was way different to the stereotypes I had of nuns. She didn't wear a habit and she didn't walk about spouting the gospel. Instead, she was dressed in non-descript civilian clothes and was nothing but kind and supportive. One day, not long after our first meeting, she breezed in while I was there and set a fragrant paper bag down on the desk.

'I brought you some lunch, Paul,' she said. 'Hope you like KFC.'

This was an unbelievable treat, yet I'm sure I sat there with a look of profound suspicion on my face. She didn't demand I repent my sins or attend church or do anything whatsoever in return.

It was an act of kindness, pure and simple, and as such, it was another of those Galilean gravity moments. I was lucky enough to have a lot more to do with Sister Marie over the remainder of my sentence, and never failed to be moved by her generosity, sincerity, and intellectual flexibility. I have no doubt that both of them, Catherine and Sister Marie, had a role to play in turning me away from the dead-end path I had been on and toward rehabilitation. The power civilians have to positively influence those in prison is massive. A non-judgemental interaction with someone who treats you like a human being helps shift the belief that you are an unworthy and irredeemable person who will never be accepted by other members of society when released.

*

A step I had taken of my own accord around this time had a positive effect on my life in prison, too. I had been dealing cannabis, as it was the easiest way to earn the money necessary to fund my own habit. But I didn't enjoy it, in part because I despised the coterie of parasites who tended to hang around me and try to ingratiate themselves with me out of the most transparent of motives. I also wasn't that effective a dealer. You don't have to be a game theorist to know that in order to ensure everyone pays you what you are due, you have to present as a credible threat in the event of non-compliance. I simply wasn't prepared to indulge in the level of violence necessary to foster that reputation. It hardly mattered, because in the unit where I started dealing there wasn't much competition; people were obliged to source their drugs from me and mostly paid up.

I gave up anyway. I continued buying at wholesale prices, but instead of dealing the dope, I just smoked it myself. As soon as I gave up dealing, I had less money to spend on better drugs, but I was less involved in the politics of the place.

Still, it doesn't take much to get yourself in the shit in prison. I got into one of the bigger fights I was in at unit 6 over a pair of boots. To my considerable annoyance, the prison-issue work boots I used when mowing the lawns vanished from outside my cell. I went around the unit politely asking if anyone had seen my boots or taken them by mistake. I wasn't being threatening or out for revenge; I just wanted my boots so I could go to work. When I asked a Samoan guy I knew and got on well with if he had seen anyone with my boots, another Samoan guy who was with him said, in a provocative way, that he had taken them.

'Nah, he didn't,' the guy I knew said. 'We haven't seen them.'

I moved on. Later that day, I genuinely asked my Samoan friend if his mate had been kidding or whether he'd been trying to start a fight with me.

'Nah, he was just joking around,' he said.

I thought no more of it at the time, which just goes to show what a stoned haze I was walking around in in those days. Later that night after dinner I sat in my cell with two other guys getting ready to get stoned. I'd only had a couple of spots when someone started trying to kick the cell door open. Luckily I had the door jammed shut with a screwdriver. At first I thought it was the screws doing a raid, but when I looked out the window I saw the same guy trying to bust into my cell. I opened the door and stepped outside. A couple of his mates from the unit were there, too.

'What's up?' I asked.

'I want to fight with you,' the very angry door-kicker told me.

'Why?' I asked.

'My mate told me you wanted to fight me. Well, here I am.'

I explained where the misunderstanding had arisen. If I'd been more mature, it probably would have ended there. Instead, once I had set him straight, I told him I'd fight him anyway, since he'd stepped me out. He was ready then and there, but I told him we'd have to go to the carving room where the screws couldn't see us. He and another guy went down there to wait.

'What's up?' asked my mates when I went back into my cell to take my jersey off.

'One of the Island boys wants to fight me,' I said. 'I'm heading down to the carving room. Won't be long.'

By the time I'd got down to the carving room, I had a bit of an entourage: my mates, a couple of others who'd seen me pass and a Mongrel Mob member or two who'd been sent by a senior mobster I got on well with who wanted to make sure the fight was fair. There were also a bunch of people who were in the carving room actually carving, but of course they stopped what they were doing to watch.

As soon as I walked in, I went up to my opponent and delivered him a swift kick in the balls and a left cross on the jaw. My mistake was being half-hearted about it. The next thing I knew I was getting forced backwards by multiple blows to the face. I distinctly remember thinking this wasn't the plan. The guy wasn't that big, but it turned out he was quite an accomplished boxer. I slipped over on the floor and landed on my back on someone's glass painting. My opponent ended up on top of me. Fortunately, having some experience in ground fighting, I was quick to use my legs to hold him away from me so he could no longer reach me with his fists. Then I used my reach advantage, going for his throat first, and when I couldn't quite get a grip on his windpipe, I changed tactics and grabbed his balls. We were stuck like this for a few seconds, me squeezing his balls as hard as I could and him unsuccessfully flailing for my face. When it became apparent that we had reached a stalemate, those present broke us up and my opponent left the carving room.

This could have been the end of it, but he'd broken my nose in his initial flurry of punches and I was unhappy with the result. I told his mate he'd better go and fetch my opponent back for round two. But he returned saying he didn't want to come back.

'You'd better get him back here,' I said, 'or we're going to go to war.'

As Solzhenitsyn once wrote, 'Pride grows in the human heart like lard on a pig,' but it wasn't only pride. I genuinely thought this was the right course of action. I was concerned about the need to comply with the prison norms and values, which stated that an upstanding member of the prison community was one with form. In these circumstances, such a person would escalate the type and level of violence if defeated in unarmed combat.

While I waited, I had time to re-think my tactics. I'd been too cocky. Being stoned probably hadn't helped either, but I hadn't been aggressive enough. The pounding I'd taken had been sobering.

My opponent returned and it was his turn to make the same mistake. He wore the cheerful smile of a man about to administer a beating. He came at me fast, and with perfect timing I kicked his legs out from under him. As soon as he hit the ground, I stepped forward to kick him in the head. The floor was slippery, so I ended up flat on my back again. We both struggled to our feet and I managed to pull his jumper over his head and punch him a number of times in the face. I was taking things seriously this time. I had the front of his jersey with my left hand and was delivering right crosses with the other. He was trying to respond, but I was in control. Trouble was, word had got out and quite a crowd of spectators had gathered to watch through the carving room window, and this attracted the attention of the screws. Some of the staff in unit 6 were good about letting people have one-off fights to sort out their issues. They didn't encourage such behaviour, but if people were going to fight anyway, they often supervised to make sure no one else jumped in. After the winner had been decided, the staff took the combatants off to the pound.

Not long into our second round, the senior staff member on duty rushed into the carving room. We had been tipped off moments before, so we'd stopped fighting, but the blood and energy in the room spoke volumes.

'What's going on?' he asked.

I grinned.

'Me and my mate here were doing a bit of sparring. It got a little bit out of hand. There's no problem.'

He looked from my battered, bloodied face to that of my opponent and appeared understandably sceptical. To convince him, I put out my hand to shake my opponent's. He took my hand — and delivered a devastating left hook flush on my right ear. I was more disappointed than hurt.

The staff member told my opponent he would call him over to the office once he had dealt with me. He took me to the office to look for a plaster, as I had cut my thumb and back on the glass painting I had fallen on in round one.

'I'm going to have to charge you both with fighting,' he said.

'Oh, come on,' I replied. 'It was nothing. Just a bit of a dust-up. It's all sorted now. Don't charge us.'

He paused in bandaging my thumb.

'I'm worried that if I let it go, there's going to be a bloody war between the Samoans and the white guys.'

I asked him to fetch my opponent so we could agree in front of him that this would be the end of it. In my opponent came (I was happy to note he was limping). He readily agreed it was over between us. We shook hands, and this time I didn't cop a left hook. The officer agreed not to write up the incident.

*

It wasn't fighting but — you guessed it — drugs that spelled the end of my relatively idyllic existence in unit 6. One day, I was smoking in my cell with another couple of guys. We thought we'd be left in peace, as there had been a muster not long before. Musters, when the staff do a round of the cells, looking out for anyone who is up to no good, were supposed to be done every half-hour to an hour, but they were hardly ever this regular. It seemed no one had told a relatively new staff member this, and she started a muster. When she got around to my cell, we were still smoking. I wasn't impressed at being interrupted. Much to the amusement of the guys I was smoking with, I stood at the door, stoned as, and started berating her for doing a muster so soon after the last one. You'd be hard pressed to find a bigger sense of entitlement than that.

When she got back to the office, she wrote an incident report about the smell of pot coming out of my cell. This was enough grounds to invoke a urine test, so two days after the incident, me and the other two found ourselves being called out by the drug testers. It was a year and a half since I'd last been tested, so I'd had a feeling I was about due. I'd arranged a dummy sample, which involved getting someone who didn't smoke drugs to piss into a pill container. You kept this in your undies and supplied this instead of your own urine when you were tested.

I was searched before being sent into the toilets near unit 6, but I was still able to pull a swifty with the samples. Trouble was, the beaker into which you're required to piss has a temperature-sensitive strip on the side. I'd neglected to take the precaution of warming up the dummy sample — either by running the pill container under a hot tap, or keeping it tucked under my balls for an hour or two before submitting to the test — so the supervising screw readily identified it was too cold. As the motto of the Green Berets goes: 'Those who fail to plan, plan to fail.'

I was told I was on charge for tampering with a urine test, and offered the opportunity to provide a genuine sample. If this sample came back positive, I'd be charged with returning a positive test rather than with tampering.

'What happens if it's negative?' I asked.

'You'll be charged with tampering,' was the reply.

I told them I didn't see much point pissing for them since I was on a charge regardless of the outcome. It was pointed out that refusing to supply a sample or tampering with the sample were treated the same as returning a positive result for class A drugs. The penalty was seven days' solitary and 28 days' off-privileges.

Better, I thought, to be suspected of class A drug use than to be proved to be *using* class A drugs. If they tested my piss, they'd find an interesting cocktail of substances. I declined to supply a sample.

I copped the penalty, and immediately appealed, not because I thought I might beat the charge, but because I knew the penalty wouldn't begin until the appeal was heard. After dinner, I withdrew the appeal and toddled off to the pound, having dodged a few hours. When I got there, I found a mattress on the floor. Every other time I'd been in the pound, the mattress was taken away during unlock, leaving you with nothing but bare concrete, a bucket and a blanket during the day. I couldn't believe my luck, and every time a screw came to check on me, I'd get as close to the observation slot as possible to obscure his view of the cell. The pound wasn't pleasant, but it was a hell of a lot easier with a mattress. After doing this for seven days, I learned that the old regime had been deemed inhumane. Solitary now came with mattresses at all hours.

Neither the pound time nor the loss of privileges were the worst part of being IDUS: it was the non-contact booth visits. They're pointless. They don't stop you getting drugs into the prison, as there are plenty of other ways to do it. And they don't even make you think twice about the offence that got you there, because due to a quirk of human nature you're more likely to feel victimised, resentful and determined to 'get back' at the authorities than you are to feel inclined to examine your conscience. I remember spending years thinking there was no way I was going to give up drug use as a result of being deprived of physical contact with my loved ones. The prison might tell you it was a 'management tool', but it looked like a punishment and felt like a punishment. To give up drugs because of this treatment would be tantamount to endorsing the punishment. This is consistent with the account of behaviour within prisons by psychologist Erving Goffman. According to Goffman, when prisoners are subjected to what they consider to be an unfair or excessive punishment, they come to regard the actions that led to this punishment as far more justified than they did when they committed them. This disposes the prisoner to engage in further criminal or antisocial behaviour as a means of getting even.

Not a month later, I was called out for another piss test. This time I was totally unprepared. All inmates within the institution are placed in a pool and each month a certain number are randomly selected by computer to undergo urine tests. Your chances of getting called out are reasonably slim. But as soon as you become IDUS, you're also included in the pool of IDUS inmates from which additional random tests are generated. This makes your chances of being selected much higher.

Alan Carr, the unit manager, called me into his office.

'The result's positive,' he said. 'We're going to have to put you on a charge.'

Carr was a good guy. I told him I thought the random test was unfair because it had been imposed less than 28 days after the last piss test I'd done, too soon for the drugs to have cleared my system.

'That's a matter to take up at your hearing,' he shrugged.

'We both know I'll be found guilty at a hearing,' I replied. 'Don't let it come to that.'

He looked at me thoughtfully.

'I'm not making any promises,' he said. 'Leave it with me, and I'll see what I can do.'

I didn't hear any more about the charge.

Soon after this, Alan Carr was demoted because he allowed an inmate out for a temporary release, which had been forbidden higher up the management chain. The replacement manager was a right fuckwit, fresh from the United Kingdom where he had worked as a senior screw. As soon as he took charge of the unit, he decided things were too sweet for the inmates. One of his first acts was to stop keys being issued to lock doors. Allowing inmates to lock the doors to their cells hadn't been a major issue for staff because they had master keys, but it had stopped stealing, plenty of which went on. He also ordered staff to enforce laws relating to cell standards, and this even meant removing pot plants such as my luxuriant creeper.

He wasn't too happy when he looked through my file and found an unactioned drugs test tucked away in the wrong part of my file. Luckily for me, it was too late to do anything about it.

*

Cowboy, my nemesis from unit 3, was transferred into unit 6 and it wasn't long before he and I fell into our old patterns. Within a few days of our crossing paths, he wrote an incident report complaining that I had verbally and physically threatened him. A few days later, he saw another prisoner try and fail to open my door. He and another screw stormed my cell and, according to his report, they found me and another inmate in there. I was, he said, incoherent for a good 45 minutes. What they had happened upon was a member of the Highway 61 gang tattooing me. For all I know, I probably was incapable of speaking coherently: I was stoned most of the time.

On Cowboy's recommendation, I was urine tested on the strength of this incident. To make matters worse, he overheard me and another prisoner questioning his parentage. I ended up sentenced to seven days' solitary confinement and 30 days' loss of privileges for this incident. No sooner was I back from the pound than I was told I was being moved to unit 7. Cowboy happened to look in on me as I was packing, and I didn't spare him my opinion of him. We ended up toe to toe, and inevitably this became the subject of yet another incident report.

I was sent back to the pound again. The silver lining was that my university exams were looming, and the idea of spending a week in the pound with my textbook was quite appealing.

The day after I returned from solitary, I was asked if I wanted a job in the kitchen. I told the screw it sounded good but I was a full-time student, to which he replied that the unit 7 manager had decreed my studies would have to be done on my own time, since this was a working unit. In an uncharacteristic display of compliance, I presented myself to the kitchen to work. I was to be a baker. My career as a baker was short-lived, however, as a few days later, while I was working in the kitchen, the kitchen boss told me the unit manager wanted to see me. I'd been expecting this. But when the door to his office opened, there was no sign of the unit manager. Instead, there were six big screws waiting for me. I was surrounded and informed that I had returned my third positive urine test. I was to be transferred to a punishment unit in Mount Crawford Prison.

CHAPTER NINE

Make the Escape

Dreams without action remain dreams. To make your escape is to start taking steps that reduce the distance between where you are and where you desire to be.

When people fail to break free of their mental prisons, it's not usually for lack of the desire to be free: it's often because they think about change as something that occurs in some distant point in the future. This is true of the complete change, but it's not true of the process of change. Wishing yourself on the mountaintop isn't going to get you walking. If you fix your gaze on the remote prospect of the major change you want to see in your life, it starts to feel as though it's beyond your reach. It's tomorrow. Next month. Next year. There is no incentive to act now.

To make your escape, you must get specific about what you want to change. Wanting to lose weight isn't a specific goal: wanting to lose five kilograms is. Having the general idea that you want to write a book will not get you to put pen to paper. Setting a goal of writing 500 words on Thursday just might.

The research backs this up. Studies have shown that having vague goals makes it hard to start and easy to give up. Specific goals mean you can't fool yourself into believing you've 'done enough'.

Nor do you want to set yourself excessively ambitious goals. The research shows that 'stretch goals' aren't nearly as effective at bringing us closer to our ultimate dreams as smaller, manageable steps. The trick is to lower the motivation bar. Cut down your daily calorie intake by a little and go for a walk (putting out of your mind the five kilograms you want to lose). If your goal is to write 500 words a day on your book (forgetting about the 90,000 still to go), start by writing 50 words a day and then build incrementally until you have reached the 500 mark. Put one foot in front of the other, then do it again, and don't look up at the summit. After all, while being good at something is difficult, getting better is always easy.

What you're essentially trying to do is stop focusing on the goal and to create habits that are conducive to your success in achieving your goal. Habits can be thought of as a behaviour loop. According to Charles Duhigg, who has made a study of habits, they usually comprise a cue, a routine and a reward. The cue might be one of five things: a particular location, time, emotional state, interaction with a particular person or an immediately preceding event. In the example he uses — his daily habit of leaving his office to go to the cafeteria to buy a cookie, which he would then eat while chatting with colleagues — the cue was the time, the routine was the purchase of the cookie and eating it with others. In order to break the habit, Duhigg found it necessary to determine what the actual reward was, and he did this by substituting coffee or a salad for the cookie (in case it was the sugar hit that he was craving), and by taking the cookie back to his desk and eating it alone. It turned out that the reward he was seeking through his daily cookie ritual was the chance to interact with his colleagues. Once he had determined this, he found it relatively easy to break his cookie habit and substitute another routine that was more conducive to his goal (which was losing a bit of weight).

Because this is the thing: you can have good habits and bad habits. Bad habits are those that obstruct your progress towards your goal or aren't a reflection of the type of person you want to be and want your reputation to reflect. Good habits are those that enable you to achieve your goals and are consistent with who you want to be in the world. Try identifying your habits, good and bad. What rewards are you craving that have led to counterproductive habits? How can you use the same (or similar) rewards to create a constructive habit? Creating good habits can be the key to success. Suppose you're accustomed to going out in the early afternoon to meet friends for coffee. There's a good chance it's the social interaction you're craving, not the coffee. Suppose your goal is getting fit. Try asking your coffee buddies (or other friends) if they would meet you at the gym instead. After all, you're not going to get fit the first time you go to the gym. But if you get in the habit of going to the gym, you're well on your way. The research suggests that creating new habits generally takes 90 days. This means the goal for the first 90 days is just getting to the gym. What you do there and how hard you work doesn't matter. What matters is creating the habit of going to the gym.

Remember, you don't have to do it all alone. You can find yourself a mentor or, failing that, a role model. When I was struggling with my dreams and goals, I found it useful to read about how others had succeeded against the odds. Around that time, I read the story of the bullfighter El Cordobés. He was a poor kid who often went hungry and had no links to the usual aristocratic circles of the matadors, and yet he became the greatest bullfighter of his generation. Growing up next to a farm that raised fighting bulls, he dreamed of becoming a matador. Rather than merely dreaming the dream, he took action, sneaking into the bull paddocks at night to teach himself how to fight bulls. The animals were not the only or even the greatest danger he faced: the farmers would have shot him if they'd caught him, because fighting bulls learn about as much from their experience as bullfighters do. Training with a fighting bull taught it how to fight.

One thing you must confront when you plan your escape is that making your escape comes at a cost. It might be as little as your psychic comfort. It might be as much as a whole way of life for you that has to go if you mean to have the future you prefer. If you do want to lose those five kilos, you can no longer consume more calories than you burn. If you do want to make a start on that book, then you'll have to face the fear that your writing might not be any good, and sacrifice time that you could be spending on easier things. If you do want to see the view from the summit, you're going to have to endure a hard climb. In the end, it comes down to sacrifice. Tony Robbins is fond of saying that the only limit to your ambition is the amount you're willing to sacrifice. Research shows that human beings naturally focus on what they stand to lose. Indeed, according to the work of Daniel Kahneman, loss aversion is the single greatest driver for people. The way to leverage this loss aversion to your advantage is to become clear about what you stand to lose if you don't start striving towards your potential, if you don't start taking action now.

Many people in prison talk about what they'll do when they're released, how they'll take better care of their kids and live better lives, but life and change are all about what you do right now.

Time is a different commodity when you're serving a long prison sentence. To survive psychologically, you need to forget about the outside world, to accept that this is your new life, and to focus on the present. Living my life in the present was key to making my escape. I didn't worry about what I was or wasn't going to do in some uncertain future: I just focused on what I could do that day, on what I could do right then. So I stopped smoking weed and started studying fulltime. Together, these practical steps enabled me to successfully complete my undergraduate degree and — as a bonus — massively reduce the amount of time I spent in solitary confinement.

Research suggests that the ability to seize the moment makes you three times more likely to achieve your goals than if you merely indulge in dreams of a better future. To seize the moment, you need to know in advance when, where and with whom you will get the opportunity to start taking the small steps that will make all the difference.

*

I walked into the reception area of Mount Crawford Prison with a creepy sense of déjà vu. This was where the whole prison experience had begun for me — four years earlier, when I'd arrived as a scared, sickly kid. I was 22 years old now and the prison environment had become my home, my comfort zone, the place I knew best and was most used to. Finding myself back at the start brought on some strong emotions. I remembered how scared and desolate I had been at the start. In the intervening years, prison had hardened me a great deal. I didn't feel as scared or uncertain now. I felt attentive and battle ready. If I'd had the maturity, I'm sure I'd have felt disappointed that once again I had managed to sabotage my own well-being, but such levels of accountability and maturity were still in the distant future for me at this stage.

They took my box of study materials from me. I told them I needed them, as I had my exams coming up, but they replied I would need permission to have them.

'When can I get that?' I asked.

'Tomorrow,' the guard replied.

It was a physical wrench walking away from them.

They led me through the visiting room to the door that connected to wing three. The first face I saw on the other side was familiar and friendly, despite being completely covered in tattoos. It was Hammer, a Mongrel Mob member I had got on with really well back at unit 6 at Rimutaka.

He flashed his eyebrows at me.

'Paul,' he nodded. 'Good to see you, bro. Everyone's here. All the old crew are here.'

He was right. There were familiar faces everywhere: a Nomad I had known well in Pare, and Mark, a cheerful, well-educated guy I had been mates and drug buddies with back in unit 6, along with heaps of others. Due to the 'three strikes' policy Rimutaka was running with regard to drug use, all of the drug users were being shipped to Mount Crawford. So here we all were.

A lot had changed about the physical set-up of wing three since I was last there — the screws' office had been extended, the laundry had been moved, and prisoners now did solitary in the observation cells instead of the pound, which had been declared both unsanitary and inhumane — but much else was just the same. With all the drug users concentrated in one place, the inevitable consequence was that drugs were freely and copiously available. I was celled up with a young bloke I knew from Rimutaka and with whom I got on very well. He shared my passion for getting wasted — so did the guy who replaced him when he was released soon after my arrival — so I spent just about every day of my time back at Mount Crawford getting stoned and playing a board game named Risk.

The other thing that hadn't changed was the violence. Soon after I settled in, a busload of guys from Waikeria Prison were transferred down. Typically, some of these young guys felt they had something to prove. We were still having compulsory yards in the morning in those days, and on the first day the new boys were out in the yard with us, a vicious fight broke out among a few of them. It's amazing to me now, but I just carried on walking up and down the yard with another guy as this fight went on. That's how habituated to the sight of violence I had become: the spectacle of a bunch of guys trying to kill one another didn't even cause me to break my stride.

It wasn't too long after this fight that one of the guys involved got into debt he couldn't pay. He took the standard exit route of ratting out everyone he could to prison authorities, and going into protection in one of the former observation cells in the caged-off area. It turned out he wasn't immune from the wrath of those he'd betrayed: one of them managed to put a high-pressure fire hose under the door of his cell and flood it out.

*

On 1 November 1999, a few days after arriving at Wellington Prison, I was issued with the charge sheets for the positive urine result at Rimutaka Prison. I went up on charge for this three days later. The prison superintendent asked for my plea, and I pleaded not guilty — not because I imagined I had any leg to stand on with regard to the urine test, but because I felt unfairly done by with the process, and in particular the timeline. The superintendent noted that this was a Class A drug offence and my third IDUS, so he referred the charge to the Visiting Justice — on the grounds he considered the charge serious enough to warrant a punishment harsher than he was permitted to impose.

I duly appeared before the VJ, Justice Henwood, who not only gave me a very sympathetic hearing, but who also handed down a set of unusually lenient sanctions as a punishment. I received eight months' booth visits, and a week of being locked up early (at 5.30 pm). I was rapt! It was the first time in a very long time I had been up on a charge without receiving a sentence of solitary confinement, and apart from the early lockup time I wouldn't suffer the deprivations usually associated with being off-privileges. And even then, because I had a cellmate, it wasn't practical to lock me up early.

Looking back, it's little things like this that helped change my attitude. Being heard respectfully, being treated with humanity ... the softening on their side probably helped to work a softening in me.

But the real change came about as the direct result of my studies. I was given permission to carry on studying for the two first-year psychology papers I had enrolled in. A few months after I arrived, my mate Mark was released and I was allowed to move into his single cell, which was far more conducive to reading and thinking than sharing with a dedicated doper. On my first night in my new accommodation, I heard a furtive noise and realised I wasn't alone. There were mice in the cell — I eventually counted at least seven — and whereas most people wouldn't be thrilled about living in a vermin-infested cell, I liked the company, and actually used to save little bits of Weet-Bix from breakfast to feed them.

Once the authorities became convinced I was serious about my studies, I was given access to an empty visiting room in the evenings. I was loving learning. It's true what they say: first free the mind, and the body will follow. I was still tightly locked up, but when I was immersed in my books and papers, my mind roamed freely. The Latin from which we derive the word 'educate' is *e ducare*, 'to lead out of', reflecting the ancient idea that to be educated is to be led out of darkness.

All the same, I wasn't yet ready to put my studies above all else. One evening, while I was reading in the visiting room, Alan Carr, the unit manager who had 'misplaced' my positive drug result, came in. He had been demoted and was back in uniform, working over on the segregation side of the prison. He expressed pleasure at seeing me working on improving myself, and he suggested I ask to be placed on segregation, where I would have more time and fewer distractions. I could see the attraction, but as yet I was too fully institutionalised to accept. The universally held opinion among prisoners was that segs was strictly for scum, for inmates who were weak or had done something so awful that their safety couldn't be guaranteed among the general population. I didn't have the maturity to see past the stigma to the advantages. I declined Alan's offer.

One day, around the time I appeared before the Visiting Justice, I was summoned by a screw and taken over to the prison library to sit my exams. Whereas I had gone into the hearing with hardly a qualm, I was nervous as hell going into the little room where the books were kept. The civilian worker in charge of Progammes at Wellington Prison was there to supervise. I'd never done any proper exams at school, and it was a strange and uncomfortable feeling sitting some now.

After they were over — they seemed to go well, but I had no real way of gauging it — I had to wait a few weeks before I got the results. I remember the excitement and dread with which I received the envelope. Who knew what it would contain? It could either be validation of my efforts and the dreams that I was just beginning to dare to have or it could deliver confirmation of the low opinion the system encouraged me to hold of myself and my abilities. The stakes were that high.

I gently eased the paper from the envelope and unfolded it. The grades leapt out at me. I had passed both papers! Not only that, but I had scored a B in one of them. Later in my academic career, I would be gutted to receive a B, becoming accustomed to scoring nothing lower than an A. But I smile now to recall the unbridled joy with which I received that B. Not only was I able to pass university-level papers, I was able to do so with a degree of competence. I had always thought I was a certain type of person with particular limitations, but this experience was evidence I was capable of more. It was evidence I could learn and grow if I were prepared to do the work and show perseverance.

Thus encouraged, I resolved to enrol in four papers the following year, including a creative writing course — an inspired move, as it turned out, as it largely equipped me to produce a coherent piece of writing for the first time. And I continued to read. Much of what I was reading fuelled my growing conviction that there were better possibilities for me: I read Alexandre Dumas' classic *The Count of Monte Cristo* and Nelson Mandela's *Long Walk to Freedom*. It seemed ludicrous to feel I was hard done by in comparison to what these people, fictional and real, had suffered, and they provided me with examples of people who flourished in spite of long terms of imprisonment.

And one day, I happened across Robert Frost's famous poem *The Road Not Taken*, which contains the lines:

Two roads diverged in a wood
And I, I took the road less traveled by
And that has made all the difference

I got goosebumps. I recognised I was at an existential crossroads. I was surrounded by examples of what my life would look like if I carried on the way I had been going, but I wanted better for myself, and I had been shown another path. I think I began for the first time to imagine a life after prison — not the life I'd imagined in my escape fantasies, but a life that seemed possible now that I was making progress in my studies. I resolved then and there to kick my drug habit and devote myself to securing a Bachelor of Arts degree, so that when I left prison, it would be with a sense of accomplishment rather than with regret for all the time I had wasted and lost. I imagined how different my future could be on release if I followed this path and achieved this outrageously ambitious goal. If I carried on doing drugs and living the standard prison lifestyle, I felt I would be unable to associate with normal people on my release. I had gone into prison at 18 and would likely be released in my mid-30s and I would only have a shameful period of imprisonment to show for all that time. This shame would drive me to seek the company of others who would not judge me, others who had been in prison or who led antisocial lives. But if I persevered and got a degree, I would have something positive, something I could be proud of, which would enable me to associate with a different group of people, who, thanks to my degree, would see me in a different light.

*

Things soon started to change in the wing. Like so many of the great ideas prison management have, the notion of a punishment wing exclusively for IDUS inmates fell by the wayside as pressure for the space came from a muster blowout. The wing started filling up with people of different classifications, and one complication of this was that many couldn't be unlocked together for safety and security reasons. The crude solution was to increase the amount of time we spent locked up, to the point where we were unlocked for only a few hours a day. Needless to say, this wasn't well received, and a meeting was called in the caged yard out of the earshot of staff to discuss the possibility of having a riot. I found myself in a strange situation. A few short years earlier, I had been in this same prison trying to *start* a riot. Now I was one of the guys arguing against one. The reality of our situation, as I pointed out, was that a riot wouldn't improve our lives. All that would happen was the guards would use the goon squad to deliver a serious beating to those involved, who would then be shipped up to Paremoremo. Reason prevailed at this meeting, but I am not sure how long peace would have lasted had not the prison decided to give up on the IDUS punishment wing idea and start sending people, including me, back to Rimutaka.

*

Just before I was sent back to Rimutaka, a guy I'd been shooting up drugs with told me he had contracted hepatitis C, a highly infectious viral disease of the liver that usually progresses to cirrhosis, liver cancer and an early death. I was grateful to him for sharing this information. He and I had been sharing a needle. I was aware it was theoretically possible to request syringes from the prison nurses, but such was my level of mistrust of them — they had invariably acted more like custodial than medical staff, in my experience — I had never put it to the test and asked for one. It seemed pretty certain I would have picked up hep C as well.

I submitted myself for a blood test, and received the devastating (if hardly surprising) news that I was positive for hep C. I was called into the doctor's office to have the meaning of the result explained to me. The doctor told me the next step was to find out what strain of the disease I had, which would involve a trip to the hospital and a more comprehensive set of tests.

The appointment was made, and it was with this shadow hanging over me that I returned to Rimutaka. I was pleased to be going back. Certain features, such as the grass in the lower security compounds and the views of the surrounding hills from parts of the prison, made it a far less depressing place than Mount Crawford.

I was placed back in unit 6, which didn't exactly go down well in the unit guardroom, where the problems I had caused were still fresh in some people's minds. My old antagonist, Cowboy, was still on the unit, and no one was relishing the prospect of a re-match. The staff member in charge told me it was a mistake I'd been assigned to unit 6 and I would shortly be moved.

'Look,' I said. 'Please give me one more chance. Things are a bit different now. Most of the trouble I used to get in was because of drugs. I'm not involved in that shit anymore.'

He looked at me doubtfully but agreed to consult the other staff to see what they thought. While I was waiting for the decision, I spied John Barlow walking around in the unit, the first time I'd seen him since Paremoremo. I waved, and he waved back. It was good to see him.

The staff member came back.

'Well, everyone who's on is prepared to give you another chance. But Cowboy's off today, and it's only fair we give him the final say. He comes back in a couple of days, so we'll let you know.'

'Thanks,' I said, genuinely grateful.

'Don't get your hopes up,' he said. 'And I wouldn't unpack my bags if I were you.'

A couple of days later, I was called into the unit manager's office, where the acting unit manager and Cowboy were sitting.

'We hear you've turned over a new leaf, and you want a second chance on the unit,' the manager said.

I told them I was focused on my studies and doing my best to stay clean. I asked that we put our past differences behind us and make a fresh start on this basis.

'What do you think?' the manager asked Cowboy.

My old foe and I locked eyes. Our mutual dislike and history lay between us. Both of us could feel the power he had over me in that moment.

'OK by me,' Cowboy said. 'I'm prepared to give him another go.'

It was a true act of magnanimity, and from the last place I would have expected. I was moved by it, and grateful. We shook hands on it, and I went and unpacked my boxes.

*

Once settled into unit 6, I was escorted by a couple of prison officers to Wellington Hospital, where I provided a blood sample for a comprehensive test for hep C. The doctor explained that if the test was positive, my prognosis would largely depend on what strain I was found to have been infected with. Another appointment was made for me in a month's time, and I was told I would receive the results of the test in the meantime. He gave me some literature to read: there wasn't much good news in there. An early death beckoned, and because hep C is so readily transmitted, it was considered irresponsible for a sufferer to have sexual contact with another. An early death after the sexless remainder of my life ...

I did my best to put the dread I felt aside, and I focused on weight training and study. Fortunately, this wasn't too hard. The most effective way to survive an environment as hostile as prison is to disconnect from your emotions. Over the years I'd been inside, I had become better and better at deadening my emotional experiences. One of the ironies of prison is that the very things that must be fostered to enable prisoners to eventually become contributing members of society, such as compassion and empathy, are the things that are most stunted within the prison environment. Prison is such a predatory environment that it would be a ceaselessly unbearable trauma for those with a finely tuned capacity for empathy or compassion. To survive in this environment, you must harden your heart.

There were no gym facilities to speak of at Wellington Prison, so it was a real pleasure to get back among it at Rimutaka. I suppose at a subconscious level the impending bad news about my health renewed my determination to treat myself properly. I was highly disciplined about what I was eating, and I did heaps of weights. I put on muscle mass: at my peak, I was 6 foot 2, I weighed in at nearly 105 kilograms, and none of that was excess body fat.

As the time for my follow-up appointment neared, I began to wonder what had happened to the test results. I imagined the worst: the news was bad, so they intended to tell me in person. The day itself rolled around, and I was taken to hospital again, where after an anxious wait, I was seen by a doctor.

'I suppose you're wondering how it happened,' he said.

'How what happened?' I frowned. I knew perfectly well how I'd picked up hep C.

'How you managed to shake it,' he replied.

There was a moment's pure confusion. But once we'd cleared it up, I learned that the results of my test had been sent to Rimutaka, where in characteristic prison fashion, they simply placed them on my file without notifying me. So it was sitting there with the doctor that I learned my blood had tested negative for hep C. The first test had merely screened for the antibodies produced when your body detects the virus, and of course, having shared a needle with a carrier, I had been exposed. Because it is so infectious, there's only a miniscule chance you'll fail to develop the disease once exposed. But, in a small number of cases, the body successfully defeats the virus. My luck was in. I appeared to be a member of that tiny minority.

*

The central tenet of Stoic philosophy, that the path to happiness and fulfilment lies in mastering one's attraction to pleasure and aversion to pain, had real resonance with me. One of the virtues Roman Stoics — and Victorian schoolmasters centuries later — extolled was the notion of *mens sana in corpore sano*: a healthy mind in a healthy body. I was doing the best that prison allowed to live up to that ideal, with my weight training and my studies.

I was shifted quite soon after I'd settled into unit 6, which had become something of a dumping ground for prisoners who weren't wanted in other units but who weren't classified as a high enough security risk to warrant being placed in high medium. My place was wanted for others, so I was shifted to unit 9. This was a good thing, because unit 9 had been set aside for those who were undertaking a nine-month non-violence course run by a psychologist and a rehabilitation worker. There weren't many inmates to start with — 30, as opposed to as many as 60 in the other units — and those who were there spent most of Monday to Thursday attending the course in groups of 10 to 12. This made the unit very quiet and gave me the space and peace I craved for my work.

Even better was the fact that another guy in the unit was studying and had been allowed a computer. I had tried for some time to get permission to have a personal computer in to the prison, but had never been successful. In unit 9, I couldn't be fed the usual 'computers aren't allowed in the unit' line.

I was visited by Henare, an old friend from my youth. I remembered admiring him for the fact that he used to work a full day and then study at night, which certainly made him unusual among the people I had hung with back then. I told Henare that I was now studying and was trying to get permission for a computer.

'Bro, if you get permission, I'll give you a computer,' Henare said.

This was an incredibly generous offer and, true to his word, as soon as I was granted permission, Henare gave a computer to Dad to pass on to me. It made a huge difference, having unlimited computer access. I still had no internet access, of course, but I was able to work more efficiently and greatly increase my workload.

The other factor that worked in my favour was that I was receiving support and encouragement from others. While in unit 6, I had renewed my acquaintance with John Barlow, who was highly enthusiastic about the change I was working towards. Not only would he proofread essays for me but also he recommended books and was happy to engage in conversation on any number of topics. We started meeting regularly for coffee and biscuits in his cell, and we'd often watch the news together and talk about what we saw on TV.

Once in unit 9, I was fortunate to be supported and encouraged by some of the staff, too. Doug, one of the COs (Corrections Officers, as I was beginning to call the screws in my own head), used to proofread my essays before I sent them out, which was a great help to me — I'd learned what every writer learns, which is that you can be as careful as you like, but you'll never pick up the mistakes in your own work that your eye has become accustomed to skate over. One of the psychologists in the unit also helped me out. She had worked as a marker during her own postgraduate study and she offered to read my assignments for me before I sent them off. This was a very generous offer, but when the senior psychologist of unit 9 heard about this, she put a stop to it. She told me the prison psychologists had better things to do with their time than to help me with my schoolwork.

The unit manager of unit 9 at this time was a guy named Nick Straughter, whom I always found to be a personable kind of man. It was he who gave the green light to my having a personal computer, and when in due course I was shifted back to unit 6, I was fortunate enough to find that Nick was now there as unit manager. I was able to bring my computer with me, and with John Barlow still ensconced in unit 6, we resumed our coffee-and-biscuits routine.

*

I was finally following my brother Jon's advice, and had become a 'grey man'. I probably didn't feature on the radar of most inmates in unit 6: I kept my head down and didn't get into fights, I wasn't involved in gangs, gambling, dealing or even consuming drugs, so there was no reason for anyone to pay me any attention. I liked things this way. But it's not enough to behave well in prison:

you have to guard against becoming associated with others who might get you into trouble. Consequently, I tended to isolate myself and stick to the few people I felt I knew and trusted. John Barlow, by contrast, is the kind of person who compulsively helps others, and he liked to collect waifs and strays from among newly arrived inmates. As much as I admired him, I resented John for his tendency to introduce potential risks into my carefully controlled environment, and I often viewed his new mates with suspicion and (probably) outright hostility.

All the same, some of the guys I met through John's soft-heartedness became friends. One such was a Burmese guy named Bo. Bo was a thoroughly nice guy who had been educated at a good school but had managed to get himself involved in the Auckland drug scene, dealing ecstasy in nightclubs. One day, deciding to extract himself from this way of life, and with $10,000 stuffed in a sock and a small stash of ecstasy and amphetamines left over from his dealing days, he moved to Wellington. His attempt at making a new life didn't last more than a few hours. He and his travelling companions were having a coffee in a café in Wellington when one of his friends opened Bo's bag and pulled out a dildo that was shaped like a long-barrelled pistol. They were having a good laugh when suddenly there were cops everywhere. Another patron at the café had phoned them to say someone was waving a gun around. Bo was searched and then found himself serving a three-year sentence for possessing class B substances for supply.

Bo was finding prison quite a culture shock. One day, he and I were chatting when a hit went down on my old mate Manu. A group of four guys, having wrapped their faces in t-shirts, barged into Manu's cell and stabbed him multiple times with a shank made from a long nail mounted on the end of a short, rounded piece of wood. Manu had extensive experience on both ends of a shank, and he managed to fight his attackers off — but not before he'd recognised them as representatives of an unholy alliance between a group of the Samoan inmates and the Mongrel Mob.

Manu stepped out of his cell and immediately picked a fight with the first Samoan he laid eyes upon. A crowd gathered to watch. The staff got wind of it but then freaked out and locked themselves in an office while they waited for backup to arrive. Bo and I were among the circle of people watching as Manu and the Samoan guy squared off. Both were competent fighters, so the kicks and punches thrown from both sides were pretty clean. Inevitably, though, another inmate tried to jump in to help his Samoan mate. Around that time the cavalry arrived and the staff moved in to break up the fight.

As everyone began returning to their cells as ordered, a Māori inmate started abusing every Mobster and Samoan he could see for what he thought was a gutless hit on Manu. Such were the strong terms in which he was stepping them out, it was inevitable one of the Samoans would take exception. In this case, it was someone who'd had no involvement in any of the earlier incidents, but tribal honour is tribal honour. Bo and I found ourselves with ringside seats for this bout, too. The Samoan guy was big and muscular, but the Māori guy was a quick and competent boxer. It made for a great fight. The smaller, quicker man ducked and weaved while the bigger man tried largely unsuccessfully to pin him and bring his size advantage to bear. Who knows which way it would have gone. The screws had to abandon locking people up to come and break up this fight and restrain the combatants.

I had enjoyed the fights, so acclimatised was I to violence. But I caught a glimpse of Bo's face. He was aghast.

*

A few months after my return to unit 6, John Barlow was moved to unit 4, a 'harmony unit', so-called because to be housed there, you had to sign up to a code of conduct in which you agreed not to engage in violent or intimidatory behaviour. Harmony units are populated by prisoners who wouldn't be safe in the mainstream, as well as mainstream inmates interested only in doing their own lag and avoiding the politics of the wider prison. They are, in effect, a slightly watered-down version of the segregation wing at Mount Crawford Prison, and much the same stigma is affixed to its inmates by the general population.

A week later, I was told I was being moved to unit 8.

'No way,' I said. 'I'd rather be put in the pound.'

Unit 8 was a relatively settled environment, but the trouble was I knew the manager, and I knew he wouldn't permit me to have my computer in his unit. This just wouldn't fly with the workload I had lined up. Luckily for me, the staff member who had told me about the move was sympathetic, as he believed me when I said my reluctance to comply arose from a desire to keep working on improving myself. He told me he would see what he could do, and when he called me back to the office an hour or so later, he told me I could instead go to the harmony unit.

'You mean four?' I said.

'Yes,' he replied. 'Unit 4.'

In effect, I was being offered exactly what Alan Carr had offered to arrange for me around a year earlier: a place where I could have my computer, be a fulltime student and, as a bonus, be reunited with John Barlow. I would have to sign a harmony bond, and I would be looked down upon by everyone in the mainstream. But I didn't hesitate, and that was proof, right there: I was making progress.

I was caring less about what people thought of me and more about what I wanted for myself. Because we are social animals, we are hard-wired to try to fit in with a tribal group. But as evolutionary psychologists have argued, human civilisation has evolved at a far more rapid rate than our psyche: we live in an age when we can be (almost) whoever and whatever we want to be, yet we still spend an inordinate amount of time worrying about what other people will think of us and our choices. This amounts to handing over a good deal of the control of our lives to others. As soon as we begin to listen to our 'authentic voice' and do what's in our own best interest, we can wrest control back.

CHAPTER TEN

Fight to Be Free

The Ancient Greeks weren't big on happiness as we know it (or think we do). The word they used, which gets translated as 'happiness' is *eudaimonia*, which meant subtly different things in the writings of different philosophers but which was more like the harmony or balance of the different elements of the soul. It usually contained notions of fulfilment, living a moral and virtuous life and realising your potential. The original Greek meaning of happiness is best understood as 'the joy that you feel as you strive for your potential'.

A key requirement of striving towards your full potential is working out where to direct your efforts. The new path I had embarked on didn't involve me abandoning who I was in any fundamental sense but simply shifting my understanding of the world and the focus of my energies. My need to be seen and valued by others didn't change, but I discovered that instead of achieving that goal at the expense of others, I could gain even greater recognition and respect by doing things that harmed no one and only further increased my sense of competence and self-worth. The importance I placed on strength, toughness and courage didn't change either, but how I conceptualised those attributes was radically transformed. Previously I had thought that the way to demonstrate these values was through violence, showing no vulnerability, and not backing down. Now, thanks to the critical thinking tools and insights I had gained through education, I realised that being strong, tough and courageous meant accepting and managing your vulnerabilities, placing greater importance on your own wellbeing than on the views of other people, and doing what was right rather than what came easily – regardless of the circumstances and actions of others. While not requiring a fundamental change in who I was, this redirection of focus did involve a massive struggle to resist a lifetime's worth of habitual responses and desires.

The Stoic concept of *eudaimonia* is about just such self-mastery — resisting your impulses and desires. Everyone knows what a struggle this is. Psychologists have proved in the laboratory that the average person spends a quarter of their waking day resisting their desires. One experiment gave people beepers to carry as they went about their daily business, and when these made a noise (at random intervals), they recorded any desire they might happen to be battling at that moment. The kinds of desires they were battling will be familiar to everyone: in order of the most common, they were the desires to eat, sleep, perform a leisure activity (for example, doing a Sudoku puzzle instead of working on a memo), give in to sexual urges, or indulge in other social activities (such as checking email, surfing the internet, using social media, listening to music or watching television).

The Stoics maintain that unless we learn how to master our selves, we are slaves to our desires. To be free, you need to fight, and your most formidable foe is your self.

For me, giving up drugs was a major battle with my desires and, like most addicts, I didn't win a single, clean victory. I had many relapses at first, as addicts, particularly those who don't address the underlying causes of their addiction, typically do: it gets called the 'recovery relapse cycle'. It took a very long time before I was free of the desire to get high. But like most things we learn in life, self-discipline requires practice, and the more you practise, the more naturally it comes to you. That's why, when presented with obstacles to my studies in prison, I was increasingly able to overcome them. Tenacity is a habit you can learn.

It is actually through overcoming obstacles that we build our capacity for change and the willpower required to make it happen. Contrary to the widely held belief that willpower and self-discipline are qualities you either have or you don't have, research shows they are developed through practice and application. They're just like muscles.

But as with most things pertaining to the mind, exercising willpower is far from straightforward. Denying your desires is useful, up to a point. A team of researchers once set a group of people a task (attempting to solve a puzzle that was, in fact, unsolvable) and supplied them with chocolate cookies they could eat if they really wanted to. But they asked everyone to exercise restraint, and refrain from eating the cookies. Whereas you might expect the group who were able to resist their desire to eat cookies to be more tenacious in trying to solve the puzzle, the opposite proved to be the case. Those who kept their sticky fingers out of the cookie jar only worked on the puzzle for an average of eight minutes, whereas those who happily munched on cookies stuck at it for an average of 20 minutes. Exercising willpower actually seemed to be sapping the will to perform the task.

The researchers called this effect 'ego depletion', where willpower ebbs and the intensity of feelings (including cravings) increases. They concluded that the cause of ego depletion in the experiment was physiological. Resisting the craving for sugar meant the cookie-free group suffered a decline in their glucose levels. Glucose is responsible for the creation of the neurotransmitters used in the parts of the brain responsible for willpower. If the amount of glucose available is reduced, the activity of neurotransmitters in other regions of the brain become more pronounced (which probably accounts for the increased emotional intensity experienced).

The moral of this story? Feed the beast! Don't do tough things on an empty stomach. Also, when you are tired, sleep. Sleep deprivation impairs the processing of glucose. Furthermore, don't think you can do everything you want at once. Focus on just giving up one thing or changing one habit at a time. Small changes make a big difference over time – play the long game!

Other factors can help you become more proficient at exercising willpower, too. Don't set yourself conflicting goals, for example, and try to pre-commit to achieving a goal rather than relying on your willpower to overcome obstacles as they arise. If you decide not to drink this week, for example, you will more likely be able to resist temptation when your workmates invite you across the road for a glass of wine than if you have an unfocused, general desire to cut down on alcohol. It can help if you establish a set of rewards for yourself if you achieve your goal. Celebrate those little wins.

It's also important to focus on the reasons for your goals, rather than merely on the goals or the individual acts of self-denial they entail. You might be cutting down on alcohol for health reasons, for example: better to focus on these reasons than on the drink someone is offering to pour you.

Buying into the reasons for self-denial makes self-denial much easier. That's why, when dealing with teenagers, it's far better to get them to help in drawing up the rules rather than merely imposing them, Moses-style, from on high. If the rules feel to a teenager more like a personal commitment, the unpleasant ramifications (self-denial) will be far easier to swallow.

And quite apart from the acts of self-denial required to achieve a goal, work on your self-control more generally. Make things deliberately harder for yourself (improve your posture, use your left hand for routine tasks if you're right-handed, change your speech habits, saying 'yes' not 'yeah' or 'yip'). Self-control is a habit that enables you to form other good habits and to break bad ones.

The way your working (or living) environment is set up can both hinder and help your efforts to achieve your goals. Make sure you leverage your environment. Remove distractions from your work area, turn off notifications on your phone, make a rule you will only check your email at a certain time, pin reminders of your goals and your strategies for achieving them in places where your eye will light on them when it goes roving looking for entertainment. It's all about making self-control easy for yourself.

Here's a list of things that assist in the development and exercise of self-control. I call it 'Willpower 101':

- Know your limits. Your supply of willpower is limited, and you use the same resource for many different things.
- Watch for symptoms. There is no feeling like depletion. Do things seem to bother you more than they should? Are emotions felt more strongly than usual? Are you having difficulty making decisions? Are you more reluctant to make a decision or exert yourself mentally or physically?
- Pick your battles. Make changes during periods of relatively low demand.

- Make a to-do list. Once you make a specific plan, your subconscious will be mollified and this will cause you less stress.
- Beware the planning fallacy. This is the tendency to grossly underestimate the amount of time required to complete a task.
- Don't forget the basics. Sleep, food, exercise and a tidy environment.
- Use postponement strategies when denying yourself something (I'll see if I still feel like this chocolate cake in 15 minutes instead of having it now).
- The 'nothing alternative' against procrastination. If you set yourself a task to complete at a particular time, allow yourself to only work on that task — nothing else is permitted for that period.
- Keep track. Monitor your progress.
- Reward often. When you set a goal, set a reward for achieving it.
- Remind yourself that when you use your willpower, you are exercising a muscle that will get stronger and easier to use as a result.

It's not going to be easy. But as it's been observed throughout human history, nothing worth having comes without a fight.

Your freedom is there for the taking. All you need to do is fight.

*

'No, no, no,' John Barlow was saying. 'You can be as educated as you like, but if you don't sound like an educated person, you'll never be taken seriously.'

All I had done is remark that someone had walked through a door, but in those days, I pronounced the word 'through' as 'frew'.

'Through,' John said slowly and distinctly. I watched his mouth.

'Frew,' I repeated.

He shook his head, grinning.

John was good for me, sanding down my rough edges. Being well-spoken himself, he taught me to pay attention to my pronunciation and diction. When we watched the TV news, he would challenge my assumptions about the way the world worked. And I remember once, quite early on in our association, when someone had overstayed his turn on the telephone and been beaten up for it — a common occurrence — I was of the opinion it had served him right. I said as much in John's hearing.

'You think?' he said. 'Did the punishment really fit the crime?'

It would never have occurred to me to question it, left to myself. But when I thought about it, the violent response to what was a relatively minor inconvenience was not warranted.

Now that I, too, was housed in the harmony unit, it was easier to see the distorted moral code of prison more clearly. The harmony unit was the most relaxed environment I'd been in since my conviction. Many of the people in there weren't hardened criminals and didn't live the criminal lifestyle. They preferred to use methods other than violence to resolve disputes. After so many years reflecting wistfully that there had to be a better way, it was good for me to be among people who believed there really was.

In unit 4, I began showing no curiosity about what people had done and what sentences they'd received to get where they were. It was less relevant. In the stauncher parts of the prison system, this information helps you make an assessment of the 'form' of other prisoners and of the threat your fellow inmates pose, but now it was easier to take people as I found them. I decided that treating others with respect and consideration was more important, and more of a reflection of my new attitude, than finding out what crimes they had committed and how much they deserved to be there. And I was lucky enough to fall in with a couple of guys who encouraged me in this pro-social way of thinking. One was a guy called Hwee, who had committed a violent crime at a time in his life when the pressure of running too many businesses had sent him off the rails. Another was Craig, who, while he had been pretty violent (and still got into the odd fight), was one of the most unflinching critics of his own behaviour I have ever met. Self-honesty was a new concept to me: for all his faults, Craig was a terrific role model to stumble upon at this stage of my life.

I did weights with Craig and Hwee, I had regular coffee, biscuits and news sessions with John, and the three of them gently corrected my occasionally inappropriate and immature behaviour. And meanwhile, I really knuckled down to my university work. I was given a job in the kitchen. Unlike the kitchen boss in unit 8, Mark, the boss in unit 4, was a humane individual, not given to exploiting the power he had over others. He was sympathetic to my studies. At first I spent much of the morning washing pots, but he soon arranged it so that my duties were making toast in the mornings and doing the dishes at night, leaving most of the day for studying.

*

One of the things I was learning from my philosophy papers is that it is morally wrong to behave in ways that have foreseeable and unnecessary negative consequences for yourself and others.

Naturally enough, when I ran that rule over my past, I found my life wanting in quite a number of areas. I was determined to do better, but some of the conclusions I was driven to seemed pretty hard to accept, at first.

One of these, and undoubtedly the most momentous decision I made while in unit 4, was realising I had to end my relationship with Tania. Just after I was sentenced, I'd told her she should forget about me and get on with her life. She refused, for which I was eternally grateful. I was in love with her in those days — a love that was sort of complicated by the fact she had shared my first experience with IV drugs, and we continued to use IV drugs together. But for whatever reason, my feelings for her had ebbed away, and I was left with far less admirable reasons for maintaining my relationship with her. Life for me was much easier with her in it than without: she deposited money in my account, she brought me stuff, and she visited me most weekends. While I was using drugs, she enabled my habit. Although I had quit, she was still using, and there was a very good chance I would relapse if I maintained my relationship with her. But my decision wasn't solely based on my determination to stay clean and the obvious challenge she posed to that choice. It would now quite simply be wrong to pretend to act like nothing had changed in our relationship.

I made a bit of a hash of extricating myself from the relationship, however, and telling Tania I didn't think we had a future together was one of the hardest things I've had to do. Understandably, she took it badly. She had devoted years of her life to me, and here I was telling her it was over. And what made it harder was I seemed to be sending her mixed signals. She kept visiting, and out of misguided kindness, I was warm and affectionate. It took me a while to realise this wasn't constructive or fair on her.

What made it especially hard was that breaking up with Tania pretty much meant an end to my relationship with her daughter, Gemma, to whom I had done my best to be some kind of dad, based on the little I knew about that role. I really loved her, and when eventually Tania and I decided she wouldn't come and visit me anymore, one of my deepest regrets was that I wouldn't see Gemma either. We wrote to each other, and one of the proudest moments of my life came when Gemma told me, shortly before I was released, that she had done a school assignment on me and the changes I had made in my life when asked to write about someone she admired. I was surprised, touched and humbled.

*

Long before this, I had indicated to the prison authorities that I was interested in talking to a psychologist, as another step on my road to improvement. But nothing had happened. I put in a form to request an interview with the unit manager, Dr Rainer, to discuss the lack of action. The interview was granted promptly.

Dr Rainer was the first genuinely educated person I had come across in a position of authority in the prison system. She asked what papers I was taking at Massey and nodded approvingly when I mentioned philosophy.

'I used to teach Descartes in my previous life,' she chuckled.

Needless to say, Dr Rainer had no difficulty seeing the value in allowing me to consult a psychologist, and as luck would have it, a Department of Corrections psychologist walked past her office just as the interview was winding up. Dr Rainer popped her head out the door and asked him if he'd be able to fit me into his busy schedule. His name was Alex, and he said he would sort it out.

Soon after this conversation, it was decided that unit 4 would be reserved for those on segs, and everyone else would be redistributed. I was sent back to unit 6, which I found highly uncongenial. In fact, being back among the predatory and brutish general prison population had an immediate negative effect on me: Fish, whose path had crossed mine many times since primary school when he taught me to shoplift, offered me a joint, and I accepted. I knew it was wrong on every level, but like most recovering addicts, I was still susceptible to temptation. Interestingly enough, I overheard another inmate in the unit, Guy Brusey, taking Fish to task for offering me weed when he knew full well I was trying to quit. It was quite novel to hear this conversation — one of the first times I had heard someone in real life expressing the idea that you should act in the best interests of those you associate with, not just your own.

I might have been prepared to forgive myself this single lapse, but strictly according to Murphy's Law, I was selected for a random urine test the next day. The test was positive, and I was duly charged; it was the first blot on my copybook for some time. I was furious with myself, but my luck was in. I managed to have the charge dismissed on a technicality — too much time elapsed between the laying of the charge and when it was heard — I dodged the pound, and I gained an insight into how precarious your handholds are as you climb out of the pit of addiction. The near-miss renewed and reinforced my resolve to stay clean.

Good things happened during this stay in unit 6, too. My brother Jon got married, and he brought Cristiane, his Brazilian wife, to meet me. I was intensely nervous in the days leading up to this encounter, because I had always bled for my brothers when I imagined them having to explain my circumstances to anyone with whom they got involved. I had no idea what my new sister-in-law thought of me, and how she would react.

I had arranged a special visit for Jon, Cris and Dad. When the three of them entered, I shot a glance at Cris. Her expression was difficult to read. Jon introduced us, and I put out my hand to shake hers. My experience of South American greetings led me to expect her to clasp my hand and offer her cheek for me to kiss. Instead, she held her own hand out as far as her stiffly extended arm would allow, and as I took it, she averted her face and leaned away. I was just about ready to die with embarrassment when suddenly a beautiful smile broke across her face and she drew me in for the customary kiss on the cheek. It was, I would come to learn, typical Cris: she didn't know me, knew only that her new brother-in-law was a convicted murderer, but she came armed with a plot to pull a prank on me. The ice was broken. The four of us had a lovely time of it.

Jon must have gone away impressed with the sincerity of my efforts to turn my life around, because he described my endeavours to an old family friend, who had been the best man at his wedding, Dr Paul Englert. Paul was sceptical. He had been a social worker in our area when I was a kid, and he knew me and how I'd behaved before prison, so he decided to come and see for himself.

Paul is a highly educated man with multiple degrees, and was then running his own company, which provided psychometric testing, leadership development, and other psychological consulting services for organisations. He was an expert in the very stuff I was learning through Massey, so we had an interesting time talking psychology, politics and moral philosophy. He was also the first person I had spoken to since embarking on my studies who had sound vocational advice to offer. At the end of this visit, Paul, too, was convinced I was a man on a mission to improve himself. He promised to pass on some books for me to read and to come and see me again.

*

Word came through that I was to be transferred again, this time back to unit 9. I was happy, as it was far more conducive to study than unit 6. Not everyone was thrilled, however. Ana, the principal corrections officer of unit 9, remembered me from my days in unit 3, and she wasn't looking forward to renewing our acquaintance. Or so she told me when I'd been in 9 a few months and she'd had the opportunity to see how I had changed.

As soon as I arrived, I put my name down on the waiting list for one of the two cells for handicapped inmates in the unit. Although there are very few handicapped prisoners, each prison is required to incorporate handicapped facilities in any new section built. Such cells are about twice the size of normal cells, which means there is plenty of room for a desk. My wish was granted. It was great having a proper desk to put my computer on, although it took me a few days to get used to all the extra space!

I began counselling sessions with Alex. I found Alex to be a very likeable guy — a key ingredient in a successful therapeutic relationship is the rapport between psychologist and client — and this half of the battle was easily won. A major advantage was that Alex was already acquainted with my case, having discussed it with a Wellington solicitor who was a friend of his and who thought I had been poorly served by my trial counsel and had possibly suffered a miscarriage of justice as a result. This probably disposed him to be more sympathetic towards me than other prison psychologists might have been. He'd also been involved in counselling some of the victims of Boyd's sexual offending, some of whom had ended up in prison. It meant I viewed Alex as someone genuinely interested in assisting me rather than as a typically adversarial prison psychologist. The work I did with Alex laid the groundwork, and I was eventually able to come to grips with my own experience of abuse and the role it played in my overreaction to Boyd's attack when I started working privately with a psychologist after release. While it did not excuse what happened, I came to understand that it had influenced my reaction, and this in turn helped me take responsibility for Boyd's death and stop painting myself as an innocent victim.

Working with Alex also helped me start to view the challenges I had faced and was still experiencing as opportunities. Whereas most of us have heard of post-traumatic stress disorder, we tend to hear less about post-traumatic growth. I was definitely suffering from PTSD when I first entered prison. But when I decided to turn my life around, the status of the trauma I had suffered became the impetus for change.

Alex could clearly see the benefits of my studies, and he encouraged me and did whatever was in his power to facilitate them. Because I was looking beyond my degree — the final exams for the last papers were looming — I could see the demands of my academic work could constrain my time in the lead-up to my parole, when I would be expected to undergo the obligatory violence prevention course. Accordingly, Alex agreed to support me in an application to do the course a year earlier than was normal.

The prison authorities assented, but many of the Department of Corrections psych staff were against it. One even thought if my studies clashed with the VPU, it should be my studies that went on the backburner. Fortunately, she didn't have the final word. The decision was made by the unit's new chief psychologist at the time, a man named Neville Trainor, with whom I got on very well. Nev saw the merit of my application and supported it. I was given permission to embark on the programme a year early. I was delighted, not only with the result but also with the fact I had stuck my neck out and asked for it in the first place. I was becoming a participant in my life rather than the victim I had supposed myself to be. I had learned the value of risking my psychological comfort — the literal truth of the motto on the SAS badge Jon had given me all those years ago: Who Dares Wins.

*

It was during this time that the unit kitchens were phased out, replaced by a centralised kitchen for the whole prison. The size and quality of the meals reduced noticeably. Mindful of how this would go down with prisoners, the size of the plates was also reduced, so that they would still look full of food. No one was fooled. What's more, once the centralised kitchen had taken over the distribution of a national menu, we no longer received desserts with our dinner. Instead, we received a piece of fruit each night, generally squishy kiwifruit or floury, bruised apples. If we were lucky, someone would over-cater on the fruit and we'd receive extra apples or kiwifruit. If we were luckier again, we would get bananas, a rare treat.

One day, the two guys working in the servery substituted kiwifruit for the bananas we were supposed to be getting with our dinner. No one was any the wiser until someone who worked in the kitchen came back to the unit that night and asked how the bananas were. That we had been robbed spread like wildfire. A screw heard about it, conducted a quick cell search and found a rubbish bag full of bananas in one of the servery men's cells. Needless to say, the two servery men were removed from the unit before they could receive a good beating.

I certainly noticed a decline in the quantity of food. I was training just as hard at the gym, but I was losing weight because I couldn't consume enough protein to maintain my muscle mass. I was training with a guy called Aiden at this time. Aiden was a member of the Road Knights Motorcycle Club and was in prison for beating someone he had caught trying to steal from the back of his trailer. When this happened, he had only just been released from prison for a gang-related act of violence. With a young family at home, he was committed to completing the violence prevention programme, leaving the gang and staying out of trouble in the future.

Besides Aiden and John Barlow, who had been moved to unit 9 at the same time as me, I was hanging around with some of the most notorious prisoners in the New Zealand system. One I will call Pit Bull. At only 17, he had seen his father die of a gunshot wound as he himself lay bleeding from a gunshot wound to the thigh. He'd gone on to commit a murder two years later. Once convicted, he'd done a long stretch in Paremoremo, during a particularly turbulent period in that institution's history. Rather than be ground down by the system and those within it, Pit Bull had decided to take a stand against it. He had cowed his fellow inmates by meeting fire with fire, and he had earned the grudging respect of the staff by never backing down. Consequently, he had quite a reputation. If it was true, one testimony to the kind of mana he had was the prison rumour that a notorious criminal, Graham Burton, had actually killed someone to be reunited with his friend Pit Bull. Soon after Pit Bull had been imprisoned, Burton, according to the story, was thrown out of a nightclub. The next day, he turned up and asked the first person he saw, a contract electrician, if he worked there. Fatally, the sparky said that he did, whereby Burton drew a knife and stabbed him to death.

I really liked Pit Bull. He tended to run any prison he found himself in, but unlike most king pins or shot-callers, he had a code and he stuck to it, without fear or favour. He never put up with bullying, and always treated people fairly. He struck me as an intelligent and capable individual, who would have done well in whatever he'd undertaken, if life hadn't dealt him the cards it had. Instead, he found himself a key player in prison's prestige economy, where the way to get ahead was through violence and showing no fear. He excelled.

He had mentioned me to another long-term prisoner I'll call The Chameleon, who presently arrived in unit 9. My first impressions of him weren't that great: he was about 6 foot 2, muscular, and with a number-one haircut, which made him look like a white supremacist. He happened to be present when I had what was to be my last, pointless dispute with prison staff.

After the construction of the new high-medium security facilities, known as the PODS, all visits, which had previously taken place in visiting rooms within each unit, were conducted in a centralised visiting area. Part of the new visiting regime required prisoners to wear bright orange, death-row-style overalls, designed to make prisoners easy to identify and make the secretion of contraband more difficult: they zipped up at the back, with the zip secured by a plastic tie, while the neck, wrists and ankles had tight-fitting cuffs. The visiting room was heavily wired with closed-circuit television cameras, with seats designed with maximum security in mind, although their designers appear to have also made them as uncomfortable as humanly possible. Like everyone else, I was pretty disgruntled with the new set-up. But what set me off that day was that the overalls I was issued were far too small for me, so that whenever I attempted to sit, the crotch seam would threaten to castrate me. I drew this to the attention of the staff, pointing out that if a minimum security, non-IDUS prisoner really did have to be treated like this, the least they could do was provide overalls that fitted.

In an admirable display of Stoicism, the staff members to whom I directed my tirade listened but refrained from commenting — at least until I'd moved through and the next prisoner arriving for processing heard their freely exchanged views on what kind of beating I deserved for being such a smart bastard. That prisoner was The Chameleon and after visiting was over he sought me out and we had a good laugh about it.

I got to know The Chameleon pretty well. Like me, he came from a good family background but had got into trouble with drugs as a teenager and had ended up in prison. He had worked as a bouncer for a number of nightclubs in Wellington, but got mixed up in the use and distribution of ecstasy. His associates were a heavy bunch. They were implicated in the murder of a man named Trevor Heath (aka Terri King), whose body was discovered near a burned-out tramping hut in the Tararua Ranges north of Wellington. An associate of The Chameleon's was arrested for the crime. At his trial, however, a pair of South African thugs appeared as witnesses for the prosecution. They were the debt collectors in the drugs operation, both huge, hard men, crew-cut and steroid-pumped, who had once belonged to a South African black ops unit named The Crowbar, which had carried out assassinations of opponents of the Apartheid regime in neighbouring African countries. The jury — mild-mannered, middle-class Kiwis all — stared at these two, aghast. One of them was asked by defence counsel whether he had ever killed anyone.

'Yes, of course,' the man replied. Then, appearing to realise how this sounded, hastened to add: 'But only in the line of duty.'

It didn't take much for the defence to build up a counter-case that these men, not the accused, could have been responsible for King's death. He was acquitted. I met the South Africans during my time in prison. I'll always remember one of them saying, 'It doesn't matter who you are, the first six or seven people you kill, you feel bad, man.'

The Chameleon's drug habit had got him into considerable debt. When the debt was called in unexpectedly early, he couldn't pay up. He was given two options: he could have his legs broken or he could take part in an armed robbery. Understandably, he chose option two.

The Chameleon executed the armed robbery without a hitch. His debt was paid off and the police had no idea who was responsible. He got on with his life. But, unfortunately for him, the guy assigned to drive for him was pulled in on another matter, and as a bargaining chip to get himself out of trouble, he gave The Chameleon up.

The Chameleon was arrested and charged with armed robbery. After his depositions hearing, he knew he would be going down. The police had recovered a baseball cap from the scene, with a drop of sweat inside it that matched his DNA. As he was a first offender, he was bailed. Once again, The Chameleon found himself faced with two options: he could flee the country or he could spend around ten years in prison. He chose option one.

The Chameleon managed to pull off the first step necessary to skipping the country: obtaining a false passport. Gone were the days, though, when you could simply go to a graveyard, locate the headstone of a deceased child and steal their identity. In the modern age of information, it was hard to find someone alive and kicking who had never applied for a passport. But having identified such a person and obtained a passport, The Chameleon was free to make a new life for himself overseas — as long as he could afford that new life.

He decided on another armed robbery to set himself up. Once again, all went well. The security guards handed over the money without demur. He dumped his getaway car and jumped into another, knowing there'd be police checkpoints on the roads out of Wellington for the first vehicle. The trouble was, the description the police were given was vague, so they were pulling over everything that remotely resembled the first car. The Chameleon wasn't 20 kilometres into the 650-kilometre drive to Auckland International Airport when he was pulled over on the Hutt Motorway east of Wellington. He played it cool until he was asked to open the boot, whereupon the rubbish bag of money and the wig he'd been wearing were found. The Chameleon knocked the constable unconscious, grabbed the money and ran off into the bush. He was cornered a few hours later. There was to be no bail this time. He was sentenced to 12 years in prison, subsequently reduced to eight on appeal.

What I really liked about The Chameleon was how he wanted something better for himself. He wasn't into sitting around with other hard-arse prisoners telling self-aggrandising stories of crime and violence. He was enrolled in a degree course at Massey University and was a committed student, apparently determined to live a profitable and straight life upon release. Once I'd satisfied myself of his sincerity, I did what I could to help him. I often edited his essays before he sent them off. Once, conscious of how surreal it was, I took my t-shirt off and draped it over my head like a road worker to shelter me from the sun as I crouched in the yard, heavily tattooed and half naked, to edit his anthropology assignment on structuralism.

It was The Chameleon who first got me into jogging. He was a real fitness freak, even by prison standards, where most people spend a large portion of their day training in order to present a credible threat and be combat-ready when violence is called for. He was very good about easing me into this, but due to my competitiveness and stubborn refusal to quit, it wasn't long before I literally had blisters on top of blisters. We would run for half an hour on Tuesdays and Thursdays before breakfast, and for an hour on Saturdays. Jogging became a major part of my workout regime. By the end of my sentence, I would run 5 kilometres every weekday around the yard, and do 10 to 15 kilometres on Saturdays — in addition to the weight sessions in the gym every evening.

John Barlow and I maintained our routine of regular catch-ups. John is a far more gregarious soul than me, and whereas by this end of my sentence I was concentrating on doing my own lag and avoiding unnecessary connections with others, he was always helping people out by repairing their electronics, providing advice or just making himself available for a chat. I often told him he was laying himself open to guilt by association if any of the lame ducks he took under his wing did anything to draw down the wrath of the prison authorities. John was always cheerfully dismissive of these concerns.

*

In truth, you don't have to court trouble to find it in prison. It can just as easily come your way. One day a middle-aged Māori guy passed me as I was on my way to make a phone call.

'Fucken white cunts!' he yelled.

I turned around and saw him staring at me.

'Yeah, you, you fucken white cunt,' he snarled, advancing on me. I had never spoken to this guy before in my life and had no idea what his problem was. None of that mattered. His intentions were clear from his balled fists and his lowered brows. In a clear demonstration of putting into practice the non-violence I was learning about, I put a handrail between us and raised my hands, palms outwards, to show I meant him no ill will. I told him to calm down.

Who knows whether it would have worked. As it was, the screws heard him shouting. When he saw them approaching, he took himself off to his cell. I later learned that he had wanted to see Sister Marie, but found she was talking to John Barlow. Neither of them was aware he was waiting outside her office, so they carried on chatting while he grew more and more agitated. Finally, he stormed off, furiously angry at John in particular and Pākehā in general. So when unsuspecting white guy Paul Wood mooched past him, he decided to vent his frustration. Such displacement is not an uncommon psychological phenomenon. Indeed, the generalised antipathy you feel directed towards you as a white guy in prison is probably the displaced expression of the resentment felt by the predominantly Māori and Polynesian prison population towards the system — the system that sees Māori and Polynesians far more likely to fail to thrive, to be pulled over by the police, to be convicted of crimes and to end up in prison. It really isn't a level playing field and I only began to appreciate what it's like to be a minority-group member in society when I experienced it in prison.

Another time, The Chameleon and I were about to start our Saturday morning jog around the compound when a well-built man whose full facial tattoos proclaimed him to be a Mongrel Mob member approached. He was new to the unit, and I didn't know anything about him; nor did he, so far as I knew, know me.

'Fuck you,' he growled, his voice and the set of his shoulders oozing aggression. 'Fuck you shutting all those windows and the curtains.'

I was taken aback, but I was conscious I couldn't afford to appear frightened or even apologetic for whatever he was accusing me of having done. I was also conscious of the need to keep in check my own deeply habitual tendency to meet aggression with aggression. Even at the time, I was surprised at the level of self-awareness and control I had acquired.

'You got a problem with my stereo, you have the balls to come and tell me to my face,' he said, pointing to the library windows.

I suddenly realised what he was talking about. As part of the non-violence programme, we had yoga sessions every Friday morning, which finished with guided relaxation.

'Nah,' I replied. 'We were doing yoga. We always close the windows and curtains at the end and turn off the lights to do a relaxation exercise.'

He glared at me doubtfully, fists still balled.

'Nothing to do with me playing my stereo out here?' he gritted.

'Nah, bro. We do it every session.'

He continued to stare at me. Then he nodded, apparently satisfied.

'Lucky,' he said, 'coz I was going to stab you.'

He turned and walked off.

The Chameleon, who had disappeared on this guy's approach, reappeared beside me, his hand in his pocket.

'All good?'

'Yeah, sweet,' I replied. 'Misunderstanding, that's all.'

'Sweet,' The Chameleon echoed. I then saw the pair of scissors he'd fetched from his cell when the guy had bailed me up. It was good to know he had my back.

I was just glad the guy who approached me had thought to ask me to explain rather than simply attacking me or throwing a chair through the window. The fact he had approached me at the first opportunity that morning indicated he had spent the previous day and all night dwelling on it. A different guy, or the same guy with different demons in his head on the day, and who knows where this incident might have left us all. It also showed I had largely shrugged off the fear you acquire in prison of appearing weak if you don't respond with maximum violence when stepped out.

There were plenty of other examples of how you could keep your head down and yourself to yourself and still fall foul of the troubled souls in prison. While I was in unit 9, I got in contact with one of the other lifers I had resided with in unit 4. Rex was a lovely bloke. He was about nine years into his life sentence and was doing everything right. He had never been a career criminal: he was in prison after shooting his wife and failing to end his own life, a failure that resulted in him blowing half his face off. He was an excellent bone carver and for a small fee completed a couple of customised carvings for my family. The results far exceeded my expectations.

Soon after he had carved them for me, he was murdered. He was in the faith-based unit at the time, which is a unit run according to Christian values. He was working as the unit's maintenance man, and to this end, he had his own space out the back where he could keep his tools and do his carving in his spare time. One day, a middle-aged guy also serving a life sentence for murder came and asked if he could borrow a screwdriver to open his radio. Rex knew this would likely be detected. All electronic appliances within prison have tamper-proof stickers so the staff can readily see when they've been opened. Accordingly, Rex told the guy he couldn't lend him the screwdriver, as it was against the rules and he stood to lose both his job and the privilege of being out the back. The guy was very unhappy with this response.

A couple of days later this guy was allowed out of the compound to work in the garden. Instead, he armed himself with a sturdy garden fork and went around the back of the unit where Rex was working in his room. He struck Rex repeatedly with the fork before driving it through his neck with such force that it was left embedded in the asphalt beneath Rex's lifeless body.

As I say: you don't have to go looking for trouble in prison for it to find you.

*

I had been in unit 9 for several months when I sat the final exams of my undergraduate degree. I was sure I'd done well — I was much more confident now than when I'd apologetically presented myself to the library at Mount Crawford to sit the exams for my first two papers. In this final year, I sat 12. The more I used my brain, the stronger it became.

I not only passed them all, I scored an A average. I had to pinch myself: I was now a university graduate, with a Bachelor of Arts and a double major in Philosophy and Psychology. It seemed ironic that prison had provided me with an opportunity to realise something about myself I would have been unlikely to discover otherwise.

My case manager, Jim Reed (or JR, as he was generally called), was nearly as pleased as I was. So, too, was unit manager Bill Henderson, who had known me when I was a thorn in the side of the prison authorities and who had seen the changes I'd made. They thought they might be able to arrange some kind of ceremony for me, since I would be obliged to graduate in absentia. JR suggested a morning tea with sausage rolls — an unimaginable treat for prisoners. It would acknowledge my achievement, they reasoned, and be an excellent public relations exercise, too. But when they promoted this idea to the site manager of the prison — the same woman who had sneered at me in the classification cells when I first arrived at Rimutaka — she wanted to know who had given me permission to study to the level I had achieved. There were to be no sausage rolls or morning tea.

*

As the seventh anniversary of my mother's death loomed, I felt it acutely that I had never visited her grave. Because I had been arrested so soon after she died, I had missed the funeral, and I had never seen where she had been laid to rest. So I put in a request for compassionate leave to go there. My application was recommended by JR and by PCO Ana who, thankfully, had become a wholehearted supporter (she was a fierce enemy if you crossed her). Thanks largely to their advocacy, my request was granted.

JR also kindly agreed to be my escorting officer, and Sister Marie joined the party. It was a strange experience driving along the motorway towards the city, but winding up into the hills to Karori, the suburb I had grown up in, was positively surreal. Everything seemed much smaller, the buildings less imposing, the distances much shorter than I remembered.

We picked Dad up in Karori and drove to the end of the suburb, where the road takes a right-hand-turn, over a saddle and into a valley that leads out to wild, stony Makara Beach. As soon as you reach the summit, it's as though you've left the city behind and you're in heartland New Zealand, with gorse-covered banks and green paddocks where sheep, cattle and horses graze. And not a single razor wire fence in sight.

Halfway along the road, and not that many kilometres short of the property where I was born, you take a left and climb a short driveway to the cemetery. We arrived and got out of the car. The sun was warm on my back and shoulders, although there was a brisk wind blowing. The outside world fitted me like a favourite coat I hadn't worn in nearly a decade: I was conscious both of its familiarity and its strangeness.

Sister Marie and JR waited a respectful distance away as Dad and I walked to my mother's memorial plaque in the lawn cemetery. We paused. The whole scene swam as tears filled my eyes. Neither Dad nor I spoke. I would never have found the words to express what I was feeling. I wasn't used to feeling anything, but now I felt a deep, nostalgic ache for my gentle, loving mum, along with acute shame. I couldn't begin to imagine what it must have been like for her watching me tread the path I was on as her illness took hold. I was glad (if that's the word) she never lived to see where that path had taken me. But I also dared to imagine she would have been proud of me and the path I had lately begun to tread. It was towards the kind of life she would have wished for me. I silently vowed to her that I would keep walking it, regardless of the obstacles or challenges.

It was an emotionally draining afternoon, and at the end of it, I was relieved to be heading 'home' — along the northern motorway to Rimutaka Prison.

CHAPTER ELEVEN

Living Free

Freedom is a journey, not an event. It is a condition that requires effort to maintain. Self-help books and programmes often fail because they don't acknowledge the demands of living free and the ongoing commitment it requires. Real, sustained positive change and growth are not things that you achieve, tick off your list of things to do, and walk away from. The price of freedom is ongoing effort. A useful analogy is fitness. You don't exercise and get fitter, then stop exercising and just stay fit. It requires ongoing effort. Furthermore, being fit doesn't mean physical challenges are easy: it just means you can cope with more before you get fatigued, before you lose your effectiveness and ability to persevere. Living free is about having 'character fitness'. Maintaining and increasing your character fitness doesn't mean life's challenges and stresses are easy: it just means you can endure more before being derailed or demonstrate behaviour you wouldn't want your reputation to reflect. I know 'character' is an old-fashioned word these days, but it's a word we should bring back into fashion. Having character is about having desirable mental and moral qualities. Having character is about being able to do the right thing rather than the easier thing. It is about being able to remain effective in the face of adversity.

'Keeping it real' is what living in freedom is about; the difference between the illusion of a quick fix and the effort required to truly live free. It involves acknowledging that sometimes we're weak. We're not always going to progress in a straight line towards our goals. Sometimes we'll slip back into old habits. Sometimes we'll fall short of our ideals. Yet such failures are opportunities for us to grow. They provide us with a chance to reflect and identify the chinks in our armour. We fall, so that we can learn to pick ourselves up again.

Contrary to the glossy magazine depiction of it, life isn't meant to be easy. We are naturally equipped to deal with stress, anxiety, adversity and failure. We are less than we can be unless we are called upon to deal with such things, and the life we're leading is less than meaningful if it doesn't stretch and challenge us. Facing adversity — even the ordinary adversity of a relatively ordinary life — requires mental toughness and grit.

The best way to think of the strength and resilience you need to live free is by building on this concept of character fitness. The mental toughness and resilience required to deal with life's adversities constitute one's 'emotional fitness'. There is a common belief that emotional fortitude and the ability to cope with and bounce back from adversity are traits you're either born with or you're not. In reality, emotional fitness is a process, not an attribute. You can develop more of it in exactly the same way you can develop physical fitness — by deliberately working at it.

There are four areas in which you can work to develop emotional fitness. One, your relationships. We are social animals, and we are at our best when we are enmeshed in strong, fulfilling

257

relationships. Most of our psychological stability comes from our primary relationship (in adults, this could be a bond with a partner), but the importance of other relationships cannot be underestimated. You've seen how important mentors and role models have been in my life. Make sure you're open to the benign influence of others in your life. Join sports clubs and take up hobbies that create meaningful connections with others. That will give you a sense of community and belonging.

Two, your thinking. When you're suffering from stress or from the turmoil that accompanies a knock in life, it is essential that you're thinking straight about things. It can be easy to get things out of perspective, and attribute greater significance to adverse events than they warrant. You might be inclined to use a reversal of fortune as evidence in a prosecution against yourself, or you might interpret things in ways that are unconducive to bouncing back. Sometimes, just focusing on the solution to problems rather than on the problems themselves helps. Mindfulness, finding a task that will fully occupy your faculties for the duration you're performing it, can help to reset your focus. And ensure you test your thinking, to make sure the thoughts causing you distress are accurate and proportionate. Involving others who know you well can make this difficult exercise much easier.

Three, look after yourself physiologically. Often in times of turmoil, we neglect to eat, sleep or exercise properly. All three are essential to maintaining or getting back on an even keel.

Four, your environment — your immediate work and living environments, and the wider world. There's nothing to make you more inclined to see the bigger picture than getting outside, away from your usual routines, especially if you can get into the outdoors — a beach, the hills, the bush, the mountains. It's important to surround yourself with things that make you feel good and are conducive to helping you be the best version of yourself. Even something as simple as tidying up can be useful, as it's an exercise in what psychologists call 'controlling the environment'. It's a little demonstration to yourself that you can work positive change.

Emotional fitness has to be built up and then constantly monitored and maintained. My wife, Mary-Ann, once pointed out to me that my habit of using audiobooks while I run is not a sensible one, as they distract me from the signals my body is sending me as to whether I can go harder or should ease up. We use this kind of distraction all the time. We respond to emotional stress by lavishing treats upon ourselves — alcohol, drugs, pornography, gambling, over-eating — but all we achieve is short-term distraction from the symptoms of more persistent problems. These signals should not be ignored. There are times during physical exercise when we need to slow our pace to avoid fatigue. If you're properly tuned into your emotional state, you'll recognise when you need an emotional break, too. Learn to recognise the signs you are becoming emotionally drained and that your resources, like your physical stamina, are reaching their limit. 'Self-care' is a discipline, not a luxury.

*

Shortly after starting the academic year, my place in group 19 of the violence prevention programme was confirmed. Before it kicked off, I was subjected to a psychological assessment and a number of psychometric tests intended to determine my propensity to violence and susceptibility to other pathologies.

After this, the eight-month course began. For four hours, four days a week, we did classroom time, working our way through a number of modules, including mood management, victim empathy, communication and problem solving, and offence chain, which helps you understand what choices led to your offending and how to avoid putting yourself into high-risk situations again in the future. Given the level to which I had already studied psychology, I wasn't expecting to learn much, but to my surprise, I learned a good deal. Some of the most interesting insights I gained were into the cognitive distortions people employ, which can result in anger and enable violence — everyday examples of which you could see in prison, but which aren't in short supply outside prison walls, either. One example is over-generalisation, where you can come to believe a particular incident is typical of a much wider range of human interactions. You might be stared down just before you're attacked, for example; then you form the mistaken assumption that anyone who looks at you too long or too hard is about to attack you. Another is 'reward thinking', the unrealistic expectation people have that they will be rewarded for good behaviour. As with many other aspects of human cognition and behaviour, psychologists break the pattern associated with thoughts and violent actions down into a triangle, the 'triad of violence'. In the case of rewards thinking, the triad comprises entitlement, victimisation, and righteous anger. If you expect to be rewarded but those rewards aren't forthcoming, you feel victimised, and you react to that victimisation with anger. This really resonated with me, not only because I'd seen this pattern around me in prison, but also because I had indulged in it myself. Simply being aware of the ways in which disordered thinking can lead to violence is an excellent way of preventing escalation. Understanding the dynamic also helped to explain why I had managed to mellow my behaviour so markedly over the last three years. If philosophy teaches you nothing else, it certainly teaches you to challenge your own assumptions, including convictions as deep-seated as your sense of entitlement. And philosophy, particularly Stoic philosophy, had taught me much. A fundamental tenet of Stoicism is that virtue is its own reward; a true Stoic doesn't have a sense of entitlement at all.

The only module of the violence prevention programme I had difficulty with was the empathy module, which entailed sitting in the classroom alone with the two facilitators, one of whom was a prison psychologist, and reviewing your offence and how your victim must have felt. Now I don't doubt that I'm by nature an empathetic person: the tears I've shed while watching *Extreme Makeover: Home Edition* are proof! But convincing the assessors was another matter, and I don't think I can take all the blame for this. We knew that every Wednesday, an observer would listen in, using microphones placed in the classroom, to monitor the quality of delivery of the course. No one could object to that. But partway through the programme, one of the participants got hold of a photocopy of the notes the observer had made, which showed that the observer was also commenting on what we were saying. Everyone was annoyed, and I was doubly incensed, as I didn't feel the comments attributed to me were a fair reflection of what I had said.

After this revelation, I couldn't shake the thought of the observer sitting there, listening and interpreting. So it was hardly surprising if I came across as distracted and less than fully engaged. Although I couldn't accept it at the time, they were probably right that I lacked empathy. As I mentioned earlier, to survive for any length of time, especially a long time, in prison, you have to shut down your empathetic side. It's a necessary adaptation to that environment, and the fact the psychological staff failed to allow for this is what psychologists call a fundamental attribution error — making the mistake that a certain negative attribute is a general fault of the subject, rather than something that can be explained by circumstances.

Other prisoners to whom I spoke used to do their best to cry, because this is what the assessors expected. I couldn't do that, and was therefore adjudged to be lacking in empathy. To address this flaw in my personality, I was directed to do a number of one-on-one sessions with the psychologist. I thought this would be a good thing: I was wrong.

*

Meanwhile, I continued to study. On completion of my bachelor's degree, I had to decide which of my major subjects to carry on with. Psychology was my first choice, but, to my dismay, I discovered I couldn't do the graduate programme from a distance. The School of Philosophy invited me to study at graduate level, but when I phoned the Head of the School of Philosophy, I discovered it would be impossible to put together a degree programme from their distance learning offerings, too.

It looked as though I would have to put graduate school on hold. But recognising how important to my personal growth and progress my university study had been, I was reluctant to just stop. I had always been interested in Greek mythology — the stories Dad told us at bedtime had seen to that — and I had enjoyed a course in ancient Greek history that was part of my undergraduate degree, so I decided to do a postgraduate diploma in Classical Studies until it was possible to resume my first choices.

I had already signalled to Massey University that this was my intention when I received a timely visit from Paul Englert. When

I told him my plans and the problem I'd had finding suitable psychology papers in the distance-learning faculty, he asked why I hadn't considered enrolling to do the research paper for an honours degree. An honours is usually a two-year degree, and most fulltime students complete eight papers in their first year, then produce a research paper and complete a number of papers in their second. Paul was proposing I tackle it in reverse order. He even offered to supply the data I could use for such a project. It was a brilliant suggestion.

When I phoned Christina Stephens, the Head of the School of Psychology to see whether it would be possible to put that plan into effect, she was most encouraging. 'Who are you thinking of as a supervisor?' she asked.

I was momentarily stumped by this one. But I had recently phoned the school to find out why I had received a lower mark than I had been expecting for one of my papers, and I had been sympathetically heard by the lecturer in charge of the paper.

'How about Dr Haberman?' I ventured.

'I think he'd be a very good choice, if he's willing,' Professor Stephens said warmly.

She warned me that my marks in psychology, which weren't as high as those I'd scored in philosophy, meant I would need dispensation from the postgraduate committee to enrol for the research paper. But with assurances from Paul Englert that he would support me, the committee were happy to give me the green light. And Gus Haberman was willing to supervise. I was over the moon. My academic career was back on track. This level of support from people like Dr Englert and Dr Haberman significantly set me apart from other prisoners and gave me a huge advantage.

After a brainstorming session with Paul Englert, I decided to study the relationship between intelligence and personality traits among New Zealand job applicants. This was a fascinating project and I launched myself fully into it.

I worked very hard, with the result that, whereas most honours dissertations weigh in at around 10,000 words, mine was nearer 60,000. Giving the final draft to Paul to read, he suggested I consider requesting it be upgraded to a master's thesis. Gus Haberman also said he considered my work to be of a quality commensurate with a Master of Arts thesis. The university accepted the upgrade. I couldn't have been happier. Here I was halfway to a master's degree already.

The thesis was worth so many academic points, but after completing it, I was left still needing 100 points to achieve my master's. Unfortunately, there were only 25 points' worth of papers that could be completed as special topics that didn't require attending lectures at the university. Massey University were unbelievable. They said they would let me complete all 100 points as special topic papers, as long as I could find lecturers who were willing to take me on as a special topic student in addition to their normal workload. I managed to find lecturers, and by the end of 2004 I had completed the requirements for the degree of Master of Arts.

*

One thing that contributed to the quality of the academic work I produced was that most of my master's was done in the conducive surroundings of unit 9. But as my final exams loomed, I knew I would be moved out of there after finishing the violence prevention programme. Between JR, my case officer, and I, we began looking at options for me to keep my computer. One of these was unit 7, the faith-based unit, reserved for low security inmates who were practising Christians. Although I found much to admire in Christian ethics, it became plain during an interview that I didn't fit the bill. Unit 7's brand of Christianity seemed far more fundamentalist than the ecumenical, Unitarian creed I thought I could live with: after all, a portrait of Charles Darwin took pride of place on my cell wall. So after a couple of days' deliberation, I declined to take up a place; I simply couldn't live the lie.

That meant my only option was unit 6, which was still a dumping ground for prisoners who didn't fit in other units and which still saw its share of the kinds of random acts of violence I had come to abhor. Worse yet, I was initially placed down the end of the unit, in an area known less-than-affectionately to its residents as The Bronx, where the gangsters were housed. It was in a cell here, with stereos thumping, tattoo needles buzzing, abuse being yelled and fights breaking out all around me, that I studied for my exam in a paper on multivariate statistics, the last written exam of my academic career. I had been in prison for eight years. I nominally had two years left before becoming eligible for parole, and my thoughts were turning toward my eventual release.

When the prison psych staff sat down to discuss the results of my non-violence programme assessment with me, I couldn't believe half of what I was reading, especially the conclusion: that I was deemed to be at moderate to high risk of reoffending. This was higher than I'd been assessed to be at the beginning of the programme!

Shocked, I asked for time to consider the draft report before I responded to it. I took it away, read and re-read it, and determined that one of the psychologists responsible for it — the one with whom I had done a number of one-on-one sessions to address my supposed lack of empathy — seemed to have got me completely wrong. I had confided to her that I had for some time been exploring legal avenues to have my conviction for murder overturned and replaced with manslaughter. She interpreted this as a failure on my part to take responsibility for my offending. In retrospect, I can understand her concern in this respect, but there were other things she was undoubtedly less justified in interpreting as negatively as she did. For example, in my efforts to be allowed to remain in unit 9, I had argued (on my case officer's advice) that I would be an ideal mentor for others in the unit. She interpreted this to be indicative of a sense of entitlement to special treatment. Indeed, she had attended a meeting at which I was told the Department of Corrections was no longer going to offer financial assistance to me in my studies because she had been expecting me to react angrily, perhaps even violently. She must have been wrongfooted by my actual reaction. Dad had initially paid for my study out of his pension, and both of us had been surprised when we'd learned, early on in my academic career, that there was assistance available, because it was signally the only encouragement the prison system seemed to offer inmates who wanted to study to university level. We continued to be surprised every time we applied for assistance and it was granted. Far from feeling entitled to it, I was immensely grateful and not a little amazed to receive it. When the funding was finally withdrawn, I was perfectly unsurprised. At the meeting, with the psychologist present, I told the site manager that I accepted the decision and was very grateful for the assistance I had received thitherto. The report indicated the psychologist suspected me of harbouring a sense of thwarted entitlement, nonetheless. I really couldn't win with this person.

I shared the report with my case manager and with the principal corrections officer. Both JR and Ana were indignant on my behalf, and so too was Sister Marie when I told her I was supposed to be incapable of empathy. I had lately been helping her write answers to children who wrote to Santa Claus about their Christmas wishes. She had noted I had taken care to personalise every letter.

Input to the final draft of the report from those who actually knew me was not only discouraged but actively resisted, but my supporters — PCO Ana chief among them — managed to have the record set straight somewhat. But I remained deeply unhappy with the prison system's perceptions of me. Nor was the report the only evidence I had of these misconceptions. It was possible, under the regulations governing parole in those days, for lifers to apply to appear before the Parole Board after serving only nine years of their mandatory ten-year sentence. This kind of early hearing wasn't in order to secure an early release on parole: rather, it was an opportunity for prisoners to hear what the Parole Board would need from them in a year's time, when they became eligible. Naturally, I had applied, believing the turn-around I had made in my life, and especially my academic achievements, to be the kind of 'special circumstances' that would make me eligible for an early hearing. But in early 2005, my application was declined. The chairman of the Parole Board noted and praised my efforts but couldn't find anything special about my circumstances. In retrospect, I can understand this decision, as although it wasn't clearly outlined, I think the kind of special circumstances they had in mind were terminal illness or the like.

At the time, though, release from prison seemed to hover before me like a mirage, always receding as I seemed to be drawing nearer.

*

Perhaps because he felt badly for me, the unit 6 manager not only agreed to my request to be moved to a cell near John Barlow at the quieter end of the unit but also expedited it. This was important to me, as I had just received word that my proposed topic for a PhD thesis in psychology had been accepted by the doctoral research committee of Massey University. Building on the work done for the master's degree, my proposed topic focused upon how differences between people in intelligence, personality and integrity could be measured in combination, and how these findings could be used to improve selection decisions and performance in the workplace. The title of the dissertation was 'Psychometric Relationships and Measurement'. Doctors Haberman, Hill and Englert agreed to act as my supervisors.

It was great being back in close proximity to John Barlow again. And soon after shifting there, I made a couple of friends who fitted well into our regular coffee, biscuit and news sessions. We became quite a clique. JD was an Australian who was doing time for fraud. I serendipitously learned he had a PhD in Mathematics just as the licence for the statistics software I had been using for data analysis expired. JD happily walked me through the functions in Excel spreadsheets that would enable me to perform the same number-crunching, without the need to pay the steep cost of renewing the licence. JD was also a keen jogger, and he helped me take my jogging to the next level, encouraging me to run distances in better and better times rather than simply running for a set period, as I'd been doing.

My other new mate was my next-door neighbour. Stevo, also an Australian, had been convicted for his role in trying to ship a large quantity of cocaine through New Zealand to Australia. He was my age, and had just started studying philosophy at Massey, so we were always going to hit it off. We spent a lot of time discussing and debating philosophy and philosophers. You had to be careful where and how you did this. One day, while we were walking in the yard and Steve was holding forth about some philosophical theory or another, a patched Black Power member who was walking just in front of us loudly remarked to his mate that some people thought they were better than others. I heard it for the warning it was, and I signalled to Steve we'd better tone down our talk. When I got a chance, I explained to him that I'd seen plenty of examples of how any effort you made to better yourself was resented by some people who had chips on their shoulders, often with violent consequences. I made a point of seeking the Black Power guy out, introducing myself and getting yarning, just so he could be sure I didn't think I was better than he was. This seemed to soothe his ruffled feathers, but I always kept a wary eye on him afterwards. A year or so after this incident, and some time after he was transferred, I heard he was murdered in another prison.

Violence, rule-breaking and general lack of consideration surrounded us, even at the better-behaved end of the unit. Nor was it only the inmates. Sometimes the instigators of problems were the staff. One such staff member was a man I'll call Ed, who had recently transferred from Paparoa Prison in Christchurch. He immediately established a reputation among prisoners and his colleagues alike for being over-zealous, especially when it came to cell searches.

Another area of his responsibility in which he was over-enthusiastic was in performing the muster when he was on night shift. The strict regulations meant the officer on duty was supposed to sight every prisoner as they did their rounds. To this end, the curtains that hung over the windows of our cells in unit 6 had a corner clipped off so that the staff could get a clear view into the cell. Most prisoners blocked this gap at night to keep out the light, and considerate staff members would usually content themselves with making sure the cell doors were secure, particularly where it came to old-timers such as myself. Ed wasn't one of those prison officers. He made a point of shining his torch directly into the face of every prisoner on his rounds.

One night at around 11 pm, I heard Ed order a gang member celled up near me to clear a larger space in his window.

'Fuck off,' was the predictable reply.

'Don't you talk to me like that,' Ed snapped back. 'Do as I say, or I'll have your cell opened.'

'Go ahead, asshole.'

Ed summoned help, in the shape of four other officers. I heard the standard instruction issued.

'Prisoner, stand to the back of your cell, hands against the wall.'

I heard the cell door open, and the sounds of a struggle.

'Fuck off! Fuck youse!'

The gangster repeatedly stepped Ed out, challenging him to a one-on-one, but I heard no response from Ed. The prisoner decided to have a crack at him anyway. With five on one in the cramped confines of a cell, he had little chance of success. The noises soon became the pained sounds of a prisoner being subjected to control and restraint tactics. A chorus was rising from the residents of other cells. Someone threw a thermos flask at the officers as they dragged the still-struggling gangster off to the observation/punishment block.

It wasn't just the inmates who felt Ed had overreacted. After all, the prisoner was plainly in his cell, and therefore doing everything he was obliged to do at 11 o'clock at night. He reappeared the next day, with no punishment entered against him, an indication of the authorities' opinion on the matter.

A common sanction prisoners took towards staff members like Ed who overstepped was to 'put them on the coat', which basically meant you pretended they were invisible and you couldn't hear them when they spoke. This was a far more effective measure than you might suppose. But in Ed's case, things had gone too far. While the prison authorities (above unit management level) generally approved of his attitude — they said so in an email — they were worried that his methods might provoke a violent reaction. When credible intelligence reached them that a hit on Ed had been offered and accepted, with money changing hands, it was deemed prudent to shift him out.

It was towards the end of this, my latest (and last) stint in unit 6, that I witnessed one of the most disgusting things I ever saw, either in prison or outside it. Because the unit office was nearby (next door to John, who was next door to me), one of the Mongrel Mob members a couple of cells along in the other direction was moved away to make room for a middle-aged guy with health problems. He was under a cloud as soon as he arrived. He claimed he was in for fraud, but this wasn't widely believed. Unless it's well known what you're in for (as it was with John Barlow, for example), old guys are always suspected of being child molesters. Threats and taunts are the least you can expect: violence is more likely, unless you have someone who can vouch for you or you can produce actual paperwork to say what you're in for. This guy was lucky that Pit Bull was in the unit (for a limited time only, until he was busted with drugs a short time later). He put the word around that the old guy was to be left alone.

Nevertheless, simmering suspicions remained. When, in the evening a couple of days after he arrived, he began to have a heart attack, several of the young guys in the vicinity of his cell began yelling.

'You dead yet?'

'Hurry up and die, you old cunt.'

The screws were soon in his cell, trying to help. They told the yellers to shut up, but two Mob associates, whom John and I privately referred to as Dumb and Dumber, kept it up, barking and telling the poor guy to die.

'Can I help?' I asked, more to let the sufferer know that not everyone around him was an asshole than anything else. Under normal circumstances, I never interfered with other people's dramas, but on this occasion I felt it needed to be done, even though it might not be appreciated by the mobsters.

'Thanks, Paul,' one of the screws said. 'We've got it.'

The unit was locked down at 8.20 pm, ten minutes early, which only aggravated the situation.

'Why couldn't you have your heart attack after lockup, you old cunt?' someone yelled.

'Just die, motherfucker,' shouted another.

An ambulance arrived, and the paramedics came down the corridor, to the accompaniment of abuse, swearing and animal noises. It made me physically sick to think of what the poor man was suffering, hearing this. I had seen and known people stabbed, beaten, burnt and raped while in prison. This was about as awful as anything I had witnessed.

*

I hadn't yet appeared in front of the Parole Board; a date, December 2005, had been set, but it was several months in the future when a prison officer came to my cell during the afternoon lockup and asked if I would be interested in moving to the self-care units.

'Why?' I asked.

'No reason,' he replied. 'Just asking.'

'Yes,' I said. 'Of course I would.'

I didn't think too much of this approach. Self-care was the pinnacle of prison life, the closest you could get to liberty without actually being released. You were supposed to be in transition to the outside (having received a release date from the Parole Board) to be eligible. On these grounds, I wasn't.

Asking around, I learned a number of others had been asked the same question, including John Barlow and a Mongrel Mob member who had, earlier the same day, returned a urine test positive for drug use. It seemed to John and me that it was nothing to get excited about: it was more than likely just another prison rumour.

Consequently, two weeks later when my afternoon constitutional around the yard with Stevo and John was interrupted by a call to the guardroom, I thought nothing much of it.

At the guardroom, there were two officers whom I knew from my time in unit 9.

'Excited?' asked one of them. 'We're here to interview you for your shift to self-care.'

I made a face.

'Not excited?' she said, surprised.

'Well, in prison you soon learn it's like Mark Twain said: "It pays not only to look a gift horse in the mouth, but under the tail as well." There's a rumour going around they just need to shift a few bodies to self-care to make room in here.'

'Nope,' she replied. 'It's the real deal.'

I stared at her. Right then and there, my palms began to sweat. I wanted so badly for it to be true. Yet I had learned not to get my hopes up in prison. It just made the inevitable disappointment that much harder to bear.

In the interview — there was another inmate besides me there, who had already been before the Parole Board — we were told about self-care. The new facility at Rimutaka comprised five Lockwood-type homes, each with four bedrooms, a kitchen/lounge, a bathroom and a laundry. Each inmate lived with three others in a flatting situation, and every Wednesday, one from each unit was taken on an escorted outing to the supermarket to do the shopping. There were conditions, of course: no drugs, no cell phones, no misbehaviour.

'Do you think you can live with that?' the interviewing officer asked.

'Where do I sign?' I replied.

I asked so many questions I was in danger of irritating them. I wanted to know all about the process so I could work out how high to calibrate my hopes. I wanted to know how long I would have to wait.

'You'll know tomorrow,' they said.

'When would I move in?'

'The day after that.'

I hardly dared hope. I told John, Stevo and JD about it. I felt bad telling John. We had grown very close, and I was hugely in his debt for the mentoring, support and unwavering encouragement he had given me. I felt awful for leaving him behind — if it happened.

'Good for you, Paul!' he said, without a trace of envy or resentment in his voice. I always admired that about John. He could be genuinely happy for the good fortune of others.

I spent a sleepless night, and an anxious morning. At around 3.30 pm, while I was pacing around the yard like a caged tiger, I saw one of the interviewing officers arriving. I hastened up to the grille to talk to her.

'Congratulations, Paul,' she said. 'You'll be moving to self-care at 10 tomorrow morning.'

I was speechless.

That night, the Coffee and Bikkies Clique met for the last time. Afterwards, I began packing up my cell. Once I was done, and I'd gone through the painful process of working out what to keep and what to give away — you acquire inordinate attachments to the few possessions you have in prison — I tried to sleep.

*

Self-care seemed too good to be true. When I arrived, Hemara, one of my new flatmates, was already there. He seemed like a good sort, keen to please to the point where I imagined he would have had a hard time of it in the predatory prison environment. We wandered around marvelling at our good fortune. The units were almost new. I wasn't sure whether the four La-Z-Boys were more amazing than the huge (compared to our prison sets) television set they were arranged around. We eyed the kitchen appliances — toaster, toasted sandwich maker, fridge and oven — like members of a cargo cult. And there were other wonders. Metal cutlery! Real glasses! Crockery made of china!

The other two residents arrived. I knew Jeff from unit 4: he was another lifer with whom I got on well. Bobby, the other one, was also a lifer and seemed fine, too. We sat on the Laz-y-Boys fooling with the reclining mechanisms and discussing how we would plan our weekly meal menus and laughing at the weirdness of discussing this kind of thing at all. Several of the staff came by for a nosey, and it was immensely empowering to be able to offer to make them a cup of coffee or tea. They were as impressed by our new accommodation as we were. Then the unit manager arrived with a couple of big bags of groceries. He told us we would still get prison meals for the first three weeks. After that, we'd look after ourselves. The bags he carried contained supplies such as bread and milk and frozen pizzas. That night, after dinner, where even the prison meal seemed to taste better eaten sitting at our dining table, I made everyone chicken and cheese toasties and we watched TV.

I made a number of excited phone calls to Dad, my brothers and friends. Each of them was surprised to hear from me without the connection being preceded by a recorded message informing them that someone was phoning from a New Zealand prison, warning them the conversation was likely to be recorded and asking whether they would accept the call. They were as excited as I was about this development — this huge step I had taken towards my eventual release.

At 10 pm, we were no longer allowed outside, although the doors weren't locked. The houses were still inside the perimeter, of course, but it's amazing the psychological difference it made, just knowing the door was unlocked! The relaxed atmosphere of self-care took quite some getting used to. I decided I'd quite like to move a chest of drawers in my bedroom so there would be more room for the desk. Out of habit, I waited until I could ask a staff member.

'Fill your boots,' she said. 'You don't have to ask permission to shift stuff around in here.'

I soon fell into a routine. Every week day, I would wake up at around 5.30, get dressed and wait until 6 am, when we were allowed to leave the villa. I'd then go for a run around the perimeter of the prison compound, up the road, around the

276

outside of the unit 7 carpark, along the outside of the youth unit fence, around the back of self-care and back up the road. I worked out that six times around was roughly five kilometres. My run would be accompanied by the wonderful dawn chorus, led by a tūī that perched on the fence across the road from the perimeter.

By the time I got back, one or more of my flatmates would usually be up, cooking breakfast. After eating, I would spend the rest of the day on my PhD work, stopping only to make cups of tea or coffee, to have lunch, and to exercise again. Occasionally, I would have visitors, including official visitors — a group from the Department of Corrections' national office, a delegation of judges from Queensland, a bunch of prison officials from Singapore. I'd take them on a tour of the place, make them coffee and sometimes even bake: coffee or chocolate cakes were my forte. But for the rest of the time I was left, blissfully, to my own devices. And in the evenings, I made full use of the phone, the conversations with my family on the outside, especially my sister-in-law Cristiane, going a long way to normalising relations with those who would provide my support network when I got out.

*

A fair amount of thought had gone into who would share which self-care unit with whom. I think Jeff and I were chosen to share with Bobby and Hemara because it was deemed we would be a good influence on them. Hemara, in particular, seemed to look to me as the kind of mentor I had been fortunate enough to have already stumbled upon. When I first met him, he was barely literate or numerate, and his speech was very unclear. One day,

I was in the lounge while he and Big T, the resident of another self-care unit, were in the kitchen muddling their way through a cake recipe.

'Hey, Paul. What does "prepare" mean?' Hemara called.

'It means to get something ready,' I replied.

A short time later, Hemara piped up again.

'Hey, Paul. What does "consistency" mean?'

'It means how the cake looks and feels,' I explained.

Soon after the cake went into the oven, Big T looked at the clock.

'Shit, is that the time? I better go get ready for work.'

'*Prepare* for work,' I said, and he grinned. 'Where are you working?'

'In the kitchen up at the staff training college,' he said.

I shook my head, wondering how many times he must have been asked to 'prepare' things in the kitchen and had got on with it without really knowing what he'd been asked to do.

Because he was so personally obliging, Hemara regularly took offence at what he perceived to be the inconsideration of others, especially Jeff and Bobby. I found myself counselling him, talking him through his reactions. I quite enjoyed taking this role. It underlined for me how lucky I was in the education I'd received, and the distance I'd come from my own unexamined thoughts and reactions to slights, both real and imagined. And for his part, Hemara began to take real pride in his own progress. He told me several people had commented on how much more clearly he was speaking — I thought of the way John Barlow had improved my speech and diction — and that he had been telling the prison literacy and numeracy teacher he felt he was making progress. One of the prison officers had overheard, and remarked that Hemara had been 'spending too much time with that bloody Paul Wood'.

About two months after we'd all shifted into self-care together, Hemara turned 27. I baked a layered chocolate cake for him and, on the morning of his birthday, we presented him with the cake and a card one of the corrections officers had bought, which we and several of the staff had signed. We shared a prison hug (whereby you join one hand, with the forearms at a 45-degree angle, and put the other arm loosely around the other guy's shoulder). Hemara seemed strangely tense and quiet. Later, because his reading was poor, I sat with him and together we worked through the messages that had been written in his card. He was still subdued, and I asked him why.

'I'm blown away, Paul,' he said. 'I've never had a birthday card before.'

I was amazed, and appalled. That evening, I was talking to the literacy and numeracy teacher.

'We gave Hemara a birthday card today,' I said. 'And guess what?'

'He told you it was the first card he'd ever had,' she replied without hesitation. 'You wouldn't believe how often I hear that story.'

Poor old Hemara. One day, a staff member told me Hemara was going to be moved out of self-care. The one thing over which I'd been powerless to exercise any influence was Hemara's occasional use of cannabis, and as seemed bound to happen, he'd returned a positive urine test. I felt guilty, and wondered if I could have done more. But in the end, I was too preoccupied with my own circumstances to dwell on it. I was shortly to appear before the Parole Board.

CHAPTER TWELVE

Walking Out

I was free before I left prison, although it didn't seem that way. But I had made the walk to freedom — all five steps of it — before I stepped through the door on the day of my physical release from custody.

The first step was when I realised that the way I was living was not the way I wanted to live, and that if I wanted to change, I would need to focus on changing my inner world as opposed to anything going on in the world outside of my head. It was a slow realisation, and it required me first to make the staggering discovery that not all things were as I supposed them to be. Two objects of differing weights, released from the same height, will hit the ground simultaneously. I was a school drop-out, a drug user, a murderer, but I wasn't born any of those things. I could choose to become someone, something different. The potential to radically transform my life was already with me: I just had to recognise that my focus needed to be on changing my inner world.

The second step was having the belief that it is possible to learn, to grow, to get better, to change. Yet this isn't enough. You also need to demonstrate the motivation and courage to do so. This motivation is most present when you're focused on what you stand to lose if you don't make change. Yet it means little without the courage to risk failure and deal with the unpleasant feelings that come from stepping outside your comfort zone. One of the biggest mistakes holding people back from taking this step is the belief that you should wait until you feel more confident before doing so. But confidence only comes from taking action. In fact, some of the research suggests your anxiety doesn't drastically reduce when you get out of your comfort zone, but your courage increases significantly. Courage is the more important attribute. Our concerns rarely turn out to be justified once they are faced, and it is only through developing courage will we have the strength of character to do so.

The third step was taking real, practical steps to emancipate myself. I could have dreamed of the future I wanted for the rest of my prison term without doing a single thing to bring it closer, and the predictable result would have been that I would have emerged from prison no closer to that imagined future. But I identified the small steps I could take to move me in the direction I wanted to go. I developed the small daily disciplines that would help me maintain the course. In some ways, the structure of university study is a model of how to make your escape. Each assignment, each paper, each year's work is a step towards the lofty, ultimate goal of a university degree. The little goals are specific, manageable and require work in the here and now. Each, once accomplished, brings the prize closer. It's like mountaineering. Each step up the slope, each rope pitch, demands effort and attention. Enough steps, enough rope pitches, and you find, almost to your surprise, that the summit is at hand. We often falsely attribute people's success to natural talent or luck, but as the great Stoic philosopher Seneca said: 'Luck is what happens when preparation meets opportunity', and if you look behind any great success or change, you will see hours, days, weeks, months, years of dedicated effort. Nothing worthwhile comes easily.

The fourth step was being prepared to fight for my freedom. It's not as though the struggle to be free comes after the other steps: it's a constant throughout. None of what I chose to undertake was easy. Despite the time it allows you to focus, in many respects prison is a wholly unconducive environment for study, with a distinct lack of resources and support and sometimes even outright resentment. I had to overcome all these obstacles. I also had to overcome the more mundane obstacles we all face when confronting an onerous task, including my own desires. But self-control is something you can train for, and you get better at demonstrating it by exercising it. And overcoming challenges and obstacles just sharpens your problem-solving skills and builds your confidence that you can positively influence your own future.

The final step was living free. I took this step, but I am still taking this step. Once I had decided I wanted better for myself, to be better, I accepted a lifelong challenge. Freedom is a journey, not a destination, and it comes at the price of continual effort. Even so simple a thing as self-awareness — actually not so simple — requires constant questioning of your own assumptions, a refusal to declare 'Mission Accomplished' on self-improvement and rest on your laurels. No matter how many summits you stand upon along the way, your road is always upwards. Being free is about character. It is about being the best version of yourself possible, being the person who behaves according to their values and demonstrates behaviour they'd want their reputation to reflect. No one is sitting at the top of their mountain in this respect. No one is always the best version of themselves in all situations and with all people. And it's not until the chips are down and you are in the midst of true adversity that you get the opportunity to test yourself. When it comes to living a truly authentic and meaningful life, the goal is getting better, not being good, which is a subtle but important distinction. To be good at something requires an external comparison with others and failure implies some judgement against your talents or capabilities. To get better, on the other hand, is only relevant in reference to yourself. Who was I yesterday, who am I today, and who will I be tomorrow? This is the only relevant comparison when it comes to personal growth and improvement, and no one else has your life story, your experiences, your enablers and hindrances. Getting better is a goal that is never completely achieved.

*

I had my first appearance before the Parole Board at 9.20 on the morning of 30 November 2006. In the New Zealand system — or at least, in the system when I was sentenced — a 'life' sentence meant you served a mandatory term of at least ten years before you were considered eligible for parole — unless a non-parole period greater than ten years is mandated, based on egregious factors in the offending. Even though you become eligible for consideration at this point, the Parole Board has no obligation to release you if they consider you to be an ongoing risk to society. 'Parole' literally means release upon your word of good behaviour. Needless to say, all but the very hardest or most damaged cases will happily give their word they will behave: to determine whether there are good grounds to believe them, the prisoner and his or her referees are quizzed about their level of insight into their offending, the genuineness of their desire to make amends and live a law-abiding life, and their level of preparedness for life outside prison.

My hopes that I would leave the hearing with a release date were sky-high. I had read through the legislation governing the board's decision-making process and was encouraged by the fact a prisoner couldn't be kept beyond their mandatory term unless it was deemed necessary for the protection of the community. I felt everything I had done in recent years to address my offending and reduce the likelihood of my reoffending meant I was as unlikely as I'd ever be to reoffend. I had undertaken every non-violence and substance abuse course available to me. I had undertaken extensive psychological counselling in order to understand and resolve the issues that had led to my substance abuse and subsequent offending. I had completed a Bachelor of Arts degree and a Master of Arts degree and embarked upon a Doctorate, which had placed me in the enviable position of having employment upon my release: Paul Englert had offered me a job in his company. And perhaps most importantly from the point of view of personal growth, I had become a voracious reader. The pioneering personality theorist Gordon Allport once said that the goal of maturation is overcoming one's adolescent narcissism. Reading is one of the major ways we gain insight into the minds and condition of others. I had read 766 books in the previous four years — I knew because I had kept a record of each book and what I had learned from it.

All of this was in the written submissions supplied to the board. They also had disciplinary and psychological reports from the prison authorities, and references from others. I had excellent referees, and I could not have asked for support people of a higher calibre. At any appearance in front of the Parole Board, you're entitled to be accompanied by up to three support people. I had asked my father, his partner Alison, and my good friend, mentor and future employer Paul Englert to attend. You're also allowed to apply to be represented by legal counsel at such proceedings. I felt it might look adversarial if I brought counsel along. I was confident in my own ability to articulate my position, and my now good friend, Dr Donald Stevens QC, agreed with me.

Besides your support people, you're also accompanied by a prison officer. Usually, this is someone who will speak to your progress and behaviour within the institution. I learned on the morning of my appearance that I had never met the officer assigned. So buoyant was I that I shrugged this disappointment off.

I was escorted to the section of the prison where parole hearings took place and was shown into a holding cell with the other guys waiting to appear. We were all too nervous to talk much, but we wished each other luck. Just before my hearing, I was taken to a waiting room where Dad, Alison and Paul greeted me. It felt so good to have made it this far, and my support crew were just as excited as I was at the prospect of my release. We only had a few minutes together before we were ushered into the room. My support people were seated next to the door at the back of the room while I was seated in the centre, flanked by two corrections officers. Facing me was the board — a District Court judge and two representatives of the community.

The presiding judge, Judge Rota, introduced himself and the other two members of the board. He asked who my support people were and then, without preamble, he asked what I would like to tell the board.

The hearing was set down to last 20 minutes, but it ended up lasting 40. Most of it was taken up with to-ing and fro-ing between Judge Rota and myself. It was a rollercoaster ride. Each time I produced a compelling argument for my fitness for parole, he would counter with a cynical riposte. I felt I answered his questions with an appropriate level of sophistication, but he even found a jaundiced angle to take on this.

'Where did you learn the language you're using to talk about these matters?' he asked.

I replied I had done every course available to me that dealt with understanding criminogenic factors. I was a graduate student of psychology, and I had done extensive reading on my own account to understand my offending and the mechanisms that had led to it.

'It's just that your answers sound very practised,' he mused.

My heart sank. Here I was, a pilgrim on the road less travelled, and all he was determined to see was another recidivist on the loop road that runs from release back to prison.

He asked about the support network available to me, and my spirits rose again. I described the loving family to which I was going to return, the exciting prospect of my new job with Paul Englert's company and the stability that continuing with my studies would provide amidst the turmoil of readjusting to the outside world.

'There are plenty of drug users at university,' he said tartly, plainly referring to the importance I'd placed on substance abuse as a factor in my offending.

'I'm sure there are drug users in all walks of life,' I replied calmly. 'But I am drug free and determined to stay that way. I'm too aware of the consequences of slipping back into that kind of behaviour to allow it to happen.'

'Everyone who appears before this board says that,' he said, the ghost of a smile on his face.

He went on to observe that my behaviour in prison hadn't been that flash for the first six years. It was only since 2001 I had cleaned up my act.

'You see, the cynic in me might say you've only started behaving as your date with this board approached.'

I replied that I could see how he might form this opinion, but the truth was otherwise, and I would only be able to prove my sincerity if I were given the opportunity to do so.

My heart was in my boots again.

The judge asked the prison officer who had accompanied me, but had never met me before, why I hadn't been on pre-release home visits. She replied that she didn't know, which appeared to only further the judge's scepticism towards me.

Both Dad and Alison were given the opportunity to speak, and I dared to hope again, so eloquently did they speak of the change they had seen in me since I had begun to study and since I had turned my back on drugs. Paul Englert had seen the way the wind was blowing and strove to assure the board that the sophistication of my answers wasn't just a well-rehearsed routine for the board's benefit; it was typical of the level of conversation he had with me when he visited. He told them about the job for me, and his confidence that I would settle into life as a contributing member of society.

The other two members of the board then had their turn to ask me questions. One focused on what measures had been taken to reintegrate me, in terms of supervised leave and home visits. I could only point to a couple of outings for medical purposes, the visit to my mother's grave and another compassionate leave I'd been granted to see my terminally ill Uncle Norm before he died. The principal corrections officer was compelled to admit that while the authorities at Rimutaka had recommended I be approved for supervised shopping outings since I'd been in self-care, my applications had been declined.

The other board member seemed more interested in my level of remorse. He asked me if I knew where Boyd was buried, and when I admitted I didn't, he told me it was 'a little red flag' for him that I had only mentioned Boyd twice in all the time I had been addressing them. The VPU's opinion that I lacked empathy was suddenly at issue, and I was told the board was obliged to ensure that the public could have total confidence not only that I'd paid an appropriate price for my offending but also that it would be protected from me if I were at all likely to reoffend.

The hearing drew to a close, and I was directed to wait in the anteroom with my support people as the board deliberated. I felt I had answered their queries very well, and Dad, Paul and Alison agreed I couldn't have done better, but all of us sensed the antagonism, and none of us could claim to be confident of a positive outcome.

After what can't have been more than ten minutes — it seemed far, far longer — we were called back into the hearing room.

'Well, Mr Wood,' Judge Rota said. 'We've decided to refuse parole at this stage.'

I was numb, disbelieving, and it took a real effort to focus on what he said next. He told me the board was encouraged by what I'd told them, by the changes I'd made and by the obviously supportive environment I would eventually be released into. Even so, he couldn't refrain from allowing a little of his scepticism to show, telling me he saw only good things for me as long as what I had told them was true and not a well-rehearsed routine. He picked up on a comment made by Paul that described me as an intense kind of person who wholly dedicated himself to projects. This, Judge Rota said, could be a good or a bad thing. If I dedicated myself to finishing my journey of change, it could only be good. But if I allowed myself to become negative, I stood a real chance of lapsing into bad habits. He talked about the magnitude of change both the outside world and I had undergone in the decade I'd been incarcerated. In light of it, he said, the board's decision was for my own benefit. In the time before the next hearing, it was important I avail myself of any and every opportunity to go on day paroles and home leaves and other reintegrative activities. When I next appeared before the board, it was likely to be the extended Parole Board, and while he couldn't promise anything on their behalf, he expected they would set a date for my release. He congratulated me on the way in which I had used my time in recent years in jail, and wished more prisoners would do the same. He apologised to Dad and Alison that I couldn't be released yet. And that, as they say, was that.

Dad, Alison, Paul and I were led back into the waiting room. We were in shock. All the positive things Judge Rota had said paled by comparison with the stark reality I had been stood down for another year. This was the longest period of time the Board could defer without applying for a special extension order. It was the same period of stand-down I would have received if I'd made zero effort to change and better myself.

I felt cruelly let down. While I had been optimistic, I had known there was a reasonable chance I'd be knocked back. Never did I imagine it would be for so long. My support people were even more upset. There were tears in all eyes. Paul had a lot to say about the judge thinking himself a psychologist. He took real issue with the judge's suggestion that what Paul had described as my intensity, but was probably better understood as my level of focus and drive, was a negative that presented a risk to society. Paul saw it as exactly the tendency that had enabled me to succeed in my studies and would be the foundation of my ability to achieve on release. A desire to excel, a single-minded focus on my goals and persistence are traits that have always been with me, but now they were channelled in a positive direction. They were no longer a risk, but instead the antidote to any return of what had gone before. He sent a text to my brother Jon, which simply read: 'Short sighted and gutless.'

The waiting room was required for others, but the staff were good enough to allow us another ten minutes together via a booth visit. I pulled myself together, and focused on comforting my poor dad and pointing out to him that all was not lost. I could, I reminded him, apply for an earlier hearing. In the meantime, I would do everything I could in the way of reintegration programmes so that an application for an early hearing would be favourably received.

As I was escorted back to my unit, several corrections officers approached to find out how I'd got on. They were universally shocked at the length of time I'd been stood down. I accepted their commiserations in true Stoic fashion. Once I was on my own, I took pride in the way in which I'd managed to conduct myself in the face of this bitter disappointment. After all, cold comfort was all that was on offer.

*

It didn't take too long to recover from the blow. Partly, planning my reintegration plan helped. This involved writing up a temporary release plan for the next 12 months. Usually, a prisoner would have a couple of day leaves of about 12 hours each and then move on to overnight leaves of 24, 48, and 72 hours. You're entitled to apply for one day leave a month, until you start being granted overnight leaves, whereupon you may apply for one overnight leave every two months. Accordingly, I outlined three day leaves to be followed by three 72-hour overnight leaves.

I compiled the plan together with a corrections officer. He wrote it up and passed it on to the unit manager, who signed it off and took it to the prison superintendent. To everyone's surprise, the superintendent suggested I have two escorted day leaves each of four hours' duration before I start temporary releases. He was concerned that I had been in prison for a long time and the plan as submitted gave me too much exposure to the outside world too quickly. I had spent many years watching prisoners, including other lifers, go out on temporary releases when they became eligible for parole. I had neither seen nor heard of anyone being required to accept escorted outings before.

In the event, the unit manager objected, and told the superintendent he supported the application as it stood and wasn't prepared to change it. Happily, and largely thanks to him, when word came down from the national office a couple of weeks later, there was no requirement for my leaves to be escorted. However, the superintendent had shortened some of them, so that I was now approved for two four-hour leaves, followed by an eight-hour and then a 12-hour leave before having a 24-hour leave and finally a 72-hour leave. I could have been disappointed, but I was simply relieved I wouldn't have to have a corrections officer come along.

I also received approval for me to go shopping for supplies for my unit. As I was the only one of the four of us with the time available, I got to go out once a week to the supermarket and a wholesale butcher, escorted by a corrections officer. I'll never forget the experience of walking around the supermarket aisle. My pulse was racing and my breathing was short; it took all my self-control not to roll my head this way and that, staring wide-eyed at it all. The confectionery aisle was the hardest to bear. After the drab prison environment, decorated from a palette of colours designed not only to soothe and under-stimulate but also to avoid anything resembling gang colours, the gaudy riot of chocolate and chip wrappers was a full-on, all-out assault on the senses. I had to stop myself gawping stupidly at the technology at the check-outs — the scanners, the moving belts, the EFTPOS keypads. None of this had been around when I was 18.

My first proper leave from prison was an escorted trip in late December, before my home leaves began. It was a trip outside of the wire to visit Jon, Cristiane and their newborn baby daughter, who had all come over from Australia to see my dad. It was for six hours, and I loved it. With the CO in tow, keeping a considerably low profile, Jon and I went to the beach at Oriental Bay. I stood in my togs, wriggling my toes in the sand and feeling the Wellington sunshine on my shoulders and all that space and emptiness around me. After years of staring at blank walls never more than a few metres away, standing before the expanse of the harbour stretching to the Orongorongo Range ahead of me and with the tall buildings of the city away to my left was the epitome of freedom.

'How's it feel?' Jon asked.

'Unreal,' I replied, and looked for other, better words. 'Unreal' was all I could find.

'Last one in!' he yelled and, with a skip and a sprint, we ran down the beach and dived into the water. The shock of cold — it was mid-summer, but the water in Wellington is never exactly what you'd call warm — the feeling of the salt water on my skin ... It was like being reborn.

Then we went back to Dad's place for a meal. After the beach, it just felt right to be sitting around with people I loved, talking normally and laughing.

Soon after that, I had my first true temporary release. I wasn't escorted this time: Dad simply signed for me at the door. We had six hours before I had to be back at the prison. This time, I went and watched my younger brother compete in the street-skating final of the X-Games. Chris was unbelievable — physically talented and totally without fear. Watching him, I was reminded of Hemingway's descriptions of matadors defying the bull. Chris used the same flair and dash to defy gravity. I was so proud watching him, with the whole thousands-strong crowd on their feet, clapping their hands and chanting his name. It was one of the happiest moments in my life, excitement at its purest.

My next temporary release was again for six hours. Dad signed me out, and we drove to Oriental Parade beach where I met The Chameleon. He'd been released from prison a few months earlier, and had settled into life outside pretty well. He had his own property development and investment company. We went for a swim and had some Italian ice-cream — a revelation. Afterwards, we met up with JD, who was living at his partner's apartment off Courtenay Place while awaiting the outcome of an appeal he'd raised against an order to deport him to Australia. Dad, The Chameleon and I had a meal before it was time to start back for Rimutaka. We stopped at my cousin's house on the way.

For my third temporary release, I was allowed ten hours away from the prison in order to attend my father's seventieth birthday party. It was so good being able to be there for such an important birthday, especially as it marked the first time my brothers and I had all been together in over a decade. It was also a very good opportunity to catch up with other family members I hadn't seen in even longer. It felt important renewing these old ties. I was already sensing that I'd need everyone's support once I was released.

Among the guests at Dad's party were his piano teacher, her husband and their daughter. The husband was an ex KGB biological weapons expert who had not one but two doctorates — but when I remarked on what an achievement that was, they told me their daughter was just finishing two double degrees, planning a trip as a volunteer aid worker to Africa and meanwhile awaiting a publisher's verdict on the draft of her first novel. Any vainglorious pride I felt at how hard-working and accomplished I was vanished in an instant. I had become unaccustomed to feeling lazy! It was an inspirational meeting. It showed me it was always possible to work harder, to achieve more. Years later, I would meet the All Blacks coach, Sir Graham Henry, who puts it well in his mantra to his players in their pursuit of excellence: better never stops.

*

My home leaves were fantastic, but they were also emotionally draining, leaving me with a tinge of relief when I got back to the villa inside the prison perimeter. I didn't have to explain myself to anyone inside. I didn't have to resist the constant, nagging sense that people around me were judging me. I felt physically safe: I knew prison, and from where and whom to expect threats. Outside, even with people I knew and loved and in situations with which I was familiar, I felt insufficiently in control of my environment to relax. It was stressful.

It was probably my fourth home leave that, more than any other, brought home to me how long the process of adjusting to the outside was going to be. This one was for 14 hours, and my sponsor was my childhood friend Amy. After having breakfast we went to the Wellington City Gallery. There were two exhibitions on. One was Patricia Piccinini's *Podcast*, which used amazing chimerical sculptures to provoke consideration of genetic engineering and like issues. The other was called *The Wonder Years* and comprised a collection of highly evocative paintings by artist Michael Smither. I found those of religious subject matter particularly interesting, such as a faceless Christ on the cross, or the one of Saint Francis rolling in thorns while two large wild pigs copulated vigorously in the background. The images I saw would come back to me many times over the coming days.

In the afternoon we met up with a couple of other friends from our childhood at Dad's place. They arrived just after 4 pm, and I was initially very pleased to see them. But the conversation soon dried up, and everyone, especially me, became aware of how far apart we'd grown. They were no longer people whom I would choose to hang out with, and I didn't feel comfortable at all.

After an hour or so of awkwardness, we went to a Thai restaurant to meet Dr Donald Stevens for dinner. It was my first experience of Thai food and like sensations inspired by the art exhibition that morning, the delectation of my taste buds would stay with me for days afterwards. It felt incredibly civilised, especially compared with the dining mess in prison, or meals eaten alone in your cell. After dinner we went for a coffee. I surprised myself by finding my eyes brimming with tears as I told Donald about my trip to the City Gallery.

After the emotional rawness of the day and with time running out before I had to return to Rimutaka, I felt the closest to free that I had felt all day. I finished the leave by diving into the bitterly cold water of Wellington harbour. It wasn't a long swim, but it was glorious.

Then it was time for the half-hour drive up the motorway to Rimutaka, nestled at the foot of the dark, bush-clad hills in the spherical glow of its security lights.

I was unsettled for days after this leave. Coming back to prison sucked, because being on the outside had been so damned good. I had a desperate longing to be living a 'normal' life on the outside.

*

My fifth temporary release was for 24 hours. Dad picked me up and we went to Queensgate shopping mall with my cousin Rose. There were people everywhere, and I became hyper-vigilant, trying to keep my eye on everyone. This is a natural, adaptive behaviour in prison, of course, where there is the genuine risk of attack any time you are in an area that can be accessed by others. But whereas you can just about manage to keep your surroundings under surveillance in a prison yard or in the mess, it's not so easy in a shopping complex.

The Chameleon then collected me and we drove to Karori to fetch my younger brother, Chris, who was home from overseas. Chris had been in Melbourne making his living as a professional skateboarder since his late teens and was on the professional skateboarding circuit in Europe and the USA. We drove up Wrights Hill to admire the hill from the lookout and to commune, I suppose, with the ghosts of the youths that we had once been. Then we hit town, my first late-night foray into Wellington city as an adult. To my surprise, I felt none of the thrill I used to feel walking down Cuba Mall and Courtenay Place. Sure, it was stimulating being around so many people and I was looking forward to when I'd be able to enjoy Wellington's vibrant nightlife to the full. But I couldn't help but be struck by how superficial and shallow it all appeared. It looked more like a situation where people were alone together.

Nor was I able to feel at ease in the crowds. At one point as we were walking along, Chris stopped to roll a cigarette. I felt an acute awareness of the space behind me, such as in the mess or thoroughfares in prison, and I found a concrete wall so I could stand with my back to it.

In those days, there was an amusement ride called the Sky Screamer in Courtenay Place. This was a large frame with criss-crossed bungee cords attached to a harness in the centre. You were buckled into the harness and then, at a given moment, the anchor was released and you were hurled into the air. Listening to those 'enjoying' it, you could see why it was called the Sky Screamer.

We were walking past it when The Chameleon jerked a thumb at it.

'Wanna go?' he asked.

'All right,' I replied at once.

I don't know why, but I'd imagined the thrill was in the acceleration, and after the upward surge, I'd be lowered slowly to the ground again. Well, I was wrong. Going up wasn't so bad, but freefalling from the zenith towards the pavement far below was very scary, especially since the harness was slightly loose and felt like it might slip off. I bounced up and down several times gripping the seat beneath me with white knuckles. I couldn't remember the last time I'd been that scared. Afterwards, I was filled with euphoric adrenalin. I was alive, and it felt good! It was somewhat like the contradictory satisfaction you can get after being punched in the face.

The Chameleon had been out on the tiles the night before, so he went home fairly early. Chris was ready to pack it in at 2.30 am. I could have quite happily walked around for longer, even though I wasn't allowed to drink or even enter licensed premises. But I wanted to get up early.

After a fitful sleep, I got up just after 5 am and pushed a mountain bike to the top of Makara Peak, a hill close to Dad's house, which has been developed with a maze of bike trails. I reached the summit at 6.30, just in time to see the sunrise, if there had been a sunrise to see: instead, I hung about in the freezing mist until I thought it was light enough to see my way down. The first trail I chose was far too demanding for my bike, let alone my level of expertise, and there were a couple of moments when I reflected how ironic it would be if I broke my neck this close to getting my life back. But I found an easier trail, and I loved every bone-shaking minute of the descent.

After bacon and eggs for breakfast, Dad and I spent the morning chatting before it was time to return to prison. After he had gone and I was sitting in the villa contemplating my study materials, it occurred to me that I was getting closer to being ready for life on the outside. The time was beginning to weigh heavily on my hands.

*

Six months into the stand-down period after my first Parole Board hearing, my flatmate Jeff came up before the Extended Board for his second hearing. Jeff was a lifer, like me, but on the face of it, he was a far more likely candidate for early parole than I was. He'd had no previous criminal convictions before he'd been found guilty of the murder of a notorious gang member. He was an automotive engineer by trade, and his tools had been stolen. The police didn't seem too interested in finding out who had done it, so Jeff had asked an associate of his who had links to the shadier end of society. Word that he was making such enquiries reached a senior member of the Nomads, who showed up on Jeff's doorstep one day and told him if he kept asking questions, his family would be murdered. Jeff freaked out, and his fear drove him to take pre-emptive action. He armed himself with a shotgun and, after lying in wait, he shot the gang member dead.

Jeff had been a model prisoner throughout his ten-year term and he had spent the seven months since his first hearing undertaking the same kind of reintegrative activities I had been doing. Consequently, I viewed his fortunes with the Parole Board as a bit of a barometer of my own prospects, and I was thus delighted when Jeff returned from his hearing with the news that he had been granted a release date in six weeks.

At the same time, I was in a kind of agony. Each taste of freedom left me craving more, and I found myself getting depressed for days, even weeks, each time I returned. By far the worst was the 72-hour leave. It was just enough time living in that style to become accustomed to it, and even my once-cosy self-care villa seemed bleak as I gazed at the razor-wire upon my return.

Meanwhile, I was growing increasingly frustrated at the knock-backs I was receiving in applications for other leave. As part of my reintegration plan, I had applied for leave to visit the Massey University campus from time to time to meet my supervisors and to use the research facilities. That effort had become mired in bureaucracy, and here I was, two years into my third degree, a doctorate, and I had never set foot in a university! Some inmates were also granted leave to play sport, notably a local rugby team that was coached by corrections officers and comprised a mixture of staff and self-care residents. I was no lover of rugby union — I had always been a league man — but it sounded like fun and it was another chance to get out into the outside world. But I was refused. At first, I was told the team had more than enough players. Then as I heard from others that they were struggling for the numbers to field a side, I began to realise there were other reasons.

I decided I couldn't go on twiddling my thumbs. I decided to be proactive and applied to the national Parole Board for an early hearing. The answer came back relatively swiftly: an early hearing was granted.

*

My experience with the board this time was totally different. No sooner had I entered the hearing room in which the Extended Board, comprising five members, was seated than the presiding judge, Judge Carruthers, said, 'Look, before we start, I'd just like you to know that we're going to release you. We're going to give you a release date.'

It was as though a bomb had gone off next to me. I sat there in stunned disbelief as he began to talk in detail about what my release would entail. I barely heard him, and I was conscious that my eyes were full of tears. When you serve a long sentence, you get used to not thinking about release, because it's vital to your psychological safety. But as the day and the reality draws near, you can't help it, especially given the little measured doses that reintegration serves you up. Consequently, the Parole Board has an awful power over you, the power to grant or withhold your deepest desire. I was so grateful to him for this act of kindness — putting me out of my misery instead of drawing out the suspense and throwing up reasons why I might be denied — that my eyes still fill with tears, even now, recalling it.

I was released on 2 October 2006, ten years and ten months to the day that I had gone into prison and, incidentally, the same day that Pit Bull was released. Dad was there to pick me up, and he let me drive his car back to his house from Upper Hutt. That was freaky! And once back at his house, I spent the rest of my day setting up the room I'd be staying in while I found my feet in this unfamiliar, wider world.

EPILOGUE

My name is Paul Wood, and I am a free man.

But the thing I have learned since I was released is that freedom is always and necessarily relative. You break free of a mental cell-block, and you find yourself still within an emotional perimeter. The harder you fight to be free, the more you realise that the free life is a life of fighting to be free. It's a journey through uncharted territory, through unknown terrain.

I recently learned a bit about the history of the silver fern as a symbol. All New Zealanders recognise it as a representative sporting motif, but it's actually a symbol of leadership. In pre-European times, when Māori traversed unfamiliar parts of the country, the leaders — the scouts, the pathfinders — would mark their trail through the bush by turning over a part of the frond of the fern that has a silver underside. For this reason, the silver fern became a symbol of leadership. I love this idea: the idea that turning over a new leaf, as the saying has it, is all about leadership. Because that has been my mission since I left prison: learning the art of self-leadership.

*

I was physically free the moment I walked out of prison that October afternoon in 2006. But the real struggle for freedom had just begun. I once heard that when you're preparing for release, it takes at least one month for every year you've been inside to decompress, to detoxify. My own experience suggests that this is a good rule of thumb, but only for getting over the worst of the prison contamination. There is a lingering residue that can last for years after your release.

I lived with Dad in the first instance. Adjusting wasn't easy. Even the home leaves hadn't altogether prepared me for the sudden absence of limits. My time was my own, and not regulated by the prison routine. I could leave my light on if I felt like it, or I could turn it off. I could phone a friend. The door to my room, the door to the house: both were unlocked. I could come and go as I pleased. I could go to a pub if I wanted, even drink a pint of beer. I could go to a café and order breakfast, drink coffee. I could go outside at night.

I knew the importance to my own sanity of self-discipline, so I soon established a routine based around carefully calibrated measures of work, play and sleep. I kept up my jogging and weights, and I added mountain biking and swimming. The ocean had been there to enfold me on my first leave from prison, and it was there when I was released. I feel almost whole when I'm standing on a beach.

Contrary to what Judge Rota had predicted in my first Parole Board hearing, it wasn't the pace and technology of modern life that took so much getting used to. It was social situations. For most of my adult life, I had been practising the adaptive behaviours you develop in prison, and those were — are — hard habits to break. It took a long time before I wouldn't feel my nostrils flare and a quickening of my pulse if I entered a space where there were unstructured groups of people. Or if I couldn't find a seat in a corner of a crowded room, I would find myself ill at ease, and seek to have a clear view of entrances and exits at all times. I still occasionally find that if someone comes and sits close to where I'm sitting when there are other options available to them, it puts me on alert. I don't like conversations I'm having to be overheard by strangers. I am hardly in control of these behaviours. I don't consciously think about them these days, and less and less they occur. Sometimes it takes an active effort of will to overcome such impulses, but they are the exception rather than the rule these days. It has got progressively easier since my first days of liberty.

Another thing that took me years to shake is the sense that you are the odd one out and others have noticed your strangeness, even if they don't appear to be paying you any attention. This feeling probably dogged me in my clumsy attempts at forming relationships in the years after I got out, too. I don't think I could quite shake the conviction in those days that there was something fundamentally flawed about my personality, and avoiding any scrutiny of this possibility had become the habit of a lifetime. This didn't make me an ideal candidate for a committed relationship. Together with the fact that my socialisation had been put on hold when I turned 18, this meant the choices I made in some of those relationships were pretty poor. I spent a few years living a kind of delayed adolescence.

Sooner or later, I caught up with most of the people I'd known and associated with before I went to prison. I could see a future with some of them, but not that many of them, partly because I have walked a very different path and have little, if anything in common with them, but mostly because I made a conscious decision before I got out of prison to eliminate certain things from my life, notably violence and substance abuse, and I was determined, when released, to surround myself only with pro-social influences.

I kept track of some of those I'd been in prison with. For example, I heard that Manu's charmed but violent life had finally come to an end: apparently he was hot-shotted on the orders of a rival in the Nomads. And on the day after I was released, I visited The Chameleon. We had a coffee together, and as usual, I really enjoyed his company. He was easily the closest thing I had to a best friend at that point in my life. But as I was leaving, I told him he needed to know that if he was considering getting mixed up in anything illegal, I couldn't be in contact with him. He just grinned — and he never phoned me again. As time went by and I realised what his silence meant, I respected him for honouring my wishes, but I couldn't help but feel some regret on his behalf. He was one of the many examples I saw in prison of people who could have made a spectacular success of a straight life, but for whatever reason, chose not to.

I heard rumours that The Chameleon and Graham Burton were operating a racket standing over drug dealers and pimps. Not long afterwards Graham Burton, tragically and without provocation, shot and killed a man, the father of two young kids, as the man was mountain biking in the firebreaks above the Hutt Valley. Burton went back to prison, where he continued to be involved in violent incidents, including the attempted murder of a Headhunters member in 2008. And then I heard The Chameleon was back in prison, too — this time in Peru, where he'd been caught smuggling a large amount of cocaine.

*

True to his word, Paul Englert hired me on a contract basis soon after I got out of prison. OPRA, his company, was a consultancy offering psychological services — primarily psychometric testing — to employers seeking to determine whether job candidates were compatible with their personnel and their corporate mission. Then, fortuitously as it seemed, just as the work for which I was taken on had dried up, a consultant's job with OPRA came vacant. Paul suggested I apply, but indicated he would excuse himself from the selection process. After interviews and psychometric testing I came out as the strongest candidate, but they were unsure of how I would be received by their clients. After all, I had spent my whole adult life in prison and my social skills were still untested.

At Paul's suggestion, it was arranged that I would hold a trial client meeting with one of the company's customers, a hard-bitten Liverpudlian who had made good in business in New Zealand. The meeting went pretty well, I thought. Afterwards, Paul met the client and asked him what he thought of me.

The man slightly grimaced.

'He was all right,' he said. 'A bit of a pointy-headed academic, though. He hasn't come up through the school of hard knocks like you and me.'

After that, Paul and the rest of the selection panel decided I would be fine with the clients. Each morning, I combed my hair and put on a long-sleeved business shirt, suit and tie. With my tattoos covered, I scrubbed up into the model of corporate respectability. No one would have suspected anything at all about my background. I worked hard to deliver top-quality work and never let OPRA down.

That said, there were still many reintegration lessons to be learned along the way when it came to interacting with clients.

One such occasion involved a meeting in a hotel with a public-sector HR manager called Glenn. It was one of my first proper meetings and I was with Paul. We were all sitting in deep chairs with high arms in a hotel lobby cafe. Glenn is obviously someone who spends a lot of time in the gym and I'm not a small man myself. Paul told me after the meeting how he had noticed with interest the unconscious non-verbals of the two alpha males with him. Glenn was sitting with his arms on the high arm rests, Paul watched me follow suit. Without even realising I was doing so I then started to out-silverback Glenn by tapping my fingers on the arm rests. Paul spoke to me afterwards about the importance of developing greater awareness of my non-verbals and how they could be perceived by others. This was a lesson I took to heart and I have since developed a high degree of mindfulness when it comes to not non-verbally communicating anything that could be misinterpreted as aggressive or otherwise playing into stereotypes.

Soon after my release, I was contacted by a reporter from Wellington's *Evening Post*, who had heard of my educational achievements in prison. She told me her editor believed it would make a good story and would I be willing to let her tell it. She told me my journey was unique: no one that she knew of had ever gone into prison with such bleak prospects and emerged with university degrees.

I wasn't interested at that stage. I thought there was a real danger I would simply be scoffed at as nothing more than a highly educated criminal. I also knew I would have to resign from OPRA if my background became public. They counted the police and the Department of Corrections among their clients, and although I had nothing to do with these client relationships, it had the potential to become a political football and I wouldn't do that to OPRA. I told the reporter I knew I couldn't stop her writing about me if she wanted to, but I wouldn't cooperate at that point in my life. But I made a deal with her.

'Let me finish my PhD, which should take a year,' I told her. 'By then I'll have a track record as a contributing member of society. Plus I'll have enough work experience to stand a chance of setting up on my own if I have to resign from my job.'

She consulted with her editor and subsequently agreed.

*

I set foot on the campus of the university for the first time a few days after my release. I had met both of my supervisors, as they had been kind enough to visit me in jail in their own time, to allow me to undertake my PhD: talk about going over and above the call of duty! It was very different meeting them in their offices. It was an amazing feeling to have full access to the university library, whenever I chose. But despite my bold promise to the journalist that I would finish my doctorate within a year, I made little progress. The trouble was, I was working, and finding the work so stimulating that I neglected my studies. One year became two, then three, then four. In the meantime, I had taken a promotion and moved to OPRA's Auckland office — a move I welcomed, as Wellington was too small a community, in the end, and I was running into people who would say things like: 'I know your background, but don't worry, I don't judge you.' I felt judged. At least in Auckland, such encounters didn't occur.

That said, Auckland presented other challenges and reintegration crossroads. I remember walking down Albert Street in central Auckland listening to my iPod when three young guys stopped me. I took out my headphones and one of them asked if I knew where to get any weed. I said no and started to move off when he hit me on the chest with the back of his hand and said, 'I'll give you $2 for your iPod.' It was only a light hit, but the message and attempt to intimidate were clear. I instinctively responded by hitting him back in the same way and saying, 'Nah, but how about I give you $2 for your hat.' He said, 'Touch me again and I'll fucken waste you.' I looked at this guy and his two friends starting to square off. I knew without a shadow of a doubt I could take all three of these guys out. It would be as clear a case of self-defence as that of my brother all those years ago. And yet I knew this wasn't what I would do. I had a deep knowledge of where this situation could lead and I knew the choice I made right now would be the one that defined me and kept me on the path I had been travelling. I raised my hands in surrender and said, 'Sorry, man, my bad', and walked away while staying out of striking distance. The easy, emotionally gratifying thing would have been to teach those guys a lesson, but I knew what was in my own best long-term interests and was consistent with the person I aspired to be.

In the end, it was Paul who saw to it that I finished my PhD. He knows how to push my buttons. One day, when I casually lamented to him I hadn't made much headway on it, he said: 'Oh, you may as well ditch it. You'll never finish it at this rate, so it's just a distraction.'

Confronted with this very real danger, and that all the work had been in vain, I was stung into action. I took three months' unpaid leave and simply smashed out the remainder of my dissertation. It was the best part of a year from the day I submitted it to the viva voce, the oral examination. This was an awesome experience, and best of all, towards the end of it, a kind of conspiratorial benevolence replaced the faint intellectual hostility in the examiners' questions. Before I walked out of the room, they had as good as told me I had satisfied the requirements of the degree of Doctor of Philosophy. I was enormously proud, especially when I got to attend my first-ever graduation ceremony. The only flaw in my enjoyment of this special day was that Mum wasn't there to see it.

*

Soon after I graduated with my PhD, I had a call from the same reporter.

'We're still keen to do that story,' she said. 'Are you ready now?'

I wasn't sure. Since her initial approach, I had built a life for myself that included a strong professional career specialising in helping others develop emotional intelligence and other leadership-related skills. My background wasn't a factor and I wasn't sure I wanted to bring it into the foreground. I consulted with a number of trusted friends and the advice was mixed. Some felt that telling my story would help others, while some believed it could be damaging to me. I thought about what I had learned in philosophy and the importance of placing value on the right things in life. I could have an easier life by just carrying on with my career and keeping my background secret, but when I looked back and measured my life, I knew that the rewards of choosing to turn my experience into a vehicle for helping others would far outweigh the risks.

To avoid any fallout for OPRA I decided to resign and work for myself. So I agreed to do the story and a week before it was due to come out, I drafted my letter of resignation. It was a daunting prospect, tossing in the one thing that had provided me with a stable base. But I had faced worse things in my life than unemployment. I would live. Because I had reached a senior management position within OPRA, my resignation stood to be disruptive for the delivery of some of OPRA's work, particularly in my area of training and leadership development and they asked if I would be prepared to carry on for another six months to help them out. I agreed. OPRA continued to be very supportive of me and I contacted all the key clients I was responsible for. I let them know about the story and who to contact within OPRA if they had concerns or wanted to discuss the matter further. The mouse cursor certainly hovered over the send button on that email as I considered the potential negative reactions this news might have. But I need not have worried about my clients' reactions. After the story appeared, practically all of the people with whom I had been working contacted me to tell me it only deepened their respect for my advice, as it made plain that when I spoke about the possibility of transformative change and development, it wasn't just an intellectual concept. I had lived it, and was living it still.

By contrast with how I had imagined I would feel — stigmatised and judged — it was hugely liberating to have my background out in the open for all to see. Living with it as a secret was like walking around with the sword of Damocles hanging over me. Once the cat was out of the bag, the sense of impending doom was gone. Everything felt cleaner. I had spent a lot of time talking to people about the need for authenticity in our dealings with the world, in our dealings with ourselves, and now here I was at last, feeling authentic.

*

I was a functional, contributing member of society, but I had still to break free of the very first prison cell in which I had languished. Five years after I had been released, I still had little or no idea how to deal with or express feelings. My life experiences had made me proficient at disconnecting from my emotions. It had been adaptive within the prison environment, where the most important outcome is survival, and you need mental toughness and resilience to avoid permanent psychological damage. Yet it was a major barrier to forming meaningful relationships. My limitations became increasingly obvious to me the more I tried to enter into relationships with women. The fish doesn't see the water, and it wasn't until an unexpected relationship breakup with Chloe, my then girlfriend of three years, that I started to get an inkling that there was something amiss. Chloe was so accommodating that she didn't tend to give me much corrective feedback as a partner, but she shared some thoughts with me once we'd broken up around my lack of emotional availability, my lack of presence and the absence of intimacy in the relationship. In all honesty, I didn't really understand what she meant. I was still years away from understanding that intimacy (in-to-me-you-see) was about having an emotional connection with someone where they really know what you think and feel about things.

I had thought a relationship was only about having someone to spend time with. As any counsellor or therapist will tell you, it is the fulfilment you derive from a primary relationship that ultimately determines your psychological well-being. I had learned to maintain a high level of well-being by myself, but there was a whole other world of enrichment and joy I didn't even know I was missing. Whereas many people are completed by their primary relationship, for me the journey to becoming an emotionally available husband and father, who knows what it means to be open to being loved and fully love others, has been nothing short of redemptive.

Not that it was a smooth or linear path to walk. It would require a lot more than Chloe's feedback to get me there.

Nearly a year later, I was invited to spend Christmas Day with Mike, a friend of mine who ran a CrossFit gym. He had a number of other friends over for the day, too, including an extremely attractive, athletic, dark-haired young woman who immediately caught my eye. I found myself feeling unusually self-conscious when chatting with her. At other times I would find my gaze drawn to her. My heart sank a little when I learned she was a student in the faraway city of Dunedin studying for a Bachelor of Applied Science in Sport and Exercise Nutrition.

Throughout that day I was acutely aware of her presence. I couldn't tell whether she was aware of me, but when she would occasionally smile in my direction the world would stop. I feel slightly self-conscious and corny writing about this now, but I had never felt so drawn to someone. She was deeply tanned with striking blue eyes and a large white smile, which no doubt had an influence on me, but she also had charisma and self-confidence that significantly added to her appeal. It wasn't until later that evening that I got any inclination the interest might be mutual. When we moved to another friend's house, the subject of conversation turned to the Israeli–Palestinian question. Mary-Ann's interest in me was piqued when she heard me holding forth and outlining the complex history of the region. She later told me she was impressed that I had an opinion or two and was smarter than I looked! It was Mike who suggested I drive her home, for which I am eternally grateful. We talked easily on the short drive and she suggested we catch up again. I couldn't have been keener and was glad she took the initiative as I still felt somewhat like a deer in headlights around her and could well have missed the opportunity to seize the moment.

The following day was one of those one-out-of-the-box summer days in Wellington. I was sitting outside my favourite café, Fidel's, in Cuba Street, keeping an eye on the street. And suddenly, there she was, walking along the street towards me. She was in a summer dress and everything else stopped for me. It was like one of those shampoo commercials where traffic stops and everyone turns to look at the beauty walking down the street. We drank coffee and talked. I found out she was the niece of Lorraine Moller, a champion marathon runner and Olympic medallist, and that Mary-Ann was herself a passionate athlete. Prior to enrolling at Otago University, she had been in the army. She had wondered how she would measure up against the demands of basic training, and there had been only one way to find out. She'd spent a year in the army, and then had obtained various qualifications in adventure tourism, working as a snowboard instructor in winter and a hiking guide in summer. Then she had decided to enrol as an adult student at Otago. When she wasn't studying or pushing herself to her physical limits, she volunteered at a homeless drop-in centre. Everything I found out only increased my interest in her. Towards the end, our conversation turned to what we respectively planned to do with the rest of our holidays. I told her I was leaving the following morning to fly home to Auckland to collect my tramping boots in order to go and do a solo traverse of the Tongariro Crossing, climbing Tongariro and Ngauruhoe mountains on the way.

'Let's go together,' she replied.

I thought this sounded like a great idea and we started talking logistics. She talked me into forgetting about flying to Auckland. I could just buy a pair of tramping boots in Wellington and we could drive up to the Central Plateau in her car.

So that's what we did. The Tongariro Crossing covers 18 kilometres up and over the Tongariro volcanic massif in the centre of New Zealand's North Island. It can be a hard slog — but not hard enough, as it turned out, for Mary-Ann. As if climbing the rocky summit of Tongariro and the steep, cinder cone of Ngauruhoe wasn't enough, she suggested we run the rest of the track. I agreed, but soon wished I hadn't. I'm not really a runner. Mary-Ann is. I kept up through sheer willpower, and it nearly killed me, but the company of this delightful woman was worth every bit of pain and suffering.

That was the beginning of it. We kept up a distance relationship, her in Otago, me in Auckland, until she finished her degree, whereupon she moved up to Auckland so we could be together.

*

I owe so much to Mary-Ann. No one has had more of a beneficial influence on me. She is strong, self-confident, forthright and compassionate. It turns out these are exactly the attributes I need in a partner for my own growth and development. She was also an excellent tutor in the ways in which civilised people behave.

That very first night we met, after she had agreed to meet me the next day, Mary-Ann had Googled me. She saw the newspaper article, with its headline: 'Convicted Murderer Graduates with PhD'. She showed it to her dad Gary, and asked whether he thought she should be meeting me for coffee.

He read it quickly.

'Phew,' he said, when he'd finished. 'Thank God he hasn't just got a master's.'

315

That's the kind of guy Gary is: compassionate, open-minded and funny. I get on really well with him. Like daughter, like father: he's a runner, and in the days when I was dating Mary-Ann, I would go on long runs with him. I (mostly) kept up, again through willpower, and I think he came to admire my determination, if nothing else. He has always been very philosophical and non-judgemental about my past.

Gary is an absolute inspiration to me. His real passion is mountain biking and in 2018 he won the Masters category of the World UCI Mountain Bike Championship in Europe. He's a man who never makes excuses and knows what it means to be dedicated, and he's the man who raised Mary-Ann to be the amazing woman that she is.

Mary-Ann, too, detached herself from my past and judged me on the person I had become, not the person I had been. Living together in my tiny place in Auckland central, we soon struck problems. A major one was that I simply wasn't ready to be in the kind of committed relationship Mary-Ann wanted. I wasn't emotionally available. I was incapable of telling her how I felt about things and why, which would have meant allowing myself to appear vulnerable and also required me to be connected enough to my emotions to know what I was feeling. I was far better at disconnecting from my emotions. As much as I loved and respected Mary-Ann, I couldn't be the kind of person she wanted in a relationship and she wouldn't settle for anything less than she deserved. And so our relationship ended.

Nevertheless, we maintained our friendship. We'd go out together, and often went running. We still enjoyed each other's company. And it was after we had agreed we would just be friends that we learned she was pregnant.

We agreed to be a team for the first year of the baby's life. We wouldn't get back together, but if it did rekindle our interest in each other that would be great. When I told my youngest brother about Mary-Ann being pregnant, he astutely guessed that this was a great opportunity for me to have another chance with the woman I loved. We decided to move back to Wellington to be closer to the support of our families, and we found a place in Karori. Spending time together did rekindle our mutual interest, and we discussed the possibility of trying to make our relationship work. Mary-Ann was perceptive enough to see that the success of this second go of things would depend on seeing a couples' psychologist. Fortunately, my education in psychology meant this course of action made complete sense to me. I didn't view meeting a psychologist as some sort of judgement against me or us, but welcomed the prospect of using an expert to help guide us through some challenging terrain. A real test of courage, for many men in particular, is facing the emotional discomfort that comes with being vulnerable and asking others for support.

*

It's pretty standard when couples attend relationship counselling for both to expect to be told they're right and the other person is wrong in disputes and issues. Neither Mary-Ann nor I got what we wanted in that respect, but we got something far more precious: an insight into the fundamental dynamics of the relationship. We learned what each wanted from the other. I began learning the language you need to discuss emotions, and this was the beginning of my learning to cope with them better as they arose and to make better decisions. I learned what it felt like to open up properly, to dare to speak about my emotions, and in so doing, to leave myself open to being hurt. I glimpsed what it is like not only to really love someone but also to be brave enough to show the vulnerability needed to be truly open to another's love. This required me to examine my deepest fears about myself, including the fear that underneath and in spite of it all, I wasn't really loveable. I saw clearly that the reason I isolated myself emotionally was because I was scared of the question emotional commitment asked: could I be loved? And in asking myself that terrifying question, I discovered what true courage was.

We finished that first session on a real high and I wanted more of that feeling. More of the courage to be vulnerable, and to be rewarded with the love of the woman with whom I wanted to spend the rest of my life.

For so long, I had been a detached person who would either get angry or emotionally withdraw from challenging situations at first opportunity. Now, I had to take ownership. The most helpful way I found to look at it was in terms of the 'Jungian shadow', the notion pioneered by one of the founding fathers of modern psychoanalysis, Carl Jung, which encourages you not to pretend you have no dark side, but to both acknowledge and embrace it. Human beings are social animals, but the animal side of their nature is potentially dangerous. You can't just wish it away or pretend it's not there. Acknowledging it's there is the more authentic approach. Properly dealt with, our dark side provides us with the drive and energy we need to achieve our positive goals. We have claws: it's just that we keep them sheathed.

Philosophy also helped. One of the cardinal virtues of the Stoics was benevolence towards those who deserved it. You can interpret 'benevolence' in many ways, but it mostly has to do with the desire to do good and to be kind. And perhaps the fundamental Stoic virtue was courage, and it takes far more of that to allow yourself to appear emotionally vulnerable than to risk physical injury. Yet the most important factor was working with a brilliant psychologist who specialised in emotion-focused therapy. This therapy helped me identify the way my coping styles impacted on how I would respond to Mary-Ann when feeling emotional distress, and helped me learn to make space of my discomfort and stand strong rather than withdrawing in these situations. Time and time again, I have found that facing up to my fears of rejection and sharing my worries and vulnerabilities with Mary-Ann has just brought us closer together, has taken our relationship and love for each other to new levels — levels I didn't know existed, but now know offer the most rewarding experiences in life. With the help of Mary-Ann and our therapist, I was able to finally learn what it really means to be free.

*

Of all I have experienced in life, nothing came close to the feeling of seeing my son born and holding him for the first time: a new human life, with all its limitless potential. Braxton Sema — the second name is a family name from the Cook Islands side of Mary-Ann's heritage — was born on 28 August 2014. I cried when he came into the world. Along with the birth of my second son, Gordon Ioane, on 11 June 2017, the other major life event was my marriage to Mary-Ann in February 2016 in front of the Boatshed on Wellington's beautiful waterfront. I had thought my external achievements were the way I'd measure my life and progress, but since meeting Mary-Ann and embarking on our journey as parents of our two boys, it is my relationship with her and the way we lead the way for our boys that are my life's priority and how I will look back and measure my success in this world.

My appreciation for my dad has deepened, too. It is only now that I'm a parent can I understand how hard my imprisonment must have been for him. He visited me nearly every week for over ten years. I consider myself incredibly lucky to have been able to spend this time with Dad, to learn about his life experiences and who he is as a person. But I also think about the sacrifice involved in him coming to visit and support me. Consider how much value you place on your days off and imagine giving up half a day a week to go into an environment where you're treated with suspicion and have to see someone you love in a terrible and unsafe situation. When I was growing up, Dad wasn't big on cuddles, or saying 'I love you', or 'I'm proud of you', which are all things my boys experience plenty of. But if I become even a shadow, a pale reflection, of the father my dad was to me in terms of the support he provided me, my kids will be bloody lucky.

*

I was immensely grateful to the directors of OPRA, Paul Englert and Dr Sarah Burke, for the stability they provided me through the reintegration years after my release. But by the time I resigned, I was ready to fly the nest. One of the first things I did once my background was out in the public domain was to approach the organisers of a TEDx programme to be held at Auckland's Aotea Centre. TEDx facilitates the spread of useful ideas among communities. The organisers liked the idea of my talk. The address I ended up giving was the first time I had told people about my past face-to-face, and I did it in front of 2000 people. I had no idea, as I gazed out at the sea of faces made dim by the bright lights focused on the stage, what they were thinking, or how it would be received. The talk was based on the question 'What's Your Prison?' and in it, I sought to share the formula of my Five Steps to Freedom as the means to free yourself from root-bound thinking and to realise your potential.

Meanwhile, I began using the skills I'd acquired managing OPRA's training and development arms to build a business that specialised in leadership development and assisting people and organisations thrive through transformational change. I soon found myself in considerable demand, as a facilitator and as an inspirational speaker. When my background became public I was worried I'd never be able to work again, but people saw my background as firsthand experience of what it means to change and develop, to turn adversity to your advantage and strive towards your potential.

I spend a lot of time in aeroplanes these days, and sometimes when I'm answering emails in the Koru lounge before a flight, or sitting back in a corporate cab, or admiring the view from a hotel window, I think about how impossible all of this would have seemed as little as a decade ago. When I am taking off from Wellington airport, I like to look down at the prison where my sentence began and remember how much I longed to be in one of the planes flying overhead.

A little while back, I made one of the most difficult trips I have made since I was released. I went back to Rimutaka Prison, where I was to address a group of forty-odd inmates who were undertaking a drug and alcohol rehabilitation programme. It was a bizarre and frankly horrifying feeling being back: the place, the people and the ubiquitous show of machismo at once familiar and strange. Men swaggered around with basketballs under their arms, brows knitted, daring anyone to make eye contact with them. An inmate with whom I was briefly locked in a sally port looked down at my shoes and said, 'I reckon we better swap shoes, bro,' with a hint of menace in his eyes.

'Nah, I don't reckon,' I replied with a genuine smile.

It was in one of these sessions I was asked a question that led to a major insight for me. A Mongrel Mob member raised his hand when I asked if anyone had any questions.

'Have you forgiven yourself?' he asked.

The question made me consider for the first time the difference between shame and guilt. Guilt is what society should want prisoners to feel, because it shows they regret their behaviour and that it is open to them to behave differently. But shame runs deeper. Shame is rooted in the belief that behaviour springs from some flawed and irredeemably broken aspect of ourselves.

'Have I forgiven myself?' I answered. 'I remind myself of what a German philosopher once said: "Life can only be understood backwards, but it must be lived forwards." I still feel guilty. But I show and reduce that guilt through the way I live my life today and by trying to be the best person I can be. I'm constantly working on my behaviour, but that's not because I'm a bad person who should feel shame about being broken: it's because no one is perfect and the goal for us all is progress, not perfection. The goal is living our lives just a little more positively every day, of shifting the balance of our behaviour away from things we want to keep hidden and which make us feel weak and ashamed, to things we are pleased for others to know, which make us feel proud. Many people have heard the quote that Rome wasn't built in a day, but few of us know that the full quote is, "Rome wasn't built in a day, but bricks were laid every hour." That's the journey, my bro: laying those bricks that are each small things, small changes, but that take you somewhere completely different over time.'

Another Māori inmate then put up his hand.

'No offence, bro, but do you think being a Pākehā has made it easier for you to make it on the outside?'

'Yes, I do,' I said. 'I wish I could say our country is a fair one where everyone gets the same chances and opportunities, but I don't think this is true. We all have our own struggles to overcome on the journey to rehabilitation and reintegration, and I do believe that Māori often experience additional challenges in this respect. Yet I also believe we all have the power to make choices that can positively impact our lives and our future, whichever cards we are dealt.'

Despite the unpleasantness of that first trip back and how it reminded me of a period of my life I'd rather not relive, I continue to periodically visit New Zealand prisons. There are ways in which I'd far rather be spending my time, but there is redemption to be had by facing this discomfort in the interests of making a positive difference. If just one of those listening to me ends up turning their life around in part because of what I had to say, then the amount of discomfort it costs me to go back will be more than justified. I often think that what I actually say during these visits isn't as important as the example I provide, of someone who has been accepted back into society despite their background of criminality and imprisonment. One of the things that most demotivates prisoners from making change is the feeling it's pointless to do so, that they are so irredeemably damaged by what they have done they will never be accepted back into society. I hope to provide an antidote to this fear.

*

Another of the Stoic virtues I have come to aspire to is wisdom, which is different from knowledge. It is the ability to apply the lessons learned through experience in a way that helps you live up to your values.

Writing this book has been hard. Revisiting the past has been an intense, emotional experience, not least because I am aware there is a parallel narrative to the 'onwards and upwards' story I have told here. I discovered that it wasn't too late to dream again, and even to live some of my dreams. I have built a fulfilling career out of helping others do just this. But all the while, I live with the knowledge that I permanently denied someone the opportunity to turn their own life around. Our prison system was devised at a time when people believed we all have a 'spark of divinity' within us, that it is wrong to despair of even the most antisocial miscreants in society. This was the fundamental tenet of the abolition of the death penalty, and of the notion that prisons should seek to rehabilitate prisoners, to nurse that spark of divinity into flame. Well, results have always varied on that one, today more than ever. But it is true that anyone can turn their life around if sufficiently motivated and if given the opportunity. I denied Boyd that opportunity, and I caused lasting grief and trauma to his family. It is they who ended up serving the real life sentence.

A while after my story appeared in the newspaper, I received a Facebook message from one of Boyd's siblings asking if I would be willing to meet. The first thing I did was to look at the photographs on this person's profile. They were startlingly ordinary: photographs of a family on special occasions, Christmas, children's birthdays, family get-togethers. Of course, Boyd wasn't there.

I offered to meet his family as part of a formal restorative justice process, which they declined. I respect this, and I wish them all the best. The offer will always be there. One of my major regrets from this whole experience is that Boyd's family and my family have had to suffer as a result of my actions. The best and only real path to redemption for me is to continue to dedicate myself, day by day, hour by hour, to making myself the best possible person I can be and to making a positive contribution to society.

*

The reason I feel I can be effective in the work that I do — convincing people that adversity can be the catalyst of growth and that transformational change is possible — is because I am living proof that these ideas are true. Accordingly, my last word is for my afflicted reader. What's your prison? How badly do you want to escape from it? What are the small steps you're taking, right now, to strive towards your potential and attain your dreams? Because, believe me, they can be attained ... one small brick at a time.

Take it from me: Paul Wood, a free man.

Paul Wood and Mary-Ann Moller on their wedding day, at the Boatshed in Wellington, February 2016

Paul and Mary-Ann with their sons Gordon, aged one, and Braxton, four, at Island Bay, Wellington, 2018

ACKNOWLEDGEMENTS

First, I would like to thank my wife and source of ongoing inspiration, Mary-Ann. Without your encouragement and support, this book would not have happened. I would also like to thank my father, Brian Wood. What a journey we have been on, and where I am now is a direct result of your belief in me and your ceaseless support. There are many others who have helped me in small and big ways to become the man I am today. My brothers, Jon, Andrew and Chris, have all played important roles in inspiring and encouraging me, as have my in-laws, Cristiane and the Moller family. Many prison staff and inmates need to be acknowledged, particularly John Barlow, JR and Sister Marie Roche. Special mentions must also go to Dr Gus Habermann, Dr Stephen Hill, Professor Mandy Morgan and all the other Massey University staff who made it possible for me to study from a distance and, in so doing, find a path out of my own ignorance and perceived limitations. I am also eternally grateful to Dr Paul Englert and Dr Sarah Burke, who provided me with the employment that formed the backbone of my reintegration on release. Finally, thanks to John McCrystal, who helped turn an old prison manuscript into something readable. Success is a team effort and I would not have come as far as I have today without the support of those mentioned and many others I have left out but not forgotten.